EUROPEAN HISTORICAL DICTIONARIES
Edited by Jon Woronoff

Historical Dictionary of Latvia

Andrejs Plakans

European Historical Dictionaries, No. 19

The Scarecrow Press, Inc.
Lanham, Md., & London
1997

SCARECROW PRESS, INC.

Published in the United States of America
by Scarecrow Press, Inc.
4720 Boston Way
Lanham, Maryland 20706

4 Pleydell Gardens, Folkestone
Kent CT20 2DN, England

British Library Cataloguing in Publication Information Available

Library of Congress Cataloging-in-Publication Data

Plakans, Andrejs.
   Historical dictionary of Latvia / Andrejs Plakans.
      p.   cm. — (European historical dictionaries ; no. 19)
    ISBN 0-8108-3292-5 (cloth : alk. paper)
     1. Latvia—History—Dictionaries. I. Title. II. Series.
   DK504.37.P58   1997
   947.96'003—dc21   96-49234
                                          CIP

ISBN 0–8108–3292–5 (cloth : alk. paper)

To Brenda and Lia

CONTENTS

EDITOR'S FOREWORD

One of the most extraordinary, and gratifying, events of recent years has been the resurrection of the Baltic Republics, including Latvia. All too long (and not just during the Soviet period) the Latvians have been a people without a country to call their own. Now that they finally have a country again, in word and in deed, they can resume the arduous task of turning it into a nation. As the past few years have shown, that is not so easy to accomplish and many problems must be overcome. But they seem less formidable when one takes a longer view and considers how much was achieved under even more difficult circumstances.

This *Historical Dictionary of Latvia* definitely takes a long view. Certainly, it concentrates on the present situation, including today's problems and today's leaders. But it also examines the period of Soviet rule, the tragic era of German occupation, and the many long centuries under Russian, German, and other domination. It tells us about not only the present Latvians but also their forebears. Alongside political events and personalities, there are numerous entries describing famous artists, writers, scientists and others who made their contribution. There are sections dealing with the economy, society and culture. The essential lines of this long and sometimes complicated story can more readily be followed thanks to an extensive chronology and further readings can be found in a very useful bibliography.

Andrejs Plakans, the author, has observed Latvia from without and within. Born in Riga, he grew up in the United States, but visited Latvia while it was under Soviet rule and more recently since it became an independent state. Professor of history at Iowa State University, Dr. Plakans has taught his students about Latvia, helped educate the general public, and participated in the activities of learned societies dealing with the region, most recently serving as president of the Association for the Advancement of Baltic Studies. Dr. Plakans has also written numerous articles, monographs, and book chapters and now this guide which will be of use to all who want to know about Latvia, including many Latvians.

Jon Woronoff
Series Editor

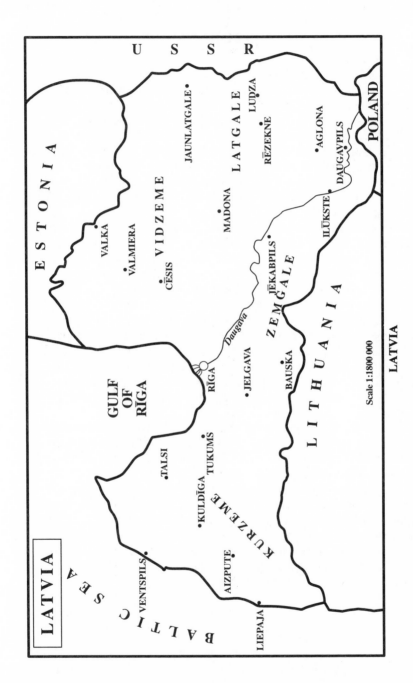

Based on A. Bilmanis, *Latvia As an Independent State* (Washington, D.C.: The Latvian Legation, 1947), p. 2, by permission of the publisher.

ACRONYMS AND ABBREVIATIONS

AABS	Association for the Advancement of Baltic Studies
ACEN	Assembly of Captive European Nations
ALA	Amerikas Latviešu Apvienība (Latvian Association of America)
ALJA	Amerikas Latviešu Jaunātnes Apvienība (American Association of Young Latvians)
AP	Augstākā Padome (Supreme Soviet)
BATUN	Baltic Appeal to the United Nations
BM	Baltic Military District
BU	Baltic University
CK	Centrālā Komiteja (Central Committee)
CPSU	Communist Party of the Soviet Union
DP	Displaced Person
DV	Daugavas Vanagi (The Hawks of Daugava)
FSR	Federated Socialist Republic
GULAG	Glavnoje Upravļenije Laggerej
IMM	*Izglītības Ministrijas Mēnešraksts (Ministry of Education Monthly)*
IRO	International Refugee Organization
KGB	Komitet Gosudarstvennoye Bezopastnosti (Soviet secret police)
LKP	Latvijas Komunistikā Partija (Communist Party of Latvia)
LLG	Lettisch-Literärische Gesellschaft (Latvian Literary Society)
LNNK	Latvijas Nacionālās Neatkarības Kustība (Latvian National Independence Movement)
LW	Latvia's Way
NATO	North Atlantic Treaty Organization
NKVD	Narodnij Komissariat Vnutrennich Djel (Soviet secret police)
PBLA	Pasaules Brīvo Latviešu Apvienība (World Federation of Free Latvians)
PSKP	Padomju Savienības Komūnistiskā Partija (Communist Party of the Soviet Union)

PSRS	Padomju Socialistisko Republiku Savienība (Union of Soviet Socialist Republics)
RFSR	Russian Federated Soviet Republic
RLA	Rīgas Latviešu Biedrība (Riga Latvian Association)
RPI	Riga Polytechnical Institute
SD	Sicherheitsdienst (Security Service)
SDP	Social Democratic Party
SS	Schutzstaffel (Nazi "blackshirts")
SSR	Soviet Socialist Republic
UN	United Nations
UNRRA	United Nations Relief and Rehabilitation Agency
VEF	Valsts Elektrotehniskā Fabrika (National Electrotechonology Factory)
USSR	Union of Soviet Socialist Republics
ZA	Zinātņu Akadēmija (Academy of Sciences)

CHRONOLOGY OF LATVIAN HISTORY

A. D. 800-1100   Tribute payments by inhabitants of eastern Latvian territories to regional Russian rulers further east; Viking raids on western Baltic coast; inhabitants of Latvian territories differentiate into Livonians, Semigallians, Couronians, Lettgallians, and Selonians

end of 12th century   First German merchants appear on Daugava River

1184-1186   The monk Meinhard begins his missionary work among Livonians and is appointed bishop of Livonia by the Pope

1196   Meinhard dies

1198   Bishop Berthold arrives at mouth of Daugava River accompanied by crusaders; Berthold killed in clash with Livonians

1199   Albert of Bremen elected third bishop of Livonia; Pope Innocent III proclaims second Baltic Crusade

1200   Albert makes peace with Livonians in Daugava area

1201   Albert founds Riga on site of earlier Livonian settlement

1202   Founding of the Swordbrothers Order

1206   Swordbrothers and their Semigallian allies defeat Livonians

1214   Swordbrothers defeat Lettgallians

1217	Swordbrothers and their Livonian and Letgallian allies defeat Estonians at Viljandi
1225	William of Modena appointed papal legate to Livonia
1229	Death of Bishop Albert
1236	Battle of Saule in Lithuania, defeat of Swordbrothers by combined forces of Lithuanians and Semigallians
1237	Swordbrothers merge with German Order, becoming the latter's Livonian branch (Livonian Order)
1242	Alexander Nevsky defeats Livonian Order on Lake Peipus
1255	Bishopric of Riga elevated to Archbishopric
1260	Battle of Durbe, Lithuanians and Couronians defeat Livonian Order
1267	Livonian Order defeats Couronians
1282	Riga becomes a member of the Hanseatic League
1290	Livonian Order defeats Semigallians
c. 1300	Riga granted city charter based on Hamburg
1410	Battle of Tannenberg in Prussia
1422	First meeting of Livonian Diet (Landtag)
1435	Livonian Order defeated in battle against Lithuanians
1452	Livonian Order and Riga Archbishopric share rule in Livonia
1481	Russian attack on Livonia

1489	Westphalian noble families become dominant force in Livonian Order
1501-1502	Walther von Plettenberg, Master of Livonian Order, together with Lithuanian allies defeats Russians
1517	Martin Luther posts his 95 Theses on church door in Wittenberg, Germany
1522	First public discussion of Lutheran doctrine in Riga
1525	Grand Master of German Order, Albrecht, becomes Duke of Prussia
c. 1530	Roman law accepted as basis of Livonian law
1546	New liturgy finished for Reformed (Lutheran) church in Livonia
1558	Ivan IV (the Terrible) launches attack on Livonia
1560	Russians defeat Livonian Order at Ērģeme
1561	Dissolution of Livonian Confederation; Master of Livonian Order pledges loyalty to Sigismund II Augustus, monarch of the Polish-Lithuanian state
1561-1581	Riga remains an independent city, not subordinated to anyone
1562	Last master of Livonian Order, Gotthard Kettler, becomes Duke of Courland and Semigallia and vassal of Polish-Lithuanian king
1563	Livonian War starts, involving Russia, Denmark, Sweden, and Poland-Lithuania
1569	Union of Poland and Lithuania
1582	Peace concludes Livonian War, Russians renounce designs on Livonia, which becomes Polish-Lithuanian territory

1600-1603	Bad harvests and famine in Livonia
1600-1629	Warfare between Poland-Lithuania and Sweden
1609	Warfare between Sweden and Russia
1629	Peace of Altmark; Sweden gains Livonia and several Courland territories, which are joined to Swedish Livonia
1630-1632	Swedish-initiated judicial reforms in Livonia
1639	Duke Jacob inherits Courland
1640	Duke Jacob obtains Tobago in the West Indies; by this date two-fifths of all Livonian estates are being held by Swedish aristocracy
1647	Treaty of neutrality between Sweden and Courland
1651	Jacob obtains St. Andrews Island in Gambia, West Africa
1654	Russians attack Polish Livland and Swedish Livland
1655	Riga has become the largest city in Swedish empire
1656	War between Sweden and Russia; Sweden attacks Courland and captures Duke Jacob
1660-1661	Peace treaties between Sweden and Poland, and Sweden and Russia
1678-1679	Swedes enter Courland
1688	Estate reduction begins in Swedish Livonia
1689	Publication of Old and New Testaments in Latvian translation by Pastor Ernst Glück

1699	Livonian nobility signs agreement with Polish ruler thus violating oath to Sweden
1700	Start of Great Northern War, involving Poland-Lithuania, Sweden, and Russia
1702	Sheremetev defeats main Swedish force in Livonia
1709	In battle at Poltava, Russia defeats Sweden
1710	Riga falls to Russians; Livonian nobility agrees to union with Russia; Courland remains under control of Kettler dynasty and Poland-Lithuania
1721	Peace of Nystadt, ending Great Northern War
1727	Beginning of Herrnhut (Pietist) movement in Livonia
1737	Ernst Biron becomes Duke of Courland, establishing Biron dynasty
1743	Czarina Elizabeth forbids Herrnhut movement in Livonia
1771-1784	Recurring peasant unrest in Livonia
1772	First partition of Poland; Russia obtains Polish Livonia (Latgale) and Belorussia
1795	Third partition of Poland; Russia obtains Courland
1796	Polish Livland and its Latvian-speaking population are joined administratively to Belorussia
1802	Peasant disturbances at Kauguri (Livonia)
1804	New Peasant Law in Livonia
1816-1819	Serf emancipation in Estonia (1816), Courland (1817), and Livonia (1819)

1822	Founding of *Latviešu Avīzes*, first regularly appearing newspaper in the Latvian language
1841	Famine in Livonia
1845	Bad harvests in all of Baltic provinces
1846-1847	Mass conversions of Lutheran peasantry to Russian Orthodoxy
1849-1860	New land laws make peasant ownership of land possible
1856	Publication of Juris Alunāns's *Dziesmiņas* -- traditional starting date for Latvian "national awakening"
1861	Emancipation of serfs in Latgale
1862-1865	Publication of *Pēterburgas Avīzes*, first explicitly nationalistic Latvian-language newspaper
1868	Founding of Riga Latvian Association
1873	First general Latvian song festival in Riga
1876	Abolition of office of Baltic governor-general
1882-1883	Inspection (revision) by Senator Mansein of conditions in Baltic provinces; prelude to "Russification" period
1883-1894	Agricultural crisis in Baltic provinces
1887	Introduction of Russification measures in Baltic provinces
1900-1915	Publication of *Latvju dainas*, compiled by Krišjānis Barons and Henri Wissendorf
1904	Founding of Latvian Social-Democratic Workers Party

1905	Revolution in Baltic area directed primarily against Baltic German landowners
1906	Punitive expeditions by Baltic German and Russian authorities against suspected participants of 1905 revolutionary activity; Latvian Social Democrats unite with Russian Social Democrats
1912	Bolshevik-Menshevik split in Russian Social Democratic Party
1914	August 1. Start of World War I
1915	Congress of Latvian refugees in Petrograd
1915-1917	German front stabilizes just south of Riga
1916	Founding of Latvian Rifle Regiments in Russian Army
1917	March. Revolution in Russia
	November. Bolshevik coup in Petrograd
1918	March. Creation in the Red Army of Latvian Riflemen Division
	November 18. Declaration of independent Latvia, with provisional government headed by Kārlis Ulmanis
	December 17. Declaration of Soviet Latvia, with Pēteris Stučka as head
1919	January 4. Red Riflemen occupy Riga
	May. Latvian Soviet government defeated, withdraws to Russia
1919-1920	Creation by Latvian provisional government of an armed force; defeat of and withdrawal from Latvian

territories of all armies opposed to creation of Latvian state

1920   April. Election of Latvian Constitutional Convention.

August. Peace treaty between USSR and Latvia

September. Start of agrarian reforms, creating some 54,000 new family farms over next decade and a half

1921   September. Latvia becomes member of League of Nations

1922   February. Latvian Constitution adopted

July. Elections for first Saeima (parliament)

1925   Elections for second Saeima (parliament)

1928   Elections for third Saeima (parliament)

1931   Elections for fourth Saeima (parliament)

1932   Non-agression pact between USSR and Latvia

1934   May 15. Coup by Kārlis Ulmanis, leader of Agrarian Union Party; establishment of Ulmanis's presidential rule

1937   Latvia concludes agrarian reforms

1939   August. Molotov-Ribbentrop Pact

October. Mutual assistance pact between USSR and Latvia; establishment of Soviet military bases in Latvia

1940   June. Ultimatum from USSR to Latvia

June 17. Soviet Army enters and occupies Latvia

August 5. Latvia annexed to Soviet Union

1941 June 13-14. First mass deportations of Latvians to various sites in Soviet Union

June 21. Germany invades Soviet Union

July 1. German Army arrives in Riga

1942 February. Hitler assents to formation of Latvian Legion

1944 October. Soviet Army reenters Riga

1945 May 8. Germany capitulates to Allies, ending World War II

1946 First Five-Year Plan in Latvia

1949 March 25. Major deportations in connection with agricultural collectivization

1950 Collectivization completed of 95 percent of farms in Latvia

1953 March. Death of Stalin

1955 General amnesty; about 30,000 deported return to Latvia from various locales in USSR

1956 Khrushchev's condemnation of Stalin at 20th Party Congress

1959 Purge of Eduards Berklāvs and other Latvian communists for "bourgeois nationalism"

July. Arvīds Pelše becomes First Secretary of Latvian Communist Party

1964 Fall of Khrushchev; Brezhnev and Kosygin become leaders of CPSU

1966	Arvīds Pelše to Moscow; Augusts Voss becomes First Secretary of Latvian Communist Party
1971	Publication in the West of letter signed by "Seventeen Latvian communists," and condemning Russification of Latvian life
1977	Boris Pugo becomes KGB head in Latvia
1983	Crackdown on dissidents in Latvia
1984	Augusts Voss to Moscow; Boris Pugo becomes First Secretary of Latvian Communist Party
1985	Mikhail Gorbachev becomes General Secretary of Communist Party of the USSR (CPSU)
1987	February 17-20. Gorbachev visits Latvia and Estonia to promote his new policies
	March. Language festival in Riga turns into celebration of Latvian language
	June 14. First mass demonstration in Riga to commemorate 1940 deportations
	August 23. First large demonstration in Riga to mark signing of 1939 Molotov-Ribbentrop Pact
	November 18. First large demonstration in Riga on anniversary of 1918 independence declaration
1988	March 25. Mass demonstrations in Riga to commemorate 1949 deportations
	April 27. Demonstrations by Latvian Green Movement against a Riga subway; project is shelved
	June 1-2. Plenum of Latvian Writers Union, now seen as starting date of "third awakening" in Latvia

June 14. Demonstrations to commemorate 1940 deportations

July 11. Founding of Latvian Popular front proposed

June 26. Founding of Latvian National Independence Movement

August 23. Mass demonstrations marking Molotov-Ribbentrop Pact

October. Boris Pugo, first secretary of Latvian Communist Party, reassigned to Moscow and replaced by Jānis Vagris

October 6. Antolijs Gorbunovs becomes chairman of Latvian Supreme Soviet; Vilnis Bresis becomes chairman of Council of Ministers

October 8-9. First Congress of Latvian Popular Front

November. Joint meeting in Riga of independence movements of Estonia, Latvia, and Lithuania

1989   February 18-19. First congress of Latvian National Independence Movement

April. Citizens Committee movement formed

May. Second Congress of Latvian National Independence Movement calls for independent Latvia

October. Second Congress of Latvian Popular Front proclaims national independence as goal

December. Latvian Popular Front candidates win majority of seats in municipal elections, including Riga

Latvian Supreme Soviet eliminates "leading role" of Communist Party from Latvian Constitution

1990   February. Latvian Supreme Soviet denounces 1940 incorporation of Latvia into USSR

March 17. Elections for Supreme Soviet return a 23-deputy majority for Latvian Popular Front and Latvian National Independence Movement

May 4. Latvian Supreme Soviet passes resolution to renew independent Latvian state on basis of 1922 Constitution

May 12. Joint Council of Baltic Republics established to coordinate move toward independence

May 14. Gorbachev declares Latvian and Estonian independence declarations illegal

July. Three Baltic states declare they will not participate in drafting of new all-Union Treaty

1991   January 13-26. Reacting to Soviet attacks on Lithuanian television facilities, Latvians erect barricades around public buildings in expectation of "crackdown" from Moscow. A pro-Moscow "National Salvation Committee" declares it is assuming power in Riga.

January 20. "Black Berets" attack Latvian Interior Ministry, killing five and injuring eleven persons

March. Referendum on independence finds large majority in Latvia in support

August 19-23. Unsuccessful coup against Mikhail Gorbachev in Moscow; Supreme Soviet in Latvia activates independence declaration on August 21

September 2. U.S. announces diplomatic recognition of Baltic states, including Latvia

September 6. Soviet Union recognizes independence of Baltic states, including Latvia

November. Fourth Congress of Latvian Popular Front

December 25. Mikhail Gorbachev resigns as president of USSR; USSR dissolved

1992   January. Beginning of drawn-out negotiations between governments of Latvia and Russia over withdrawal of Russian troops from Latvian territory

February. U.S. Vice President Dan Quayle visits Latvia

July. Latvian ruble, a transition currency, becomes legal tender in Latvia

August. Meager grain harvest threatens winter food shortages

October. Russian president Yeltsin censures Estonia and Latvia for not observng human rights of their Russian-speaking citizens

1993   March. Latvian *lats* becomes legal tender, forming parallel currency with Latvian ruble. Formation of "Latvia's Way," an electoral coalition in preparation for June parliamentary elections

June 5-6. Election of fifth Saeima (parliament), which replaces Supreme Soviet as the national legislature; Latvia's Way wins plurality (34) of seats

July. Saeima (parliament) elects Guntis Ulmanis of Agrarian Union party as President of Latvia; Latvia's Way forms coalition government with Agrarian Union, with Valdis Birkavs as prime minister

September. Three Baltic states sign trilateral free trade agreement. Pope John Paul II visits Latvia

1994   February. Latvia signs "Partnership for Peace" agreement with NATO

March. Latvia and Russia conclude agreement on troop withdrawal by August 31 and on Russian use of the radar installation at Skrunda until 1998.

Saeima suspends five deputies, including popular Foreign Minister Georgs Andrejevs, for alleged past collaboration with KGB

June. Nationalist bloc wins plurality of votes in local elections, signaling growing unpopularity of Latvia's Way coalition

July. U.S. President Bill Clinton visits Latvia; Government of Valdis Birkavs resigns, as Latvia's Way coalition partner, Agrarian Union, abandons coalition; Saeima (parliament) in a special session passes final version of citizenship law

September. Latvia's Way forms new Cabinet, with Māris Gailis as prime minister

1995   October/November. Second post-1991election, producing a parliament incapable of forming a cabinet

December. President Ulmanis asks Andris Šķēle, a Riga businessman, to form a cabinet. The Šķēle government receives 70 votes in the parliament.

1996   June. Parliament elects President Guntis Ulmanis to a second three-year term

INTRODUCTION

Latvia's Physical Features and Borders

The Republic of Latvia is situated between 55° 40́ 23˝ and 58° 05́ 12˝ North latitude and 20 ° 58́ 07˝ and 28 ° 14́ 30˝ East longitude. On contemporary European maps, the country has a common border on the north with Estonia, on the south with Lithuania, and on the east with Belorus and the Russian Federated Soviet Republic (RFSR). On the west and partially on the north Latvia borders on the Baltic Sea and on the Gulf of Riga. These borders have remained relatively unchanged since 1918 when the country first acquired independence, although in 1945 a small district called Abrene, in the northeastern corner of the country, was separated from the area that from 1945 to 1991 was known as the Latvian Soviet Socialist Republic and added to the territory of the RFSR, where it remains today. With that exception, the borders of present-day Latvia became fixed in the post-World War I years, after the country obtained its independence from the Russian Empire. The political borders established at that time generally corresponded to the ethnographic and linguistic borders that had defined the principal area of settlement of Latvian speakers for the past century or more.

Latvia lies on the northeastern extension of the Great European Plain so that its physical features consist mostly of gently rolling land crossed by five major rivers (Daugava, Lielupe, Venta, Gauja, and Salaca) and the tributaries of their catchment systems. The country is also dotted with lakes, with the largest and most numerous located in the southeastern part of Latvia (Latgale). In the distant past, much of the country was covered by coniferous and mixed-wood forests, but in the twentieth century the forest cover has been reduced to about 25 percent of the total area. These physical features, and the fact that Latvia has few mineral deposits, determined for centuries the primary occupations of its inhabitants -- entrepôt trade, agriculture based on cereals and livestock, forestry, and fishing. In the twentieth century the importance of diverse manufactures and service occupations has increased substantially, but the traditional forms of livelihood have maintained their significance.

1

Recent History

Latvia is one of the three so-called "Baltic states" on the eastern littoral of the Baltic Sea. The other two are Estonia to the north and Lithuania to the south. Although Latvian-language popular discourse had used the term "Latvia" even in the nineteenth century, the designation gained official status only in 1918 when a Republic of Latvia was proclaimed amid the turmoil of the post-World War I years. The country existed as an independent and sovereign state during the 1920s and 1930s alongside the other two Baltic states, but in 1940 the three were occupied and annexed by the Soviet Union. After a period of German occupation (1941-1944) during World War II, Latvia was again occupied by the USSR. From then until 1990, Latvia, as well as Estonia and Lithuania, were de facto Soviet Socialist Republics and constituent parts of the USSR, but their de jure status as independent states remained unchanged since many of the great powers of the western world refused to officially recognize the incorporation.

The status of Latvia changed once again in 1990, when on May 4, amid the perestroika period in the Soviet Union, a newly elected Latvian Supreme Soviet (Parliament) re-proclaimed Latvia's independence as a political goal for the near future. The final act in this recent drama came on August 21, 1991, when during the abortive Moscow coup against Mikhail Gorbachev the Latvian Supreme Soviet issued an announcement that Latvia's ties with the Soviet Union were completely severed as of that moment. By mid-September 1991 the country had been recognized as an independent state by most of the major powers, including the Soviet Union, and had been admitted to the United Nations as a sovereign entity.

Political History: Eighteenth and Nineteenth Centuries

Though small both in territory (about the size of West Virginia) and in population (1989 population 2.8 million), Latvia has had a complicated history. In fact, it is historically inaccurate to speak of a "Latvia" at all before the 1918 independence proclamation because during the preceding centuries the territories--and their residents-- that merged into an independent state in 1918 were separate poli-tico-administrative units. The inhabitants of the pre-1918 "Latvian" territories resided in what then were called the Russian "Baltic provin-ces" of Livonia (Ger. *Livland*) and Courland (Ger. *Kurland*), and in the western districts of the province of Vitebsk adjoining the Baltic provinces proper. In Livonia, the Latvian-speaking population lived in the southern districts of the province; the northern districts were populated by Estonian-speakers.

The Baltic provinces were separate entities in the Russian Imperial administrative system, and each had its own unique history. Livonia was acquired by the Russian Empire from Sweden in 1710, as a result of the latter's defeat in the Great Northern War. The Russians obtained the Latvian Vitebsk territories during the second partition of Poland in 1772. Courland was added to Russia in 1795 when the last Duke of Courland relinquished his family's rights to that office in return for a cash payment from Catherine the Great. Thus, by the end of the eighteenth century, all the territories that in 1918 became the Republic of Latvia had become constituent parts of the Russian Empire.

Political History: Twelfth to Eighteenth Centuries

Before the arrival of Russian hegemony, the political history of the region was more complicated still. In the twelfth century, the territories that in 1918 were to become Latvia were inhabited by tribal societies--Semigallians, Selonians, Couronians, Lettgallians, Livonians--that already had a political structure, with their leaders (kings) living in fortified places. These peoples had become permanent residents of the region during the seventh and eighth centuries, though the borders of the specific areas each occupied are difficult to reconstruct. At the end of the twelfth century, however, these territories came to the attention of both the Papacy as well as German traders because most of the indigenous peoples were not Christian but did live in an area that appeared ripe for economic exploitation.

Some Christian influences had come into the Baltic region from the east already in the eleventh century, but systematic efforts to Christianize the Baltic peoples began with the arrival in 1196 of the Augustinian monk Meinhard from the German lands of the Holy Roman Empire, and continued under the leadership of Albert of Bremen who during his 30 years as bishop of the Livonian territories succeeded in establishing there a permanent German presence. His efforts were helped by the issuance of a bull by Pope Innocent III calling for a crusade against the Baltic "barbarians," By the end of the thirteenth century, the western Europeans--principally the Germans-- had consolidated their hold through the establishment of "Livonia," a collection of territories governed by the Livonian Order and the Church (represented by the Archbishop of Riga). These institutions controlled virtually all land and redistributed it as fiefs to their supporters. Throughout this process, the indigenous peoples lost their leaders and gradually during the late medieval centuries turned into a peasantry that, as peasants elsewhere in Europe, comprised the base of the entire Livonian feudal edifice.

Coexistence between the Church and the Order was riddled with conflict, and by the mid-sixteenth century Livonia, at the moment in the throes of the Protestant Reformation, seemed promising to the expansionistic Russian Tsar Ivan the Terrible as well as to the rulers of the Polish-Lithuanian Commonwealth to the south and to the budding Swedish empire. The ensuing Livonian Wars (1558-1583) and Polish-Lithuanian War (1600-1629)--immensely destructive to noncombatants--brought an end to the medieval Livonian state and the Livonian Order, and left the territories in the control of Poland-Lithuania and Sweden. The German-speaking upper orders--the landowning nobility and the urban merchants and tradesmen-- remained in place, however, and adjusted to their new sovereign lords.

From the 1630s onward, the territories inhabited by the Latvian-speaking peasantry formed (in the south) the semiautonomous Duchy of Courland, with its dukes being vassals of the Polish-Lithuanian monarch; in the east, so-called Polish Livonia, which was governed directly by the Polish-Lithuanian kings; and in the center and north, Swedish Livonia, the history of which in the seventeenth century was directly linked to the colonial policies of the Swedish Vasa dynasty. This distribution of control remained unchanged until 1700 and the beginning of the Great Northern War (1700-1721) between Sweden, Poland-Lithuania, and Russia, from which Russia, now under the leadership of Peter I the Great, emerged as the decided victor since it gained control over Livonia. The rest of the Baltic territories were added to Russia later in the eighteenth century.

Latvian-Language Culture

From another viewpoint, one can say that there was a Latvian-language culture in the eastern Baltic littoral long before there was a state called Latvia. But the Baltic area was layered culturally just as it was politically. The permanent "high" culture used Latin during the centuries when it was connected with the Church, and German after the sixteenth. Polish and Swedish also played significant roles during the sixteenth and seventeenth centuries, but their importance receded as the area came under Russian dominance. In the first half of the nineteenth century, the languages of administration were Russian and German (predominantly the latter), while German also dominated urban culture and virtually all of the written word.

In terms of the spoken word, however, the weight of significance was reversed, because the vast majority of the people (using the total population of Courland, Livonia, and Polish Livonia [Latgale]) spoke Latvian. In the centuries since the sixteenth, an interesting genre of written Latvian had also come into being, as German-speaking clergymen translated the Old and New Testaments, hymnals, liturgies, and prayerbooks into the language of their parishioners. These efforts, lasting until the mid-nineteenth century, in effect, created a literary Latvian language. On their side, the Latvian-speaking peasantry, excluded from "high" culture, kept alive an oral tradition the centerpiece of which was hundreds of thousands of short folk songs called *dainas*. A secular literature in Latvian, still being written by the German-speaking Baltic intelligentsia, began to appear in the eighteenth century.

This configuration of the cultural-literary world was totally transformed with the start of the Latvian "national awakening" during the 1850s, and during the next 60 years until World War I, Latvians succeeded in ending the Baltic German monopoly over the written word in the area. By the time of the declaration of Latvian independence in 1918, a Latvian-language literary culture was inextricably a part of the the total culture of the Baltic world.

Though after 1918 hopes were high that a Latvian state and Latvian culture would continue to develop if not flourish, these hopes were dashed by subsequent events. Politically, after 15 years of existence as a multiparty parliamentary democracy, Latvia became an authoritarian state when in 1934 Kārlis Ulmanis, leader of the Agrarian Union party, founded a single-man presidential government disbanded all political parties, and dismissed the parliament. In 1940, after a half year of encroachments, the army of the Soviet Union occupied the country, dissolved the existing government, deported Ulmanis, and in August of that year, after a mock election, accepted Latvia's "request" to become a constituent part of the USSR. From 1941 to 1944, Latvia was occupied by the German army and became an element in Hitler's general plan for captured eastern territories.

In 1945, the Soviet Army returned, and from that point until August 1991, the country was one of the Union Republics of the USSR. Republic politics and all political institutions in Latvia during this period were dominated and controlled by the Latvian Communist Party, which was, in turn, a constituent part of the Communist Party of the USSR. As the Soviet Union and the Communist Party collapsed in the 1989-1991 period, Latvia regained independence, and from that moment onward has sought to rebuild its political institutions on the basis of the 1922 Constitution and other basic laws of the interwar period. In June 1993, it held its first free parliamentary elections since 1934, electing the fifth Saeima (Parliament) (the fourth Saeima having sat from 1931-1934). The newly elected Saeima in turn elected as President of the country Guntis Ulmanis, grandnephew of Kārlis Ulmanis.

Culturally, the interwar period of relatively free development was followed after 1940 by a series of damaging events. In a series of deportations and executions (1941, 1944-1945, 1949-1950) the Communist authorities "cleansed" the Latvian intelligentsia of all those who were suspected of not being totally accepting of the Communist regime, which category included large numbers of persons who had been prominent in the cultural, educational, medical, and legal institutions of the interwar period. In 1944, shortly before the return of the Soviet Army, some 120,000 Latvians emigrated to the west, and these numbers included a large proportion of the intelligentsia as well. Participants of this emigration, who did not assimilate very quickly to the cultures of the host countries where they lived after 1950--Canada, United States, Sweden, Germany, Australia, West Germany--formed a diaspora Latvian culture with its own newspapers, journals, book publishers, theater companies, and weekend schools.

In Latvia, cultural affairs after 1950 were dominated by the orthodoxies of the Communist Party, even though a period of thaw occurred in the period 1956 to 1960. Generally, though, culturally creative people had to be careful not to emphasize Latvian national culture in their work so as not to be accused of "bourgeois nationalism." Moreover, the Latvian cultural world from the late 1940s onward experienced repeated waves of Russification, during which the Latvian language became increasingly peripheral to the daily work and creativity of the Latvian intelligentsia. Those who opposed, openly or surreptitiously, the growing dominance of the Russian language were systematically vilified as being "bourgeois nationalists." all these patterns of cultural change came to an end in 1989, when the Latvian language was by law reinstated as the language of the state.

Economic Development

Similar discontinuities appeared during the twentieth century in Latvian economic and demographic development. Economically, before World War I, the Baltic provinces (including the Latvian territories) were one of the most commercially and industrially developed regions of the Russian empire. Riga, which just before the war had a population of about 530,000, was not only the most important city in the Baltic region, but in 1913-1914 accounted for a higher share of the Russian export market than St. Petersburg and stood just behind the capital in its share of the import trade.

These patterns of economic growth were disrupted by World War I and the occupation of the southern half of the Latvian territories by the army of imperial Germany. Industrial equipment and entire factories were transported to the interior of Russia, and large numbers of refugees fled north and east to escape the advancing German army. These changes were symbolized by the fact that in the 1920 census (the first in independent Latvia) the population of Riga had been reduced to about 185,000.

Much of the first decade of the independence years was spent in economic reconstruction, but the upswing at the end of this decade was ended by the worldwide depression of the 1930s. Throughout the interwar decades, the Latvian economy was mixed, with a strong free market but also statist elements. Government participation in and guidance of economic life increased substantially under the authoritarian presidential rule of Kārlis Ulmanis.

The World War II years brought another set of radical changes in the country's economy, the most important of which was the nationalization of the economy during the first year (1940-1941) by the new Soviet government. Government control over economic life was also nearly total during the period of German occupation from 1941 to 1944 as could be expected in wartime conditions.

After the return to Latvia of Soviet power in 1944-1945, the country, now the Latvian SSR, was transformed into a component part of the command economy of the USSR. Collectivization of agriculture was completed by the early 1950s. These patterns of state control, direction, and planning continued for the next 40 years until the economic changes sought by Mikhail Gorbachev under the new perestroika policy. After the collapse of the Soviet Union and its command economy, the renewed Latvian state has been diminishing its former economic role in an effort to create a relatively free market, but the government still plays a much more significant part in economic decision making than is the case in many western European countries, though not as great a role as in most of the other former republics of the USSR.

Demographic Changes

The demographic development of Latvia in the twentieth century has followed, and felt an impact from, the political and economic changes already described. In the period 1800 to 1914, the total population of the Latvian territories grew from an estimated 720,000 to 2.5 million. The tribulations of World War I reduced that number--via wartime losses and emigration--to about 1.6 million at the start of the interwar independence period. During the next 20 years, natural growth and immigration raised the total to approximately 2 million. Severe losses during the World War II years again reduced the total population to an estimated 1.4 million in 1945. Thereafter the growth of the total population was continuous, reaching approximately 2.8 million in the 1989 census.

In the post-World War II years these aggregate numbers contained a very significant compositional shift, because during the 50-years period from 1940 to 1990 the proportion of Latvians in the population of Latvia was reduced from an estimated 75 percent to an estimated 52 percent. The growth in the proportion of non-Latvians in the population of Latvia was due in large part to state-induced economic development, as a result of which many large state enterprises were built in Latvia in spite of labor shortages within the country. The labor force for these had to be recruited from other parts of the Soviet Union, with the result that by 1989 the population included some 1.1 million Slavic-speaking peoples, mostly Russians but also important minorities of Belorussians, Ukrainians, and others. This transformation of the composition of the country's population had great significance in the creation of the open dissident movement in Soviet Latvia, as well as in the rapid growth of strong separatist sentiment after 1989.

Renewed Independence

In the March 1990 elections of the Supreme Council (Soviet) of the Latvian SSR, the voters elected a majority of reform-minded deputies who were associated with the Latvian Popular Front and the Latvian National Independence Movement. These organizations had come into being in the 1988-1989 years, when Mikhail Gorbachev's perestroika and glasnost policies encouraged creation of "informal" public organizations to implement his new policies at the republic level. Though "reformers" in Latvia were by no means single-minded on the question of separation from the USSR, there was sufficient consensus to permit the Supreme Council to proclaim, on May 4, 1990, the intention of Latvia to reestablish its independence in due course. That resolution was the basis for the law-making efforts of the Council and the Cabinet of Ministers for the next 15 months, until, during the August 1991 coup against Mikhail Gorbachev, the Council declared that Latvia was a sovereign, independent state as of that moment. Though independence had now arrived formally, institutionally there remained great continuities between the pre- and post-independence periods, as symbolized by the Council itself, since it (and the Cabinet of Ministers) remained the sole law-making organs from the 1990 elections to the June 1993 elections of the new parliament (Saeima), two years into the new independence period.

During this three-year transition, the Council and the Cabinet of Ministers had the responsibility for disattaching Latvia from the USSR in every area of life and, after the collapse of the USSR at the end of 1991, for establishing Latvia as a successful entity among the many new post-communist and post-Soviet states in the European east. Because the new independence was more difficult to consolidate than the heady mood of the perestroika period had promised, the Council and the Cabinet, from 1990 onward, experienced a continuous downward slide in popularity and public support. By the spring months of 1993 only about 10 to 11 percent of those questioned in public opinion polls expressed confidence in these two bodies. The growing unpopularity of the transition government, which had come into being as a vehicle for Popular Front ideas, culminated in the June 1993 parliamentary elections in which the candidates' list of the Popular Front did not receive even the minimum 4 percent of the vote for parliamentary representation. The head (prime minister) of the Cabinet of Ministers, Ivars Godmanis, fell into the role of lightning rod for all manner of public discontent. Popular perception of the Council and the Cabinet increasingly highlighted the origins of these two organs in the Soviet period and attributed much of the unpopular but necessary transition policy to this "soviet" political elite.

While a large proportion of the political elite of the transition period had indeed been members of the Latvian Communist Party and some among them had held high rank, surrender of party membership had been rapid in the 1989-1991 period. The spectrum of political views in fact excluded those who might have wanted to argue for retention of the old Soviet-style command economy, and shifted in the direction of market mechanisms. The Supreme Council and the Cabinet of Ministers from 1990 onward had the task of piecemeal but fundamental economic reform that had to be realized amid basic political, institutional, and constitutional reform. Given the proliferation of newspapers in a new atmosphere of freedom of expression, all reform measures normally met with a barrage of criticisms, as they were proposed, during their discussion, and after they had been adopted.

One condition that colored all public discussion of reform was the continuing presence on Latvian soil of ex-Soviet army contingents, which after 1991 had formally become contingents of the army of the Russian Federation. Their numbers decreased steadily but not quickly enough for most Latvian public opinion. This situation was worsened by the lack of an agreement between the Latvian and Russian governments on a timetable for withdrawal. It was believed firmly by many that the Russian Federation was deliberately refraining from rapid withdrawal of its troops because they were to be used at an opportune moment to forcibly return Latvia to a renewed "Russian Empire," The government of the Russian Federation kept the issue inflamed by periodically linking the question of troop withdrawal to the question of how the new Latvian state planned to treat the non-Latvian component in its population. The press noted as well the relatively slow creation of a border control system, and added that to the general charge that the Latvian government was not succeeding in realizing the principle of national sovereignty.

Nonetheless, under the aegis of the Supreme Council and the Cabinet of Ministers the transformation of the Latvian state continued on a wide variety of fronts in the 1990-1991 period before the collapse of the USSR, and in the 1991-1993 period when Latvia had become one of many new post-Soviet and post-Communist states. The country's identity as a sovereign state became more firmly fixed in the international arena as it established permanent representation in the United Nations and ambassadorial offices in the major Western countries, had its applications for membership receive serious hearing in other international organizations such as the Council of Europe, and witnessed the creation of foreign embassies and information centers in Riga. To many, this was a reprise of the 1919-1921 period, when the newly created Latvian state also had had to establish an international presence and had done so successfully. Latvia, of course, did not have a corps of trained diplomats but personnel for such tasks emerged from other professions. In a number of instances ambassadorial posts abroad have had to be filled by persons of Latvian ancestry who had been living in those countries but had retained knowledge of the Latvian language and were willing to help in the rebuilding.

Urged by the World Bank and the International Monetary Fund to stabilize its currency, Latvia assigned the task to the Bank of Latvia, which began the process of withdrawing the country from the "ruble zone," The goal was to diminish the influence in Latvia of the Russian ruble, which in the 1991-1993 period lost value steadily. In 1992, a parallel Latvian ruble was introduced, which step was again a reprise of the post-1918 period, when a similar measure was taken. During the course of 1992 and early 1993, the Russian ruble was extruded from the Latvian economy, and during the summer of 1993 the Latvian *lats* (the currency of the interwar period) was introduced. The Latvian ruble and *lats* remained parallel currencies until the fall of

1993, when the ruble was withdrawn. In the interim, these monetary reforms brought inflation under control even while the ruble in Russia continued to be inflated. The Bank of Latvia kept strict control over emission of the Latvian ruble in spite of heavy pressure from many in the political arena to increase the volume of money in circulation. By the end of 1992, inflation had been reduced to an annual 10-15 percent rate and remained at that level throughout 1993.

Strict monetary control in combination with the gradual but persistent removal of price controls over many consumer goods meant a substantial diminution of purchasing power and a growing disjunction between status and income. There were repeated price increases for many goods and services that under the Soviet system had represented minimal expenditures in household budgets. Rent, transportation, and foodstuffs consumed an increasingly larger part of income, which increased minimally or not at all. Certainly by the parliamentary elections of 1993 a large proportion of the population, regardless of occupation, perceived itself as being poor. The most serious impact was felt by those who were already living on fixed incomes or entered that status during these transition years, most notably pensioners who constituted approximately 25 percent of the total population. In the 1992-1993 period there was a noticeable growth of soup kitchens in the urban centers as well as a proliferation of street musicians and beggars. In all the professions where income levels were determined by state budgets, there was an explosion of second and third part-time jobs that were now necessary to maintain living standards. At the same time, however, the competitive sectors of employment did grow and persons who had salable skills or were willing to retrain themselves to have them could compete for higher incomes and attain a rising living standard. Most frequently these opportunities arose in the commercial sector, where profit margins could at times be extraordinarily high.

The most intractable problem revolved around the principle of privatization of former state-controlled agricultural and industrial enterprises. The liquidation of sovkhozy and kolkhozy (state and collective farms) proceeded apace during the transition period, while the Ministry of Agriculture reduced its earlier functions severely. Those who benefited from these dissolutions by receiving small farms immediately ran into the problems of all small-scale producers-- shortages of start-up capital, shortages of basic equipment, absence of marketing mechanisms, and shortages of information. This process produced shrinkages in all the quantitative indicators of agricultural activity in 1992, for example, the number of cattle, hogs, and poultry on Latvian farms had shrunk to 1968 levels, and the number of milk cows to 1955 levels. The production of milk and meat in the first half of 1993 was 20 percent less than for the comparable period in 1992, which was in turn less than in 1991.

Similarly, as state-owned industrial enterprises were dissolved, broken up, or otherwise reduced, output decreased. In the first six months of 1993, total industrial production was about 43 percent of that of the first six months of 1992, and the 1992 output already represented a dropping back to 1976 production levels. These processes in turn have contributed to the growth of unemployment, which in 1993 rose to about 7 percent of the available labor force. While this is not a high proportion in comparison with western levels, it is a new experience for a society in which in the past (at least officially) unemployment was unknown. Moreover, the existing "safety net" for the unemployed--unemployment compensation and other social services--was severely underfunded, even while the Latvian government in 1993 experienced a severe budget deficit.

Though economic difficulties of this magnitude might be expected to produce dramatic political polarization as well as calls for some form of return to the old system, the parliamentary elections of 1993 showed that not to be the case. There was, to be sure, a large number of slates of candidates presented--23 in all--but the most extreme opinions of either the political right or the left were only weakly represented in this spectrum. The extreme "right" in 1993 were those who called for Latvia to become ethnically pure and agrarian with some form of economic statism; the extreme "left" were those who regretted the collapse of the Soviet Union, opposed the introduction of the free market, and demanded immediate and unrestricted citizenship rights for all current residents of Latvia, including the non-Latvian component of the population. Insofar as the Supreme Council had not adopted a citizenship law (which would also define the voting population), a special (and temporary) law defined the voting population in this election as those who had been or were descended from citizens of the interwar republic.

The result of the vote brought into the 100-person parliament deputies from eight parties or electoral coalitions, with the plurality of the votes going to Latvia's Way, an electoral coalition whose leading figures were prominent persons from the old Supreme Council and the Popular Front, as well as from Latvian émigré circles. The second largest number of deputies was elected from the Latvian National Independence Movement, the third from the Harmony party and the fourth from the Agrarian Union. Of these, only the Harmony party was "left" of center; the others were center-right. A coalition cabinet, formed by Latvia's Way with cabinet seats being awarded to smaller coalition partners, began to work in July 1993, controlling just barely a majority of the parliamentary votes. Though there were some calls for a popularly elected president of the country, the new parliament remained faithful to the 1922 constitution, which called for a president elected by the parliament. Guntis Ulmanis, grandnephew of the last interwar president Kārlis Ulmanis, assumed this post in July 1993. In October 1995 the second postindependence parliamentary election showed the political forces in Latvia continuing to be so evenly divided on basic questions that President Ulmanis had to reach outside the parliamentary arena to find a prime minister--a Riga businessman named Andris Šķēle--to form a cabinet. Šķēle received a 70-vote parliamentary majority for his coalition cabinet and in 1996 continued the task of economic reform. In June 1996, President Ulmanis was reelected by the parliament (with 53 votes) to a second three-year term, with his strongest competitor receiving only 25 votes. These conflict-free elections and nonviolent transfers of power suggested strongly the democratization of the Latvian political domain.

Compiling a Historical Dictionary on Latvia

The history of Latvia over the centuries has included the emergence of different bodies of historical scholarship, each of which, when dealing with the Latvian past, tends to emphasize the importance of events and individuals within its own politico-cultural tradition. The compilation of a historical dictionary about Latvia must be cognizant of this fact. At this writing, there does not exist an integrated history of Latvia within which these differing viewpoints are dispassionately incorporated, nor a union bibliography within which their scholarly production is listed in its entirety. The entries in the following historical dictionary have been chosen with this diversity in mind, but they cannot pretend to completeness.

THE DICTIONARY

- A -

ABRENE (also PITALOVO, PIETĀLAVA). A district of about 1,200 square kilometers, and a city in the district, at the extreme northeastern border of Latvia. In the 1920 treaty between Latvia and the USSR Abrene was included within the interwar borders of Latvia but in 1944 was administratively separated from the Latvian SSR and added to the Russian FSR. In the medieval centuries, Abrene had been included in the lands administered by the Archbishop of Riga, but later the district was under Russian control. Though fully aware of the post-World War II border changes, the government of Latvia after 1991 has not raised the issue in its discussions with the government of the RFSR.

ACADEMY OF SCIENCES (Latv. ZINĀTŅU AKADĒMIJA, ZA). Although there had been some discussion in the interwar period about creating a Latvian academy, the ZA was established in 1946 (after the incorporation of Latvia into the USSR) as the new authorities sought to place intellectual work in Latvia on the same basis that it already had in the rest of the Soviet Union. During the next 40 years, the Academy of Sciences became the dominant research organization in the country and a component part of the Academy of Sciences of the USSR. It was divided into a series of institutes and research centers, with the entire organization receiving its budget from the state. Most ZA scientists did not teach, since pedagogical work was left to the universities, but there was somewhat of an overlap between the personnel of the universities and the ZA. Since the ZA organized and funded virtually all research, the Latvian Communist Party (q.v.), which had a chapter in the ZA, was able to supervise and control the findings of research. Like other large institutions in Soviet Latvia, the ZA served the double function of sometimes protecting its leading scientists against party zealots but also making sure that Latvian research in all fields proceeded along guidelines laid down in Moscow. In 1990, the Latvian ZA separated from the ZA of the USSR, and after the re-proclamation of independence in

1991, the ZA was totally reformed to become a national honors-granting organization for personal achievement. The research institutes that had been its component parts were dismantled, became independent research centers, or were integrated into the university system.

AGLONA. The site in Latgale (q.v.) of the most renowned Roman Catholic (q.v.) church building in Latvia, donated to the Church in 1699 by a noblewoman named Ieva Zastovska. The first institution on the site was a Dominican monastery that included a wooden church, which burned in 1766. This was replaced by a baroque-style brick structure, with two 60-meter spires and ten altars. Over the nineteenth century the Aglona church became a favorite object of pilgrimages and in the interwar independence years the church had a local congregation of about 5,000 persons.

AGRARIAN REFORM. If defined as fundamental change in rural life brought about by actions of the central government, agrarian reform has been a major theme in Latvian history since the seventeenth century. With Livonia (q.v.) controlled by Sweden, the royal government in Stockholm initiated a review of the basis on which landholders in Livonia claimed to control their landed properties and, as a result, severely diminished the proportion of land under private control by placing such properties under crown control and bringing about the so-called "estate reduction" (q.v.). In the early nineteenth century, resulting from agreements between the Russian tsar and the Baltic German (q.v.) landowning nobility, a Peasant Law of 1804 regularized some aspects of serfdom (q.v.), and in the 1817-1819 period the institution of serfdom was abolished altogether. In the late 1840s, the Livonian Diet began to accept the notion that peasants, who from the emancipation onward had held their lands on the basis of labor rents, should be able to purchase land outright, and these laws eventually permitted the transfer of some 40 percent of arable land to peasant ownership.

The most radical reform came after the establishment of independent Latvia, when the Agrarian Reform Law of 1920 permitted the Latvian government to confiscate some 3.3 million hectares of land, largely from landed estates, and to redistribute it to some 144,000 persons who were landless or judged to be deserving in other ways (e.g., veterans of the Independence War). This action created a large stratum of smallholders (called *jaunsaimnieki*, or "new farmers"). In 1949-1950, after the incorporation of Latvia into the Soviet Union, the Moscow government initiated agricultural collectivization (q.v.), creating kolkhozy and sovkhozy and deporting those farmers who were judged to be actual or potential resistors. After 1991 and the reestablishment of independence, the Latvian government has begun a process of reprivatization of rural land, which is proceeding relatively slowly.

AGRARIAN UNION (PEASANTS UNION, FARMERS UNION) (**Latv. ZEMNIEKU SAVIENĪBA**). The Agrarian Union was one of the two most important political parties in Latvia during the first period of independence (1918-1940); the other was the Latvian Social Democratic Party (q.v.). It was founded in 1917 at the initiative of a coalition--called Konsums (q.v.)--of a large number of rural cooperatives and farm organizations formed in the Latvian territory of the Russian Baltic provinces (q.v.) in the years before the beginning of World War I. After the March 1917 Russian Revolution, many of the borderland nationalities of the empire, including the Latvians, perceived an opportunity for statehood and they used their existing organizations to take the first step in the process. The leader of the Agrarian Union at the time was Kārlis Ulmanis (q.v.), and he also became the first prime minister of the new provisional Latvian government after independence was declared on November 18, 1918. In the parliamentary era (1920-1934), the Agrarian Union never held the majority of seats in the 100-deputy Latvian parliament, but nevertheless succeeded in heading most of the coalition governments during the period as well as in supplying Latvia with all of its four presidents.

Though in spite of its name the Union began its existence as a national party representing the interests of both rural and urban sectors of the electorate, its party ideology did have a "peasantist" coloration that became stronger during the 1930s. Both the Union and the Social Democrats had been losing electoral support by 1934, when Ulmanis, the Union's leader, brought about a coup and suspended not only Parliament but also all political parties including the Union. In forming cabinets during the period of his personal rule, Ulmanis called upon his old Union colleagues only some of the time. In the interwar trend that created many strong-man governments in eastern and central Europe, the Union therefore never served the same function for Ulmanis as the National Socialists did for Hitler or the Fascist Party for Mussolini.

In the second independence period (after 1991) a Latvian Agrarian Union has been formed, ostensibly as the successor of the interwar Union, but its membership and electoral strength have not approached those of the interwar party. It is now, nonetheless, one of the main parties of the renewed Latvian Saeima (q.v.) (Parliament), because after the parliamentary election of June 1993, the Agrarian Union formed a coalition cabinet with *Latvijas ceļš* (Latvia's Way, q.v.), the coalition that won the plurality of the seats in the Saeima. The October 1995 parliamentary election diminished the party's strength by three seats, but it still remained an important political force in a somewhat fragmented parliament.

AGRICULTURE (Latv. **LAUKSAIMNIECĪBA**) . Agriculture permeated the lives of virtually all inhabitants of the Latvian territory until the mid-nineteenth century. Upwards of 90 percent of the population were peasants, and those social groups that were not tillers of the soil (such as the land-owning aristocracy and urban merchants and craftsmen) derived much of their wealth from the sale of or trade in agricultural products. Throughout the centuries before the nineteenth, agriculture in the Latvian lands was practiced on isolated farmsteads rather than villages, although the latter were not unknown and in fact was the dominant settlement pattern in the southeastern areas of the territory, especially Latgale (q.v.). From the sixteenth century onward, farmsteads belonged to landed estates and their inhabitants were serfs (q.v.), which meant that farmsteads and all rural activities were submitted to the discipline of estate agriculture with its obligatory peasant labor and other feudal dues.

On these estates, agriculture was relatively undifferentiated, the principal crops being rye, barley, oats, and other grains. In addition to these, the traditional crops included flax, the products from which were as important for rural self-sufficiency as for export. Two- and three-field systems existed through out the territory, and continued to be important well into the modern era. The horse, rather than the ox, was the principal draught animal, and all Latvian peasant farms possessed as well cows, sheep, pigs, and to a lesser extent goats. With the early nineteenth century and the penetration into eastern Europe of ideas from the western socalled agricultural revolution, crops (potatoes and clover), tilling techniques (improved plows), and land utilization (consolidation of fields) became more varied, albeit very slowly. The landowning elites in the Baltic tended to be conservative in spite of the fact that since the sixteenth century they had thought of their properties as producing not only for local consumption but also for both short- and long-distance trade.

Yet, the nineteenth century did break with the past in several very radical ways. Latvian serfs were emancipated (q.v.) in the 1816-1819 period and in the 1850s the landowners agreed that the now-free peasants should be able to buy outright the land they farmed. Land purchase lasted until World War I and had two consequences: the appearance of a new class of Latvian rural landowners, a large portion of them smallholders, and the revelation that, as long as the Baltic German (q.v.) landed nobility retain ownership of most farmland (just over 50 percent by 1914), a landless class of paid agricultural laborers would also continue to grow. Thus, while in absolute figures agricultural productivity increased until World War I, the social basis of the agricultural system was riven with conflicts and simmering resentments.

These conflicts were resolved by the creation of the Latvian state in 1918 and the agrarian reform (q.v.) it carried out starting in the 1920s. But the resolution was paid for with a drop in agricultural productivity. To wartime disruption, especially in Courland province, which was occupied by the German army, was added the massive adjustments required by the estimated 144,000 new smallholders created by the agrarian reform. The reform required massive state investments in agricultural modernization,and by the late 1930s mechanized cultivation was expanding rapidly. But rural electrification was expensive and did not begin in earnest until the completion of the Ķegums hydroelectric station on the Daugava River (q.v.) in 1939. Agricultural productivity did not reach pre-World War I levels until the second half of the 1930s, by which time Latvia had also developed a brisk export market for its agriculture, especially in dairy products.

Since in World War II Latvian territory was again on the eastern front, the 1940-1945 period brought the inevitable disruption of productivity and a reversal of the gains made before the war. An even greater upheaval was caused by agricultural collectivization (q.v.), which the Soviet Latvian government began in 1948 and concluded in the early 1950s when the process had created some 4,500 collective farms and had virtually eliminated the traditional system of privately owned farmsteads. Agriculture was now to operate according to the dictates and quotas of central Moscow planners.

Because of the widespread falsification of production statistics in the Soviet period, the relative success of the collective farm system is difficult to assess at this time. Mechanization of cultivation continued apace, and rural electrification was nearly universal by the 1980s. The per-hectare crop yield fluctuated over the decades, but did increase in aggregate terms in the 1955-1985 period. The increase of yield, however, has to be balanced by a substantial increase of wastage, due to inadequacies in mechanized harvesting, storage, and transportation. The most efficiently administered collective farms were models of modern agriculture; on the other hand, the small private plots farm families were allowed to maintain outside the collective system also showed greater productivity than the collectively worked fields. By the early 1980s collectivized agriculture in Latvia was demonstrating an inability to change, and even internal critics had begun to talk in terms of an agricultural crisis for which Mikhail Gorbachev's perestroika (restructuring) policy was to be a solution. Before such restructuring could be implemented, however, Latvia regained its independence in 1991.

As in other sectors of the economy, the new government's policy in agriculture since 1991 has consisted of privatization of farmland and the gradual freeing of prices. These changes, constituting a transition period, have resulted in a decline of agricultural (as well as industrial) productivity, but not to the extent of threatening Latvia's ability to produce its own food supply. Virtually all collective farms have been broken up, land nationalized in the 1940s has been returned to those claiming original ownership, and the most successful collectives have become privately owned joint-stock companies. Though many individual farmers continue to look to the government for directives about how much to plant, others have become adept at working in the context of an unplanned agriculture. Continuing state subsidies of various kinds have resulted in some agricultural products (such as meat products) being unable to compete with cheaper products imported from, for example, Poland and Hungary. As Latvia's general economy achieves tighter connections with the rest of Europe, farmers will feel the effects of greater competition and the government will be faced with the prospect of retreating from the free trade principle it has practiced so far.

AIZSARGI. Derived from the Latvian verb *sargāt*--to protect or guard. The "home guard" or "national guard" organization was created by the provisional government of Latvia in 1919 at a time when civilian authorities were not numerous enough to provide security to local inhabitants, especially in rural areas. At the beginning, service in the Aizsargi was mandatory for all males between the ages of 16 and 60, and each county (*pagasts*) was to have an Aizsargi unit. In early 1922, service was changed to a volunteer basis, and after 1925 women were accepted into the organization as well. During the rest of the interwar independence period, the Aizsargi served a wide variety of functions, such as guarding the railroad network and seacoast areas and intercepting contraband goods at borders. The Aizsargi had a quasi-military organization, usually trained with the Latvian army, and had as their commander-in-chief the president of the country.

They played a significant role in the 1934 coup of Kārlis Ulmanis (q.v.) and in his subsequent authoritarian government from 1934 to 1940. In 1940, in the last months of independent Latvia, the Aizsargi numbered about 68,000 persons. The new communist government of Latvia dissolved the Aizsargi organization in July 1940, deporting some 80 percent of its officers to Siberia. During the German occupation from 1941 to 1944 the Aizsargi were revived by the occupation authorities, but dispersed throughout the German army and police units. In 1990, as Latvia's government began the process of exiting from the Soviet Union, the Aizsargi organization was revived with approximately the same "home guard" functions.

AKURĀTERS, JĀNIS (1876-1937). A Latvian writer who became prominent in the last decade of the nineteenth century, particularly in the period surrounding the 1905 Revolution in Latvia. He wrote both poetry and prose, and in his prose works described in great detail the everyday life and psychological state of the people in the lower layers of society (e.g., *The Farmhand's Summer*). In his political writings he defended the idea of a Latvian state and Latvian rights to self-determination. In 1937, he was awarded the Fatherland Medal for his cultural accomplishments.

ALCOHOL. Judging from folkloric evidence, before the eighteenth century the most widespread alcoholic drinks among Latvians were beers of various kinds, including mead. With the eighteenth century, however, grain alcohol, apparently introduced from Russia and Poland, became widely popular and readily available. Estate owners obtained a monopoly over its preparation and used it as an additional source of income in the form of local and export sales. The spread of grain alcohol was accompanied by the proliferation of the rural taverns (*krogi*) so that by the end of the nineteenth century there were altogether 1,301 alcohol-dispensing taverns in Livonia (Vidzeme) and 664 in Courland (Kurzeme) (qq.v.). In Vidzeme there was one tavern for every 31 farmsteads.

The government of interwar independent Latvia retained a monopoly over the sales of hard alcohol, but left its preparation in private hands. From the late nineteenth century onward, the use of alcohol among Latvians has been combatted by various kinds of antialcohol and temperance movements. Alcoholism became a serious social and health problem among Latvians starting with the eighteenth century, and in recent decades it has played a major role in the decline of life expectancy in Latvia, particularly among males.

ALKSNIS, JĒKABS (1897-1938). One of a number of military officers in the Latvian Rifle Regiments (q.v.) who supported and defended the Bolshevik (q.v.) cause during the Russian Civil War and remained in the military establishment of the Soviet Union after the founding of the Latvian state in 1918. He was arrested and executed in 1938, during Stalin's purge of the Soviet military establishment, but was "rehabilitated" in the period of Khrushchev's thaw.

ALSUNGA. A district in central Courland (q.v.) that in the seventeenth century, when Courland was a semiautonomous duchy, became Roman Catholic in what was otherwise an almost entirely Lutheran province. This pocket of Roman Catholicism (q.v.) was created by the local landowner von Schwerin in 1623 when he converted from Lutheranism (q.v.). In subsequent centuries the foklore of the district continued to reflect its religious uniqueness, and its inhabitants came to be called *suīti*, a corruption of the Latvian term *jezuīti* (Jesuits).

ALUNĀNS, ĀDOLFS (1848-1912). The "father" of the Latvian theater, who began his acting career in the 1860s working for various German-language theater companies in the Baltic provinces (q.v.). As director of the Riga Latvian Theater from 1870 to 1885, he popularized theater arts among Latvian urban and rural audiences, wrote plays in Latvian, and oversaw the first production of many of them. From 1896 to 1904 he headed his own theater company in Riga and during the last decade of his life remained a prominent figure in that city's Latvian cultural scene.

ALUNĀNS, JURIS (1832-1864). Together with Krišjānis Valdemārs (q.v.) and Krišjānis Barons (q.v.), Alunāns was the best-known nationalist activist of the early phase of the Latvian "national awakening" (q.v.) He was a poet, but also devoted much of his creative energies to translating poetry into Latvian in an effort to demonstrate that the Latvian language was sufficiently developed to express the thoughts and sentiments of the poetry of other nations. In fact, the appearance of his first publication of original and translated poetry--*Dziesmiņas* (Poems) (1856)--is conventionally used to date the beginning of the Latvian "national awakening" in the nineteenth century. Somewhat later, in 1862, Alunāns and Valdemārs founded the *Pēterburgas Avīzes* (q.v.), the newspaper that became the principal vehicle of the Latvian nationalist challenge to Baltic German politico-economic and cultural hegemony in the Latvian area of the Baltic provinces (q.v.).

APGABALI. The main administrative divisions of Latvia during the interwar period. There were altogether five *apgabali*--Riga, Vidzeme, Kurzeme, Zemgale, and Latgale (qq.v.)--and each of these was subdivided into five or six *apriņķi*, which were normally named for the largest city in each. *Apriņķi* were subdivided into *pagasti*, which were the smallest administrative units in Latvia. In 1950, the government of Soviet Latvia devised a new administrative system, dissolving the *apgabali* and *apriņķi* and introducing *rajoni*. There is a strong likelihood that the government of post-1991 independent Latvia will return to the interwar system of regional and local administration.

APSĪTIS, JĒKABS (1858-1929). Pseudonym for the Latvian writer Jānis Jaunzemis, who began his literary career in the 1880s and brought into Latvian belles lettres a theme of piety and religiosity stemming from the Moravian Brethren (Herrnhut) (q.v.) tradition. The positive characters of his stories were pure-in-heart rural people, uncorrupted by urban ways and at one with nature. To portray such types, he had to stress what he believed to be the negative aspects of urban life such as greed, self-centeredness, and dishonesty. Apsītis's conservatism in the 1890s was overwhelmed by the more forceful and prolific "new current" (q.v.) in Latvian writing, and he wrote virtually nothing after the turn of the twentieth century. Nonetheless, the nonacceptance of modernity and the idealization of rural virtues continued as one of the main themes of Latvian writing throughout the twentieth century.

ARKLS. This word in modern Latvian means "plow," but historically the word also signified a measure of the value of land and is the conventional translation of the German term--*Haken*--

for such a measure. It is virtually impossible historically to establish the areal equivalent of an *arkls* (*Haken*) because the term normally referred to how much a piece of land worked with one horse-drawn plow (or a similar piece of equipment) could produce. Thus, a farmstead could be revalued from one survey to the next depending upon a determination of the value of what was produced on the arable whose areal size did not change. Over the centuries, there were numerous surveys (*Hakenrevisionen*) of farmland in the Latvian territories from the medieval period onward, but historical interpretations of them have varied because of the absence of conventional interpretations of the basic meaning of *arkls*.

ĀRONS, MATĪSS (1858-1939). A prominent journalist who began his career in the late "national awakening" (q.v.) period, Ārons worked for the newspaper *Dienas Lapa* (q.v.) (1891-1894) and then in succession edited the journal *Austrums* (q.v.) (1895-1902) and the newspapers *Balss* (1906-1907), *Dzimtenes Vēstnesis* (1910-1917), and *Valdības Vēstnesis* (1920-1937).

ASPĀZIJA (1865-1943). Pseudonym for the Latvian writer Elza Rozenberga, who was born to well-to-do farmer parents in Courland (q.v.), and very early after her secondary education (in 1884) began a writing career that spanned the next six decades. She became known primarily for her poetry and plays, with her early drama seizing on fin-de-siècle conflicts in the Baltic and transforming them into controversial art that offended conservative members of the Latvian intelligentsia but pleased the participants of the "new current" (q.v.) of the 1890s. Her first play (*Atriebēja* [*The Avenging Woman*]), 1888) dealt with Baltic social conflict; her later plays (e.g., *Zaudētās Tiesības* [*Lost Rights*], 1894), *Sidraba Šķidrauts* [*The Silver Veil*], 1905) stressed women's rights themes in the manner of Ibsen and Strindberg.

Her friendship with and 1897 marriage to Jānis Rainis (q.v.) (her first marriage ended in divorce) continued to turn her toward "new current" ideas, and after the 1905 unrest in the Baltic both she and Rainis chose exile in Switzerland, returning to Latvia in 1920. Immediately thereafter they were both elected to the Constitutional Convention formulating the basic document of the new Latvian state. In Switzerland Aspāzija had continued to work at both her poetry and drama and this creativity continued after her return to Latvia, though in this later period her themes were increasingly drawn from her own childhood memories and Latvian history and mythology. She remained a revered figure in Latvian literary culture during the 1930s (Rainis had died in 1929), and her last poetry collections appeared in 1942 and 1943 by which time Latvia had already been occupied by the armed forces of Hitler's Third Reich.

AUGŠZEME. Before 1918, the extreme southeastern part of the old Baltic province of Courland (q.v.). After 1918, when Courland was divided into Kurzeme (western half) and Zemgale (eastern half), Augšzeme became the southeasternmost region of Zemgale. It was also in the medieval centuries the home territory of the Selonians (q.v.). The inhabitants of Augšzeme spoke and still to some extent speak an identifiable dialect of the Latvian language.

AUSEKLIS. Perhaps the best known of the various temperance organizations in pre-World War I Latvian territory, Ausēklis was distinctively progressive in its political philosophy and, as an organization, became a leading advocate in the 1905 Revolution in the Baltic provinces (q.v.) of the democratization of the Baltic provincial and Russian political system.

AUSEKLIS. Pseudonym for Miķelis Krogzemis (1850-1879) who, in his relatively short lifetime, became the best-known poet of the Latvian "national awakening" (q.v.) in the second half of the nineteenth century. The son of a farmstead head, he studied for a while (1868-1871) in the teachers' training school headed by Jānis Cimze in Valka, and thereafter worked irregularly as a rural schoolteacher and tutor in Vidzeme as well as outside the Baltic provinces (q.v.). His temperamental nature and uncompromising stance on Latvian cultural matters evidently made it difficult for him to hold jobs for very long, but his publications appeared very regularly.

From the beginning of his literary career Auseklis showed himself to be a fiery Latvian nationalist in the romantic spirit and an opponent of self-Germanization among the Latvians, with his poetry celebrating Latvian history, folklore, and mythology. He also composed choral music, contributed hundreds of shorter pieces to the Latvian newspapers of the time, and authored various kinds of teaching materials for secondary and elementary schools. He tended to picture the cultural conflicts in the Baltic area as wars of the spirit, and his poetry used elaborate symbolism to promise the eventual reemergence of the Latvian "castle of light" after centuries of oppression.

AUSTRUMS. The best-known monthly Latvian-language magazine published from 1885 to 1906, first in Moscow by the group of Latvians organized in that city by Krišjānis Valdemārs (q.v.) and then in various Latvian cities of the Baltic provinces (q.v.). In the first ten years of its existence it was virtually the only regularly appearing publication that carried on the momentum of the Latvian "national awakening" (q.v.) of the 1860s and 1870s. *Austrums* was edited for the first 18 years by the Latvian philologist Jēkabs Velme, and thereafter by Matīss Ārons, Teodors Zeiferts, and Andrievs Niedra (qq.v.).

AUZIŅŠ, IMANTS (1937-   ). Having received his higher education at the University of Latvia, from the early 1960s onward Auziņš developed a strong reputation as a poet, literary scholar, and officer of the Latvian Writers' Union (q.v.), which he chaired starting in 1989. In his earlier works, rural themes predominated, but he occasionally also published collections that lamented the fate of Latvians caught between larger and expansionistic neighbors. As many other literary artists of his generation, Auziņš wrote during a period (the so-called stagnation era) when expression of controversial thoughts had to be veiled so as not to incur the charge of "bourgeois nationalism."

- B -

BALODIS, JĀNIS (1881-1965). Before World War I, Balodis was an officer in the Russian army while remaining interested in Latvian political events. After Latvian independence in 1918, he played an active role not only in the Latvian "independence war" but also in Latvian public affairs generally. In 1920, he assumed the rank of general in the Latvian national army and continued his military service until 1940. As a "political general" he served as minister of war in the 1930s, and was one of the organizers of the 1934 coup that brought to power in Latvia the authoritarian government of Kārlis Ulmanis (q.v.). He worked closely with Ulmanis until he was dismissed from office in 1938. In 1940, after the occupation of Latvia by the Soviet army, he was deported to the Soviet interior where he lived in exile and under arrest until being permitted to return to Latvia in 1965.

BALTIC ENTENTE. An agreement signed by Estonia, Latvia, and Lithuania in September 1934 calling for cooperation and consultation of the three countries in the formulation of foreign policy, as well as for periodic meetings of the three countries' foreign ministers. The agreement had been launched earlier in that year by a similar bilateral treaty between Latvia and Estonia. The Vilnius and Klaipeda questions--of immense significance for Lithuania-Polish relations--were excluded from the treaty so as not to impact on relations between Estonia and Poland and Latvia and Poland. The regular Foreign Ministers' meetings began in December 1934, and during the next several years there were indications that other countries were ready to accept the entente as a reality.

BALTIC GERMANS (also **GERMAN BALTS**). The English term used to designate those inhabitants of the Baltic area who spoke German most of the time and identified themselves as being of German nationality. In the history of the Latvian territory, the term ceased to have major significance in 1939, when the vast majority of the Baltic Germans in Latvia emigrated to Germany proper, where in post-World War II years they sought to maintain their unique historical identity through organizations and specialized publications. Before 1939, however, the Baltic Germans had played a major role in the history of the Latvian territory from the twelfth century onward. An element in the German *Drang nach Osten* of the medieval period, the German-speakers defeated and subordinated the indigenous peoples of the Latvian region and created the medieval state of Livonia (q.v.), in which they became the dominant military, landowning, and cultural elites. Though sovereignty over the Latvian territories changed during the subsequent centuries--from Polish-Lithuanian, to Swedish, to Russian--the Baltic Germans managed to retain their elite status with its special privileges.

While having age-old divisions among themselves--especially between the landed nobilities and the urban patriciates--the Baltic Germans were drawn together by the Russification (q.v.) policies of the czarist government in the second half of the nineteenth century, which was also the period of the Latvian "national awakening" (q.v.). Until World War I, Latvian nationalism portrayed Baltic German privileges as at least an equal if not a greater threat to Latvian national aspirations than was the autocracy of the czarist government. The single most damaging blow to Baltic German standing in Latvia was, of course, the founding of the Latvian state in 1918, but, within that framework, materially the most damaging event was the Agrarian Reform Law (q.v.) of 1920 under which the new Latvian government confiscated without compensation the landed estates of the Baltic German population, thus bringing to an end what had been a virtual Baltic German landowning monopoly in the Latvian territories.

BALTIC LANGUAGES. A branch of Indoeuropean languages, the Baltic language group normally includes Latvian and Lithuanian, which are living languages, and Old Prussian, which used to be spoken by inhabitants of the Baltic seacoast area roughly southwest of Lithuania but ceased to be a living language by the end of the seventeenth century.

BALTIC MILITARY DISTRICT (BMD). The BMD was established in 1945 as an organizational subunit of the Soviet Army. Territorially it included the Estonian, Latvian, and Lithuanian republics as well as the Kalinigrad oblast, and the headquarters of the BMD were in Riga (q.v.). Because of the proximity and the need for mutual cooperation, the BMD headquarters staff developed over time a very close working relationship with the upper levels of the Latvian Communist Party (q.v.) and the Latvian government organs. The meaning of the BMD for Latvian history lay not only in the fact that the Soviet military presence served as a symbolic support for civilian authorities but also in the byproducts of this military presence, because numerous Soviet military officers, upon retirement, chose to remain in Latvia. When the Soviet Union disintegrated after the abortive 1991 coup, the presence of the Soviet (now Russian) armed forces in Latvia became a legacy of the Soviet system that the new Latvian government now had to deal with.

BALTIC PROVINCES. Strictly speaking, the "Baltic provinces" in the Russian Empire were the three provinces of Estland, Livland and Kurland (qq.v.) (*Estlyandskaya guberna, Liflyandsaka guberna, Kurlyandsakay guberna*), the populations of which included only the Estonians and the Latvians of the Baltic region. Though Lithuania in the twentieth century is normally included in the "Baltic states," before 1918 they were not "Balts" in the administrative sense. Neither were the Letgallians (q.v.), whose districts were included in the new Latvian state after 1918, since the Letgallians before that date lived in Vitebsk province, adjoining Livland.

BALTIC REVIEW. The name of the trilingual journal that was supposed to have been published as a byproduct of the Baltic Entente (q.v.) of 1934. The first issue of the *Review*, however, did not appear until February 1940, when it was used as one piece of "evidence" by the Soviet Union that the three Baltic states had created a military alliance against the USSR. Several other publications of that name were published after World War I, the most significant of which was the official publication of the Baltic Humanitarian Association.

BALTIC UNIVERSITY (BU). An institution of higher learning founded in 1946 in Hamburg, in the British Zone of occupied Germany, by academics in the Estonian, Latvian, and Lithuanian refugee communities. In 1947, the BU was moved to Pinneberg where it continued its work with the help of 53 professors, 50 docents, and 48 lecturers who were organized into nine "faculties" (departments) (philology, law and economics, mathematics and natural sciences, agriculture, medicine, architecture and engineering, chemistry, mechanics, and art). In 1946, the BU was teaching 996 students; in 1947 1,052 students; but, in 1949, only 468 students. In 1949 the BU was closed after nine semesters of work, by decision of the British military authorities. By that time it had granted 50 diplomas, largely to students who had begun their studies during the war in their homelands. Many students who were instructed at the BU transferred to German universities and finished their degrees there.

BALTIJAS VESTNESIS (BV). Baltijas Vēstnesis (*Baltic Messenger*) was published from 1868 until 1906. It was the successor to the *Pēterburgas Avīzes* (q.v.) in furthering the goals of the Latvian "national awakening" (q.v.), which task it performed well though in a less confrontational way. Its editorial positions reflected the viewpoint of the Riga Latvian Association (q.v.), which was founded in the same year. First appearing twice weekly, in 1880 it became a daily newspaper. Closed by czarist authorities in 1906, the BV found lineal successors in the newspapers *Balss (Voice)* and *Dzimtenes Vēstnesis (Homeland Courier)*. Representing a moderate nationalist point of view, the BV opposed what it saw to be the excesses of the "new current" (q.v.). Its founder and editor until 1892 was Bernhards Dīriķis (q.v.).

BANGERSKIS, RUDOLFS (1878-1958). Bangerskis became a general in the Latvian national army in 1925, but before that, starting in 1915, he was an officer in a number of the Latvian Rifle Regiments (q.v.) of the czarist army as well as in the army of the

"White" general Kolchak. After the defeat of Kolchak in the Russian civil war, Bangerskis returned to Latvia and assumed a series of high-level commands in the Latvian army during the interwar period. He served as minister of war during 1928 and 1929. During the Second World War and the German occupation of Latvia, Bangerskis worked in the "self-government" (q.v.) that the German authorities permitted Latvians to form, and from 1943 to 1945 he was the inspector general of the Latvian Legion (q.v.), one of a number of non-German military units attached to the Waffen-SS. In 1945, Bangerskis emigrated to Germany and lived there until his death in 1958.

BAPTISTS. Among Latvians, Baptist congregations first appeared in the seaport city of Liepāja (q.v.) in the 1850s and experienced a moderate rise in their numbers during the second half of the nineteenth century. Initially opposed by the Russian authorities as well as by the Lutheran Church (q.v.) in the Baltic provinces, the Baptists obtained the rights of a recognized confession in 1879. By the first decade of Latvian independence, there were some 89 Baptist congegrations in Latvia in spite of the fact that a large number of Latvian Baptists in the early 1920s emigrated to Brazil, where in the 1950s their numbers still approached about 2,000. Some 2,500 Baptists left Latvia in 1944, together with other Latvian refugees. Starting with the 1989-1990 events, Baptist congregations have experienced a revival in Latvia, where they now enjoy complete freedom of religion.

BĀRDA, FRICIS (1880-1919). Bārda received his elementary and secondary schooling in Latvia and afterward became a schoolteacher and a budding poet. His poetry appeared in the period between the revolutions of 1905 and 1917, but Bārda remained an apolitical poet, unlike most of the leading Latvian poets of this era. Bārda was attracted by the German romantic tradition and became its leading exponent in the pre-World War I Latvian cultural world. His poetry remained very popular during the interwar period, but remained largely unknown during the Soviet period because of its individualism and sometimes mystical symbolism.

BARONS, KRIŠJĀNIS (1835-1923). Barons was born in Courland (q.v.), the son of a bailiff on a landed estate, and received an elementary and secondary education not atypical of aspiring Latvian youths of his generation. In 1856, he enrolled at Dorpat (Tartu)

University, where he, Krišjānis Valdemārs (q.v.), and others began to meet regularly to discuss the consequences of their determination to be considered "Latvians." These and other meetings like them in the decades between c. 1855-1875 formed the core of the so-called Latvian "national awakening" (q.v.), which changed not only the individual self-perception of its participants but also the collective consciousness of many Latvian-speakers of the Russian Baltic Provinces (q.v.). Barons was an early participant of the movement, having started his activities in Dorpat and continuing them at St. Petersburg University where he resumed his studies after 1862. In St. Petersurg, Barons, Valdemārs, and Juris Alunāns (q.v.) edited and published a newspaper called *Pēterburgas Avīzes* (*St. Petersburg Newspaper*), which was among the few Latvian-language periodical publications of the time that directly challenged Baltic German (q.v.) cultural and political hegemony of the Baltic provinces and as a result was closed by czarist authorities in 1865.

After these events Barons lived almost continuously in various places outside the Baltic in Russia, working as a private tutor and periodically writing pieces for the Latvian-language press. In the late 1870s he took over from Fricis Brīvzemnieks (q.v.) the task of collecting, sorting, and arranging the Latvian *dainas* (q.v.)--the typical four-line Latvian folk song. His efforts in this domain of the Latvian oral tradition established his image in the history of Latvian culture. In 1893, he returned to Riga (q.v.) and in the period 1894-1915 published a six-volume *daina* collection (containing 217,996 songs), which fixed the *daina* as the centerpiece of Latvian folklore, inviting analysis and further collecting activity. By the time Barons died in the early years of the first Latvian republic, the study of the *daina* had become the central preoccupation of Latvian folklorists, and his memory was linked perhaps more to it than to his earlier activism as a "national awakener."

BAUMANIS, KĀRLIS (1835-1905). Baumanis participated in the Latvian "national awakening" (q.v.) in the nineteenth century as an activist but, relatively speaking, as a minor figure, because his real interests lay in music and composition. He composed much of the Latvian choral music that was sung by his contemporaries. One of his compositions, done in 1873-- "Dievs, svētī Latviju" (God, Save Latvia)--eventually became and remained the anthem of the Latvian national state.

BELS, ALBERTS (1938-   ). After a somewhat disjointed series of jobs that had little to do with literature, Bels emerged as a serious and talented writer in 1966 with a collection of stories and was accepted for membership in the Latvian Writers' Union (q.v.) in the same year. During the next three decades, his productivity grew and some of his novels represented a stylistic turn in Latvian writing by employing the stream of consciousness method of presentation and dealing with the harsh realities of life in Soviet Latvia. As so many writers of his generation, Bels was frequently challenging the limits of officially permitted expression both in style and content. In 1990, he was elected to the Latvian Supreme Soviet, as a deputy from the Popular Front (q.v.).

BELŠĒVICA, VIZMA (1931 -   ). Belšēvica is among the most accomplished and respected poets and literary figures in Latvia. Born and educated in Riga (q.v.) with additional study in 1961 at the Gorky Institute in Moscow, she began to publish poetry in the late 1940s but really did not hit her stride until the mid-1950s with the publication of her first book of poems. From the beginning her poetry exhibited a preoccupation with the connection between personality and society and with the problems of self-esteem and national consciousness. Such themes meant, predictably, that a strong undercurrent of her work from the 1960s onward was a critique of the despoliation of Latvian culture by the Soviet Russian presence: "Shout, my nation! Twist in your agony! I will continue to pour salt into your wounds so that you will forget nothing! Turn your pain into sanctified hatred, which is holier than the gentleness of forgiveness." Though such direct language tended to be unusual for the times, Belšēvica belongs to the first post-Stalinist literary generation in whose mature work worry over the future of Latvian culture and language continues very close to the surface.

BENDRUPE, MIRDZA (1910 -   ). Bendrupe belonged to a generation of literary artists who began to write and publish during the independence period in the late 1930s but for various reasons chose not to or were unable to emigrate in the last years of World War II and therefore continued their literary careers in Latvia during the Soviet period. Her poetry and prose tended toward philosophical treatments of their subject matter, and she also became known as a translator into Latvian of the classical writers of Russian literature as well as a writer of poems and stories for children.

BENJĀMIŅŠ, ANTONS (1860-1939). Though he worked for various newspapers in Latvia before World War I, Benjāmiņš became famous (and wealthy) in the interwar period as publisher (with his wife, Emīlija) of *Jaunākās Ziņas* (*Daily News*) (from 1919) and the popular magazine *Atpūta* (from 1924), both of which were the largest publications of their type during the 1918-1940 period. Both publications were stopped in 1940 by the new Communist government. Antons Benjāmiņš died in 1939, and his wife was deported to Siberia in 1941.

BERGS, ARVĒDS (1875-1942). Bergs's lifetime spanned the crucial decades of pre-independence Latvian political activity as well as the interwar independence period, and he remained an active participant in virtually all the important events of his time. From 1918 to 1921, he served as the interior minister of the provisional government of the new Latvian state, and was a member of the Constitutional Convention as well as of the Latvian Saeima (q.v.) (parliament) in the 1920s. In 1921, he founded a political party called the National Center Party and, from 1921 to 1934 was the publisher of the increasingly ultranationalist newspaper *Latvis*. Generally speaking, in the interwar independence period he became one of the leading figures of the ultranationalist right wing of the Latvian political spectrum and, in 1941, together with many of his political allies, he was deported to Siberia by the Soviet authorities.

BERKLAVS, EDUĀRDS (1914-). Berklavs was an active member of the illegal (and therefore underground) Latvian Communist Party (q.v.) during the late 1930s, and began to play an increasingly active role in party affairs in Latvia after the Second World War. Sometime during the later 1940s and early 1950s, as he reports, his views on the viability of communism began to change, but he remained an important figure in the Latvian party. In the 1950s, he was deputy chairman of the Council of Ministers of the Latvian SSR, which position he (and like-minded) colleagues used to challenge what to them appeared to be a systematic Russification (q.v.) of Latvia. Such opposition led in 1959 to a purge of the Latvian party of "bourgeois nationalists," and Berklavs and numerous others were exiled to other parts of the Soviet Union until 1968. Returning to Latvia, he resumed life as an ordinary laborer but at the same time participated in various surreptitious actions against Russian hegemony in Latvia.

Berklavs reemerged in the public eye in 1988 as a founder of the Latvian National Independence Movement (LNNK) and of the Latvian Popular Front (q.v.) (in which he was a member of the board of directors). In the political spectrum of the perestroika period, Berklavs's LNNK was on the "right wing." demanding immediate independence for Latvia and the elimination of all Communist influences from Latvian affairs. Berklavs was elected a deputy to the 1990 Supreme Soviet (q.v.), which governed Latvia during the last years of the existence of the USSR and the first two years of regained Latvian independence. In 1993, he was elected on the LNNK ticket to the Latvian Saeima (q.v.), the renewed Latvian parliament.

BĒRZIŅŠ, ALFRĒDS (1899-1977). From the beginning of his political career in the late 1920s, Bērziņš was an influential member of the Agrarian Union (q.v.), the second largest political party in the interwar independence period (the largest was the Latvian Social Democratic Party (q.v.). The Union was dominated by its long-term leader Kārlis Ulmanis (q.v.), who, in 1934, organized a successful coup as a result of which the parliament was dismissed and all political parties disbanded. Bērziņš remained an Ulmanis loyalist and served in Ulmanis' personally chosen cabinets as interior minister (1934-1937) and as minister of social affairs (1937-1940). Fleeing from Latvia to Germany in 1940 when the Soviet occupation of the country began, Bērziņš remained active in the political affairs of the Latvian DPs in Germany after the war and in the Latvian émigré community in the United States after 1950.

BĒRZIŅŠ, JĀNIS (1889-1938). An active supporter of the Latvian Bolsheviks (q.v.) in the World War I period, Bērziņš assumed a series of important posts in the government of the USSR. From 1920, he helped establish the organs of Soviet military intelligence and, during the 1920s and 1930s, served in various capacities in the Soviet intelligence establishment. He also acted as a political representative of Soviet interests in the Spanish Civil War, but was executed in 1938 during Stalin's purges.

BIBLE (See ERNST GLÜCK).

BIELENSTEIN, AUGUST (1826-1907). Bielenstein was a Baltic German Lutheran (q.v.) minister and a leading intellectual of the German-speaking world of the Baltic provinces (q.v.) In the second half of the nineteenth century, producing numerous important publications dealing with the language and ethnography of the Latvian people (see Bibliography). He was chairman of the Lettisch-Literarische from 1864-1895 and a corresponding member of the St. Petersburg Academy of Sciences from 1890. Because the decades during which he was prominent coincided with the period of the Latvian "national awakening" (q.v.), the relations between Bielenstein and his Latvian-speaking contemporaries were strained and at times became antagonistic, though in due course even the Latvian nationalists recognized Bielenstein's accomplishments on behalf of Latvian self-understanding.

BIEZBĀRDIS, KASPARS (1806-1886). Biezbārdis was a well-known activist of the Latvian "national awakening" (q.v.), even though the range of his activities did not bring him into the first rank of that movement. He was particularly interested in the material circumstances of the Latvian peasantry in the middle decades of the nineteenth century and wrote several influential works on that theme, criticizing in them the monopoly over land and political power enjoyed by the Baltic Germans (q.v.).

BIĶERNIEKI FOREST. A forested area on the outskirts of Riga (q.v.) that in the pre-1940 period was frequently the site for the meetings of various illegal left-wing organizations. Then, in the period of German occupation (1941-1944), it became one of several execution sites of Jews and opponents of the German regime. It is estimated that in the German occupation period, some 46,000 persons, mostly Jews, were killed at this site.

BĪLMANIS, ALFRĒDS (1887-1948). For most of his professional life Bīlmanis worked as a diplomat for the Latvian interwar state, serving from 1932 to 1935 as the Latvian ambassador to the USSR and from 1935 to 1940 as the ambassador to the U.S. In 1940, with the occupation of Latvia by the Soviet army, the last president of the country, Kārlis Ulmanis (q.v.), granted Bīlmanis (and other Latvian ambassadors in Western countries) authority to continue to act on behalf of the pre-Soviet Latvian state. These grants of authority had considerable significance in those countries that did not recognize the incorporation of the Baltic states into the Soviet Union. Bīlmanis remained in charge of the Latvian Legation in the United States until his death in 1948, publishing a series of books on the history of Latvia and on the international ramifications of the Soviet seizure of the Baltic lands.

BIRKAVS, VALDIS (1942-   ). Birkavs graduated from the Faculty of Law at the University of Latvia in 1969 with a degree in jurisprudence, and received his doctorate in this specialty in 1993. An activist in the Latvian Popular Front (q.v.), Birkavs was elected to the reformist Supreme Soviet in 1990 and in January 1992 became deputy president of what was then still called the Supreme Council (i.e., parliament). In the 1993 parliamentary election--the first since 1934--he was a candidate in the Latvia's Way (q.v.) list, which won a 36-seat plurality. In July 1993 Birkavs was asked to form a coalition cabinet in which he assumed the position of prime minister, a position he held until July 1994 when the coalition split and he resigned. His leadership of a center-right cabinet continued the transition policies of the 1990-1993 transition government, as Latvia continued to move toward a free-market economy, finally passed a citizenship law, and began to fully participate in the transnational political structures of Europe such as the Nordic Council. Birkavs continued to serve as foreign minister in the cabinet that succeeded his.

BLAUMANIS, RUDOLFS (1863-1908). One of the preeminent Latvian writers in the period before 1918 and one of the founders of modern Latvian literature (q.v.). Blaumanis was born into a Latvian rural family, but received virtually all of his elementary and secondary education in the German language. In 1887, he came to Riga (q.v.) in order to participate in the social and literary activities of the growing Latvian community there. For reasons of health, however, during the next 20 years he alternated residences between Riga (q.v.) and the countryside. From 1882, when he published his first poem (in German), Blaumanis countinued to write in all genres of Latvian literature except the novel.

   In poetry, short stories, and especially in drama, his productivity was exemplary and, though the quality of his work was uneven, in each of these areas several of his creations have stood the test of time and changing popular tastes to become classics of Latvian literature. With respect to the theater, Latvian literary historians judge Blaumanis to have been the first modern Latvian playwright, though for organizational reasons, they also judge Adolfs Alunāns (q.v.) to be the "father" of Latvian theater. Blaumanis wrote mostly lyrical poetry, although some of his most often-quoted poems (e.g., *Tālavas taurētājs*) deal with historical themes. His best plays are set in the late-nineteenth-century Latvian countryside and explore within the context of the farmstead the universal themes of love (*Purvā bridējs*) and generational conflict (*Indrāni*), as well as the lighter side of rural social life (*Skroderdienas Silmačos, Trīnes grēki*). The last years of his productive life were spent in Riga where he played an important role in helping the development and careers of the next generation of Latvian writers.

BĻODNIEKS, ADOLFS (1889-1962). Having received his education at the Riga Polytechnical Institute (q.v.) in the period from 1910 to 1914, Bļodnieks served in the Russian army, but after the Revolution of 1917 helped to organize the military forces of the new Latvian national government. As a participant in the Constitutional Convention, he worked in its Finance and Budget Committee. In 1924, he organized and then led the New Farmers and Smallholders Party, serving in the Saeima (q.v.) as its deputy. From 1933 to 1934, he served as prime minister. In 1944, he emigrated to Germany and, in 1951, to the United States, continuing during the postwar years to play an important role in Latvian émigré politics.

*BOLSHEVIKS (*Latv. BOLŠEVIKI or LIELNIEKI*)*. This wing of the Latvian Social Democratic (q.v.) movement appeared first in 1906 and, taking its cue from the Russian Bolsheviks and V. I. Lenin, repeatedly criticized other Social Democrats for their alleged failure to perceive that the making of revolution necessitated fighting for a "proletarian dictatorship." The influence of the Bolsheviks in Latvian Social Democracy grew, creating internal divisions and sharpening the conflict within the left. By July 1917, the fifth congress of the Latvian Social Democrats was dominated by the Bolshevik wing, and by this time Bolshevik agitators had also become the principal influence on the political thinking of the Latvian Rifle Regiments (q.v.). By the time Latvian independence was proclaimed on November 18, 1918, the Latvian political left was completely divided, with the more moderate and democratic wing generally supporting the idea of an independent Latvia while the Bolsheviks, in December 1918, supported the invasion of Latvian territory by the Red Army and the effort to create a Soviet Latvia.

The Latvian Bolsheviks, led by Pēteris Stučka (q.v.), triumphed briefly during the first half of 1919, when a Latvian Soviet government was created in the Latvian territories not occupied by the German army. By mid-year 1919, this Latvian Bolshevik government and its military force was being expelled from Latvia by the military force supporting the Latvian national government and its German and Estonian allies. After 1919, the most prominent Latvian Bolsheviks and lesser supporters of the Bolshevik cause remained in the Soviet Union, working there in a variety of party and governmental posts and developing a not-inconsiderable Latvian-language émigré cultural world. In the period from 1937 to 1938, a very large proportion of them was executed during Stalin's purge of the "Old Bolsheviks." and their cultural institutions (theaters, publishing houses) were closed.

BRĀĻU DRAUDZE (See MORAVIAN BRETHERN).

BRĪDAKA, LIJA (1932 -). Brīdaka received her higher education at the University of Latvia, and in the mid-1950s began her career as a poet and prose stylist writing about the experiences of women in Soviet Latvian society. She was also employed as a teacher and as an editor, and from 1967 to 1972 worked as a staff member for the Latvian Writers' Union (q.v.).

BRIEDIS, FRIDRICHS (1888-1918). Briedis was an officer in the Russian army from 1909 to 1912 and was later assigned to the headquarters of the 25th Daugavpils (Dvinsk) regiment. In 1915, he was transferred to the Latvian Rifle Regiments (q.v.), where he advanced in the ranks to become a colonel. In 1918, during the formation of the Red Army, he was executed for allegedly participating in an anti-Bolshevik action.

BRĪVZEMNIEKS, FRICIS (1846-1907). Brīvzemnieks was among the youngest of the notable figures of the Latvian "national awakening" (q.v.) and did not begin to leave his mark on the movement with publications until the early 1870s. He was particularly interested in Latvian folklore, especially the four-line Latvian folk song called the *daina* (q.v.). His earliest (1873) publication of these began a genre of Latvian intellectual activity that, in the preindependence period, culminated in Krišjānis Barons' (q.v.) published collection and has continued ever since. Brīvzemnieks also published collections of Latvian proverbs and riddles, and in a series of writings in the magazine *Austrums* (q.v.) explained the importance of folklore for Latvian national identity and the need for systematic collections of it.

BRŪVERS, OLAFS (1947-   ). Brūvers was among the political activists--"dissidents" (q.v.)--who began to challenge various aspects of Soviet rule in Latvia, starting in the mid-1970s. After a technical education, he worked at various jobs and then served in the Soviet army for three years. In 1974, he and his brother Pāvils Brūvers (q.v) prepared a questionnaire dealing with, among other things, conditions in Soviet Latvia. This action led to his arrest and detention and a six-month sentence at a detention camp. His arrest received the attention of Western media and human rights activists and, as a consequence, he was urged to emigrate to the West and did so in 1976, first to Germany and then to the United States.

BRŪVERS, PĀVILS (1949 -). Brūvers was one of the political activists-- "dissidents" (q.v.)--who starting in the mid-1970s began to challenge various aspects of Soviet rule in Latvia. Having received a musical education, Brūvers continued with medical studies, but in 1974, in connection with a questionnaire prepared with his brother Olafs (q.v.) which dealt with conditions in Soviet Latvia, he was arrested and sentenced to one year in jail. He emigrated to Germany with his family in 1977.

BUŠĒVICS, ANSIS (1878-1943). A member of the Latvian Social Democratic Party (q.v.) since its founding in 1904, Bušēvics remained a party activist throughout his lifetime but continued to move increasingly leftward in his attitudes. In the pre-World War I period, he lived in St. Petersburg and was active among Latvian Social Democrats there; during the war he relocated to Tobolsk province; from 1918-1919, he was imprisoned in a concentration camp in Germany. Returning to Latvia after independence, Bušēvics participated in the work of the Latvian National Council and the Constitutional Convention, and was elected to the Saeima (q.v.) (parliament) on the Social Democratic ticket. As a member he was active in the drafting of the Agrarian Reform (q.v.) Law, reputedly one of the most radical of such laws in interwar Europe. Politically inactive during the second half of the 1930s when party activity was not permitted, Bušēvics emerged into prominence again in 1940 and participated in an electoral committee that brought into being the left-dominated parliament that voted to request incorporation into the Soviet Union.

- C -

ČAKLAIS, MĀRIS (1940 -). Having finished his education at the University of Latvia, Čaklais began his career as a journalist, editor, and writer in the early 1960s and maintained an impressively steady output of poetry and prose for the next three decades. He dealt with a variety of themes, including the fate of the Latvian Rifle Regiments (q.v.) in the First World War period and the problems of maintaining a Latvian identity in the modern world. As a translator into Latvian, he worked principally with German and Russian literature. In 1987 he began to serve as editor-in-chief of *Literatūra un Māksla* (*Literature and Art*), the most important cultural periodical in Latvian.

ČAKS, ALEKSANDRS (1901-1950). With the publication of his first collection of poetry in 1928, Čaks became the first unapologetic celebrant of Latvia's urban experience, in contrast with most other Latvian poets who stressed ruralism and general human emotions. Riga (q.v.), the capital city, was particularly the object of Čaks' poetic attention. From 1937 to 1939 he also published a cycle of poems dealing with the war experience of the Latvian Rifle Regiments (q.v.) in the Latvian War of Independence. During the last five years of his life, as resident of what was now the Latvian SSR, Čaks was also forced to write panegyrics to the Communist leadership.

ČAKSTE, JĀNIS (1859-1927). A professional lawyer, in 1887 the head of the Latvian Society in the city of Jelgava (q.v.), and publisher from 1888 to 1914 of the Latvian newspaper *Tēvija* (*Homeland*), Čakste established in the years preceding World War I a strong reputation as a tireless worker for Latvian causes. He was especially active from 1917, in the last year of the war, as director of the Central Committee for Refugee Relief, an organization created in St. Petersburg to aid the hundreds of thousands of refugees who had fled the Latvian territories to escape the advancing German army. He participated in the Latvian National Council, presided over the Constitutional Convention, and in 1922 was chosen to be the first president of newly independent Latvia.

CEDRIŅŠ, VILIS (1914-1946?) After spending three years of his childhood as a refugee in Siberia during the First World War, Cedriņš returned to Latvia in 1921 and completed his education in the early 1930s, thereafter becoming a journalist and writer and establishing for himself a creditable reputation as a poet whose work dealt with poetic themes and motifs drawn from Latvian history and folklore. In 1944, he was arrested and deported to Siberia, where he died (probably in the Vorkuta labor camp).

ČEKISTI. In Latvian popular parlance, the functionaries of the various organs of state security (ChK, GPU, NKVD, KGB) in Soviet Russia and the USSR. The term entered the Latvian language during the period of the First World War, especially during the first half of 1919 when the unoccupied part of the Latvian territories was governed by Bolsheviks headed by Pēteris Stučka (qq.v.) and when in Soviet Russia other Latvian Bolsheviks were playing an important role in creating the state security apparatus. During the Stucka period, the *čekisti* executed alleged "counter-revolutionaries" in large numbers, and thus the term *čekist* in the Latvian language not only came to refer to official persons who perpetrated acts of terror against any opponent of Communist regime(s) but also later retained its original form in spite of the name changes the organs of Soviet state security underwent over the decades. The threat implied in the term receded, of course, during the interwar period of independence, but returned in full force (as the NKVD) in 1940 with the incorporation of Latvia into the Soviet Union. In 1992, after the establishment of the second period of independence, the Supreme Soviet (q.v.) barred from candidacy for parliamentary seats any persons who had worked for the state security apparatus (in recent decades, the KGB).

CELMIŅŠ, GUSTAVS (1899-1968). One of the most controversial of the political activists of the interwar period, Celmiņš headed from 1930 to 1934 the Pērkonkrusts (q.v.) (Thundercross) organization, the most important openly anti-Semitic groups on the right wing of the Latvian political spectrum. Pērkonkrusts was dissolved in 1934 after the Ulmanis (q.v.) coup, and Celmiņš was imprisoned from 1934 to 1937 for antistate activities and then exiled from the country. He returned to Latvia in 1941 with the German army, but fled west again in 1944.

CELMIŅŠ, HUGO (1877-1941). A well-known politician in the interwar period, Celmins was editor of the newspaper *Baltijas Lauksaimnieks* (*The Baltic Agriculturalist*) from 1907 to 1934, minister of agriculture in 1920, minister of education from 1923 to 1924, and chairman of the Council of Ministers in the years 1924 to 1925 and 1928 to 1931. Later he was mayor of the city of Riga (q.v.) and the Latvian ambassador to Germany. Arrested by the Communist authorities in 1940 after the Soviet occupation, he was deported to Siberia in 1941.

CĒSIS (Ger. WENDEN). Because of its location athwart the valley of the Gauja River, Cēsis in central Vidzeme (Livonia, q.v.) was an important political site even before the Swordbrothers (q.v.) erected a castle there in 1206. Evidently the indigenous settlers on the site were Wends. Subsequently, Cēsis was an important residential, administrative, and military center for the Livonian Order (q.v.), and in later centuries became the most significant Livland (Livonia) city after Riga (q.v.). The region around it became the site of a series of important battles during the Latvian Independence War of 1919-1920. The population of Cēsis in the 1989 census was approximately 22,000.

CHRONICLES. The earliest and in many respects the only written historical sources about the Latvian territories and their inhabitants in the twelfth and thirteenth centuries. Before the medieval chronicles, the sources are almost entirely unwritten, i.e., archaeological. The main chronicle sources for the period to about 1600 are the *Chronicle of Heinrich of Livonia* (q.v.) (to 1225-1227), the *Livonian Rhymed Chronicle* (to about 1290), the *Livonian Chronicle of Balthasar Russow* (to the 1580s), and *Salomon Hennings Chronicle of Courland and Livonia* (to 1590). From the mid-thirteenth century onward, the chronicle sources can be supplemented by written documents produced by the religious and governmental institution of the medieval Livonian state.

CIELĒNS, FELIKSS (1888-1964). Cielēns was a loyalist of the Latvian Social Democratic Party (q.v.) and one of the better-known interwar politicians because of his active career in the Latvian Saeima (q.v.) (parliament). He served in the National Council and the Constitutional Convention, was repeatedly reelected to parliament on the Social Democratic ticket, and held the posts of deputy foreign minister (1923), foreign minister (1926-1928), and ambassador to France (1933-1934). Moved to the periphery of Latvian political life by the Ulmanis (q.v.) coup, Cielēns nonetheless remained loyal to Latvian Social Democracy, resuming his political activism in Sweden where he fled into exile in 1944 just before the return to Latvia of the Soviet army.

CIMZE, JĀNIS (1814-1881). A member of the numerically small and prenationalist generation of university-educated Latvians in the first half of the nineteenth century, Cimze was a leading figure in

Latvian educational efforts, particularly in his capacity as long-time (from 1839) director of the Vidzeme (Livonian) Teachers seminary. The seminary trained primarily rural schoolteachers, and sought to inculcate in them a conciliatory spirit toward the Baltic German (q.v.) cultural hegemony in the Latvian-language territories. During his tenure, Cimze and his staff trained several thousands of young Latvians for teaching posts throughout the Baltic provinces (q.v.), but many of them, starting with the 1860s, were influenced by the nationalism generated by the Latvian "national awakening" (q.v.).

CĪŅA. First published in 1904 as the principal organ of the Latvian Social Democratic Party (q.v.), *Cīņa* (*Struggle*) became the oldest continuous Latvian political newspaper in the twentieth century. Before World War I, the site of its publication changed frequently because for much of the period it was an illegal publication, and at times it had to be published by Latvian Social Democrats living in Western Europe. In 1918, *Cīņa* became the principal newspaper of the Latvian Communist Party (q.v.). It remained illegal also during the interwar period of independence insofar as, continuing as the central organ of the Latvian Communists, it advocated subversion of the Latvian state. In 1940, after the creation of a Communist government in Latvia, *Cīņa* finally became a legal publication, changed its place of publication to the Soviet Union during the German occupation from 1941 to 1945, and returned to Latvia in 1945 to appear for the next 45 years as the main organ of the Latvian Communist Party and the Supreme Soviet (q.v.). In 1990, as the Latvian Communist Party collapsed, the newspaper severed its party ties and, under the name of *Neatkarīgā Cīņa* (*Independent Cīņa*), continued as one of the principal daily newspapers in Latvia.

COLLECTIVE FARMS. During the first year of Soviet rule in 1940, the new authorities repeatedly announced that the collectivization of Latvian agriculture (q.v.) would not take place, but after 1945, with the country seemingly a permanent part of the Soviet Union, there began to appear with increasing frequency various descriptions of the superiority of collective over individualized farming. From 1945 to 1949, however, agricultural collectivization had minimal results. Thus, in 1949, the Soviet authorities changed tactics and in March of that year arrested and deported some 100,000 persons, mostly from rural areas, who were judged to be obstacles to the collectivizing effort. After this, the process by which the dominant pattern of individualized farmsteads was transformed into collectivized agriculture proceeded smoothly, so that by mid-1950 there were approximately 4,500 collective farms of various types (kolkhozy and sovkhozy) in Latvia. Over the subsequent decades, this number was reduced substantially as smaller collective farms were absorbed by larger ones. After 1988, insofar as the principle of collective farming was judged to go against the grain of traditional Latvian farming practices, there has taken place a process of dismantling of collective farms as well as their transformation into private enterprises.

CORVÉE (Latv. KLAUŠAS). In an inclusive sense, corvée is any kind of labor that legally constituted authorities can require of those persons over which they have jurisdiction. In its narrower meaning in relation to Latvian history, the corvée was the labor that the landed estate could demand from the peasants living on it, particularly but not exclusively during the centuries when Latvian peasants were living in conditions of serfdom (q.v.). In this sense the corvée is a major part of the history of work among Latvians.

Before the abolition of serfdom (1816-1819), the corvée had two principal forms. First, an estate owner (or renter) could require as a condition of tenure that each farmstead supply a certain number of laborers (sometimes with a team of horses) each week who would prepare, cultivate, and harvest that part of the estate lands (the demesne) that was allocated to the owner (or renter). The amount and duration of such labor was regulated through custom and tradition, but at the end of the eighteenth and the beginning of the nineteenth century various reform laws began to require that these obligations be written down in a *Wackenbuch*. Second, landed estates, which in the fifteenth and sixteenth centuries became the principal units of local administration, also required of their peasants that they contribute their labor to public needs, such as, for example, road and bridge repair. Though the amount of both kinds of corvée labor was in principle regulated (i.e., fixed), the long-term tendency among estate owners was to increase (sometimes sharply) the number of tasks and the amount of labor required of the peasantry.

With the abolition of serfdom, however, the entire labor system was reshaped, with public tasks now falling under the jurisdiction of local *pagasts* governments, and the old serf obligation becoming a form of labor rents for those peasants who could not afford to make rental payments in other forms. Though corvée labor was an aspect of normal rural life throughout the centuries of serfdom and for about 30 years after serfdom was abolished, the Latvian term *klaušu laiki* (the time of corvée) refers to the latter period. Peasants were now personally free, but access to land still required labor, which to many appeared to be no change at all. The vast majority of peasants in the Latvian territories continued to perform corvée until the 1860s, when this form of rent was abolished by the reform laws of that decade. Thereafter, if estate owners needed a labor force, they had to obtain it on a wage basis.

COURLAND KINGS (Latv. **KURŠU ĶONIŅI**). A generic term, used in medieval documents, to refer to those leaders of Livonians and Couronians (qq.v.) who became vassals of the new Baltic German territorial lords. These so-called kings apparently were able to maintain many of their earlier personal freedoms and collective privileges even as they became tillers of the soil and as other Latvian rural people were being enserfed (see SERFDOM) during the sixteenth and seventeenth centuries. The documentary record about these privileged peasant lineages is very sparse, and their best-known communities -- seven "free hamlets" (Latv. *brīv-ciemi*) --were located in the Kuldīga (Ger. Goldingen) district of west-central Courland. The lineages in them were not included in the formal register of Courland noble families. The land they farmed, however, continued to be exempt from the normal laws pertaining to rural properties until the twentieth century. In the course of time, due to in- and out-migration as well as intermarriages, the population of this special area lost its unique character, although the family names typical of the area (e.g., Peniķis, Tontegode, Dragūns, etc.) were preserved in the general Latvian population. Similar privileged peasant lineages in Livonia assimilated totally to the general peasant population much earlier, probably by the end of the seventeenth century.

COURONIANS (also **KURS**). The people of one of the tribal societies inhabiting the territory of present-day Latvia in the early medieval period (sixth to thirteenth centuries). Their language is presumed to have been Baltic. Couronian settlements actually covered most of western Latvia as well as a considerable section of present-day northwest Lithuania. Thirteenth-century written sources mention Couronians as well as place-names in their territory, but do not make clear whether the place-names signify territorial or political units. Inferences from archaeological research on castle and burial sites have led historians to describe the Couronians as a people who were socially and politically stratified, had political leaders (kings) but not a unified state, and who, living near the Baltic Sea, practiced piracy and occasionally raided Sweden. After the arrival of German merchants and crusaders in the Baltic area in the late twelfth century and the start of their efforts to subjugate the indigenous peoples, the Couronians continued to resist for several generations, until in 1267 they signed a peace treaty with the crusading orders (q.v.). In subsequent centuries the Couronians merged with the peoples of the other Baltic tribal societies to form the Latvians. Their presence in Latvian history is memorialized in the name "Kurzeme" (land of the Kurs)--the westernmost of the four traditional territorial divisions of Latvia.

CRUSADING ORDERS. Two crusading orders were prominent in the Baltic area in the medieval centuries. German merchants, clerics, and adventurers first appeared in the Baltic region at the end of the twelfth century and carried back to the Holy Roman Empire information about the pagans who lived there. The first bishopric in the territory of present-day Latvia was established at Ikšķile by Father Meinhardt in 1184, but he died in 1196 without any significant results to his efforts. His successor, Berthold, was killed in 1198 in a battle with the Livonians (q.v.). Berthold's successor, the strategically and tactically more adept Albert, not only founded the city of Riga (q.v.) in 1201 in order to give the German effort a larger anchor, but also in 1202 established the Swordbrothers (*Schwertbrüder*), a crusading order for the Baltic that was to give the effort a military backbone. In the course of the next 30 years, the interests of the Riga bishopric and the Order began to diverge as more land and people came under the control of both. Though the Swordbrothers fulfilled their mission relatively successfully, they suffered a major defeat at Saule (in Lithuania) in 1236 from a combined army of Lithuanians and Semigallians (q.v.). The Order was nearly decimated in this battle and in 1237 decided to unite with the German Order (*Deutsche Orden*).

The German Order, with its headquarters in Prussia, had gained considerable experience in the crusades in the Holy Land, but now took over the effort against the "pagans" of the Baltic. Since the German order was active in many lands, the Baltic branch of it--the former Swordbrothers--came to be known as the Livonian Order. By the end of the thirteenth century, the Church and the Order had carved out in the Baltic five small states (the Riga archbishopric, the bishoprics of Courland, Dorpat, and Ösel, and the lands of the Order), which were referred to collectively as Livonia (q.v.). During the next two and a half centuries continuing opposition to the German presence in the Baltic area fell increasingly to the Lithuanians (the Balts to the north having been more or less completely subjugated).

Though ostensibly fighting on behalf of the Church, the German Order had its own material interests and it was also a defender of the political interests in the area of the Holy Roman Empire. Predictably, this meant that during the late medieval centuries, the new political and economic superiors of the Baltic--the Church, the Papacy, the German Order, the Holy Roman Emperor--were often fighting one another as well as "pagans" and other enemies outside the Baltic area. The German Order in Prussia was secularized in 1525, and, in the course of the Livonian War (q.v.) (1558-1583), the last Master of the Livonian Order--Gotthard Ketteler--in 1561 signed a treaty with Sigismund II Augustus of Poland becoming the latter's vassal. With this act, the last of the crusading orders ceased to have an independent existence in the Baltic.

CURRENCY. Since the beginning of World War I when the currency in the Latvian territories was the Russian ruble, Latvians have experienced a bevy of different currency systems. During World War I, the principal currencies were the Russian ruble and the German *Ostrubel*, the latter being used in Courland (q.v.), which was occupied by the German army. After the declaration of Latvian independence in 1918, the new Latvian government isssued the Latvian ruble, which was in circulation until 1922, when it was replaced by the Latvian *lats* (1 *lats*=100 *santimi*). The *lats* remained as the official currency even during 1940, the first year of Soviet occupation, though alongside with it the Soviet ruble was also used. During the German occupation of the country from 1941 to 1945, the *Reichskreditkassenscheine* was used: it looked like the German reichsmark but had an imprint signifying that it was for occupied territories where the local currency had been removed from circulation.

The Soviet ruble returned after 1945 and remained in use until 1991, when the Supreme Soviet (q.v.) of Latvia began to distance the country economically from the Soviet Union as a whole. The Latvian ruble, issued by the Bank of Latvia, then became a parallel currency to the Soviet ruble until 1992, by which time the Soviet Union had disintegrated. The Latvian and Russian rubles remained parallel currencies in Latvia until the summer of 1993, when the Bank of Latvia again began to issue the *lats* (1 *lats*= 100 *santīmi*), though both the Latvian ruble and the *lats* remained in circulation until the end of 1993, when the former was withdrawn.

- D -

DAINA. The Latvian term *daina* was adapted from the Lithuanian word *dainos* by Henri Wissendorf, who with Krišjānis Barons (q.v.) during the period from 1894 to 1915 published an eight-volume collection of this genre of Latvian folk songs. The scholarly literature dealing with Latvian folk music often uses the more generic "folk song," but *daina* tends to have pride of place in common usage. *Daina* refers to a normally four-line rhymed poem, which is either sung or recited and encapsulates an observation about nature, human relations, religion, and other aspects of human existence. These folk poems were frequently used by Baltic German (q.v.) writers of the period from 1500 to 1800 as examples of the spiritual culture of the Latvian peasantry, but serious efforts to collect, transcribe, and publish them did not start until the work of Johann Gottfried Herder (q.v.) at the end of the eighteenth century. The age of this folk poetry is a matter of dispute because internal evidence from them is ambiguous, but present-day collections no doubt contain some *dainas* from the late medieval period.

After the collecting efforts of Wissendorf and Barons--especially the latter, who came to be known as the "father" of the *daina*--the *daina* became the central feature of modern Latvian folklore studies, with enhanced collections appearing periodically and with the Latvian folklore institutes of the interwar and Soviet periods continuing the work of collection, transcription, and systematization. During the past century, folklorists have recorded and transcribed some 800,000 basic texts and several million variants. In terms of cultural politics, the activists of the Latvian "national awakening" (q.v.) used the existence of the *daina* (and forms of the Latvian oral tradition) to counter the Baltic German argument that the Latvian peasantry had no culture of its own and was therefore bound to be absorbed by nations with older "historic" cultures.

DANIŠEVSKIS, JŪLIJS (1884-1938). Originally a Social Democrat, Danis̆evskis joined the Latvian Bolshevik (q.v.) cause in the pre-World War I period and worked actively to bring about Soviet governments in Russia and the non-Russian territories of the Russian Empire. In 1919, he emerged as the deputy chairman of the one-year Soviet Latvian government headed by Pēteris Stučka (q.v.). After the members of this government and the army units that supported it were expelled from Latvia by the armed forces of the new national government, Daniševskis lived in the Soviet Union and held various government posts. In 1938, he was executed during Stalin's purge of "Old Bolsheviks." but was rehabilitated in the Khrushchev era.

DANKERS, OSKARS (1883-1965). Dankers received his military education in the czarist period, and began to serve in the Russian army in 1903. In the First World War he fought on the eastern front, but in 1919 he joined the army of the newly independent Latvian state. During the interwar independence period, he continued to serve in the Latvian army, having acquired the rank of general in 1925. In 1940, during the first year of Soviet occupation, Dankers emigrated to Germany, but returned to Latvia in 1941, where he worked in the "self-government" (q.v.) throughout the entire period of German occupation and as first general director of the "self-government" in the final year of its existence (1944). He emigrated to Germany in the fall of 1944, and in 1945 was interned by the U.S. Army and investigated for a period of 22 months. Upon his release, he continued living in Germany but, in 1957, emigrated to the United States.

DAUGAVA (Ger. DŪNA; Russ. DVINA). Latvia's largest and most renowned river, the Daugava originates in the Russian FSR, traverses Belarus and flows into the Gulf of Riga (q.v.). Its entire length is 1,020 kilometers, 357 kilometers of which length is in Latvia. It was used as a major commercial artery during the medieval centuries, and has continued to play this role in the economy of the Latvian territories until recent decades when a series of hydroelectric dams reduced its long-distance commercial use. Until the creation of the Latvian state in 1918, the Daugava served as the border between the Baltic provinces of Livland and Courland in Latvia. It continues to serve as the border between

Vidzeme (Livonia, q.v.) and Zemgale (the eastern half of the old province of Courland) (qq.v.). As Latvia's preeminent waterway, the Daugava for many centuries has had immense significance in the popular culture of the Latvians.

DAUGAVAS VANAGI **(DV) (Engl. THE HAWKS OF DAUGAVA).** A Latvian war veterans' organization founded in 1945 in the POW camp in Cedelghem, Belgium, where approximately 12,000 Latvian soldiers, most of them from the Latvian Legion (q.v.), were interned. The immediate purpose of the organization was to provide assistance and relief for the Latvian veterans (and their families) who had participated in the Latvian Legion in World War II, but in the postwar decades the DV accepted as members all persons of Latvian descent (and their descendants) who had seen military service of any kind anywhere. Primarily a Latvian émigré organization with its headquarters in the U.S. but with membership worldwide, the DV increased in number of members and in significance over the post-World War II decades, establishing its own meetinghouses and retirement homes, credit unions and lending libraries. In 1990, the DV established a chapter in Latvia, where membership rules created the problem of how to deal with Latvian veterans who had served in the Soviet armed forces.

DAUGAVPILS **(Ger. DŪNABURG; Russ. DVINSK).** Daugavpils is located on the Daugava River (q.v.) in the extreme southeastern corner of Latvia and with its 127,000 inhabitants (1989) is the second largest city in Latvia. It is first mentioned in medieval chronicles in 1275 as the site of one of the castles of the Livonian Order (q.v.). Because of its location, Daugavpils throughout its history has been multiethnic in the composition of its population and in its urban culture, and as late as 1989 the proportion of ethnic Latvians in its population was less than 15 percent. In all periods of history, Daugavpils has been an important commercial center for a region that includes Belorussian, Russian, and Lithuanian territory. In the twentieth century, it has been a significant railroad and industrial center as well.

DAUGE, ALEKSANDRS (1868-1937). As a university student in the 1890s, Dauge was a leading figure in the "new current" (q.v.) and expended his energies in writing about such subjects as historical and dialectical materialism. After independence in 1918, Dauge served briefly as minister of education (1921-1922) and subsequently became a professor at the University of Latvia.

DEGLAVS, AUGUSTS (1862-1922). A popular novelist and short-story author, Deglavs began his literary career in the early 1890s. For the next 30 years he wrote in a socially realistic manner about the generational transition among Latvians from the "national awakening" to the "new current" (qq.v.) period, as well as about the social and cultural reorientations in Latvian life that accompanied rural-to-urban migration during the last half of the nineteenth century. His most popular novel--*Rīga*--was published in two parts in 1920/21.

DEMOCRATIC PARTY SAIMNIEKS (DPS). DPS is the name of the political party that received the plurality of seats in the Sixth Saeima (q.v.) after the parliamentary election in the fall of 1995. It thus became the principal rival of Latvia's Way (q.v.), the party that had dominated the Fifth Saeima from 1993 to 1995. The DPS was founded in April 1995 from two existing political groupings: the Democratic Center Party (founded in 1992) and represented in the Fifth Saeima; and *Saimnieks*, which had made a strong showing in the municipal elections of 1994 but was new to national politics. In the 1995 parliamentary election campaign the DPS was headed by Ziedonis Čevers, who had been a member of the Godmanis (q.v.) government and, after the 1995 Saeima election, was a strong but ultimately an unsuccessful candidate for prime minister. Čevers subsequently entered the coalition cabinet of Andris Šķēle (q.v.) and in 1996 the DPS remained a political force to be reckoned with.

DEPORTATIONS. In its most inclusive meaning for Latvian history, the term "deportation" refers to the practice of the Russian (later Soviet) government of forcible relocation of people from Latvia to distant parts of the Russian Empire (or Soviet Union) for punitive or policy reasons. Before 1917, deportation was a relatively normal punitive measure for sedition and other crimes of similar magnitude, and "Siberian exile" was experienced by a large number of Latvians on an individual basis while the Latvian territories were under Russian control (to 1917). In these cases the deportation was normally preceded by at least a hearing or a trial.

   The relocation of massive numbers of a given population primarily for   reasons of state policy (and normally without a judicial hearing) was first felt by Latvians on June 13-14, 1941, after the 1940 incorporation of Latvia into the Soviet Union. Some 15,000 Latvians were deported and relocated mostly to areas east of the Ural Mountains. The policy goal was to remove from the Latvian population all those who, after a year of experience, were judged to be hindrances to the new regime.

A second wave of deportations came in the summer and fall months after the cessation of hostilities in 1945. The intent then was to remove those who were judged to have been too cooperative with the German occupying forces in the period from 1941 to 1945. This action by the reestablished Soviet government caused substantial resistance in the form of a partisan movement that lasted, with diminishing fervor, from 1945 to the mid-1950s and involved over that period an estimated 10,000-15,000 partisans (q.v.). A third wave of deportations was associated with rural collectivization and took place from March 23 to 25, 1949. The intention was to remove all those (kulaks, Latv. *budži*) who were judged likely to hinder collectivization, and this meant primarily persons who owned farmland over 100 acres; by the definition of Jānis Kalnbērziņš, secretary of the Central Committee of the Latvian Communist Party (q.v.), all those who had become successful farmers in the 1930s fell into this category. In any event, in 1949, some 50,000 people were deported to various locations in the USSR. This was the last of the mass deportation actions in Latvia, although individuals continued to be deported for various loosely defined "crimes" until the mid-1980s.

DIENAS LAPA. Appearing from 1886 to 1905 in Riga (q.v.), *Dienas Lapa* was the newspaper in which the writers and journalists of the "new current" (q.v.) published their views. In the beginning its political views were centrist, but during the editorships of Jānis Rainis and Pēteris Stučka (qq.v.) the paper veered to the left and began to champion socialism and various workers' causes. Even so, it maintained its national orientation, publishing much material of interest to all Latvians while attacking what it believed to be the materially based nationalism of the Riga Latvian Association (q.v.). After 1897 and the arrest of many Latvian Social Democrats (q.v.), the newspaper returned to its earlier moderate views but, during the 1905 Revolution, became once again relatively radical. At the end of 1905 the authorities stopped its publication.

DIEVTURĪBA. Derived from the Latvian *Dievs* (God) and *turēt* (to hold). A religious movement among Latvians, starting in 1923-1924 and involving at least initially mostly intellectuals. The movement's main intention was to "renew" the original religious faith of the pre-Christian (pre-twelfth century) inhabitants of the Latvian territories, with Latvian folklore materials (especially the *dainas*, q.v.) serving as the principal religious texts. The belief was that by this means Latvians could refashion a truly "Latvian" religion and ethical system, uncorrupted by foreign (i.e., Germanic) elements of the dominant Latvian Lutheranism (q.v.). Over the interwar period, Dievturība developed its own network of congregations as well as a set of interpretative writings authored largely by the movement's ideological leaders Ernests and Arvīds Brastiņi. Though the movement never attracted a widespread popular following but remained attractive mainly to intellectuals, it generated a substantial literature dealing with the interpretation of folklore. During the World War II period most of its intellectual leaders were deported to Siberia or emigrated to the west. Retaining a small following among western émigré Latvians during the Soviet period, Dievturība has renewed its activities in the post-1991 period.

DINSBERGS, ERNESTS (1816-1902). A Latvian educator, translator, and poet whose most important work was done in the second half of the nineteenth century during the "national awakening" (q.v.) period. Staying clear of direct confrontations with Baltic German (q.v.) and czarist authorities, Dinsbergs worked tirelessly at translating the masterpieces of other literatures into Latvian and at producing schoolbooks for the rapidly increasing numbers of Latvian children in the grade schools.

DĪRIĶIS, BERHARDS (1831-1892). Dīriķis was an active participant in the Latvian "national awakening" (q.v.) and represented its practical side. He was instrumental in the founding of the Riga Latvian Association (q.v.) in 1868 (serving as its chairman from 1862 to 1870) and, in 1869, of the very influential newspaper *Baltijas Vēstnesis* (*Baltic Courier*) (serving as its editor from 1869 to 1892). In 1877, he also founded the first Latvian daily newspaper *Rīgas Lapa* (*Rīga Paper*).

DISSIDENT MOVEMENT (Latv. PRETESTĪBAS KUSTĪBA).
During the past half-century dissident movements in Latvia
directed their activities, first, during the 1940-1941 period,
against the Soviet government created after the incorporation of
Latvia into the USSR; second, in the period from 1941 to 1945,
against the German occupation government and third, in the
1945-1988 period, against what now seemed to be an irreversible
Sovietization and Russification (q.v.) of the Latvian territories. In
the 1940-1941 period, dissident activities took the form of
proposing an alternative list to the Communist-approved
candidates in the July 1940 elections, and after that of printing
and circulating pamphlets denouncing the occupation of Latvia.
In the longer 1941-1945 period, the principal form of opposition
was illegal publications, which generally called for non-
compliance with the orders issued by the German authorities,
including volunteering for service in the Latvian Legion (q.v.).

In the decades immediately following World War II, the
most important form of dissidence was the partisan (q.v.)
movement, which consisted of organized and armed units
operating out of the Latvian forests and periodically attacking
representatives of Soviet state power. The partisan movement
came to an end by the mid-1950s, and the locus of dissidence
then shifted to the Latvian Communist Party itself where Eduārds
Berklavs (qq.v.) and others made decisions aimed at slowing what
they perceived to be a planned Russification of Latvian life and
institutions. Overt dissidence in official circles was ended, at least
for a while, by the 1959 purge of the Latvian Communist Party
and governmental institutions of persons accused of "bourgeois
nationalism," In the 1960s, dissidence in Latvia, as elsewhere in
the Soviet Union, took the form of illegal groups, mostly among
the young, using the instruments of samizdat to protest
Russification and Sovietization in Latvia. There was also the
continuing appearance of forbidden national symbols (e.g., the
Latvian flag), the laying of flowers on the graves of interwar
leaders, and the circulation of illegal leaflets.

During the late 1960s and throughout the 1970s, punishment
for those accused of or caught in such acts was imprisonment and
frequently exile from the Soviet Union or confinement in
psychiatric hospitals. Though the numbers of open dissidents in
Latvia remained small, each case had wide ramifications,
especially when the dissidents came to the notice of Western

human rights organizations. Dissidence grew somewhat during the involvement of the Soviet Union in the Afghan War, and by the Gorbachev period the ideas that once had fueled dissident activities were at times discussed quite openly. The new policies of glasnost, perestroika, and demokratizatsiya quickly brought into the mainstream of public discussion all the ideas for which dissidents had been systematically punished during the previous 50 years.

DOMINICAN ORDER. One of the monastic orders of medieval Europe, founded in 1215 in Toulouse, France. The first Dominican monastery in the Latvian territories was built in Riga (q.v.) in 1234 and for the next 300 years the Dominicans were a constituent part of the religious life of medieval Livonia (q.v.). Their monastic institutions were closed and destroyed in the violence that accompanied the introduction of Protestant Lutheranism (q.v.) to the Baltic lands.

DP (DISPLACED PERSON). This English-language term became important in Latvian history as a result of the Second World War, during the last years of which some 130,000 refugees fled Latvia to escape the re-Sovietization that was expected to follow Germany's defeat and withdrawal from the Baltic area. In immediate postwar Europe, the Latvian Red Cross identified 130,000 refugees--most of them in Germany and about 3,000 in Austria, 2,000 in Denmark, and 6,500 in Sweden. They made up a small proportion of the several millions of Eastern European "displaced persons" whom the Allies and the United Nations now had to care for. Most of the Latvian DPs (or, in Latvian, *dīpīši*) lived in Germany in some 300 displaced persons' camps, the largest of which was in the American Zone in Esslingen (about 8,000 persons). Other large camps were near Lubeck (6,000 persons), Hamburg (4,000 persons), and Hannover (2,000 persons). Initially, the DPs were under the care of the United Nations Relief and Rehabilitation Agency, but later under the International Refugee Organization. During their six to seven years in the camps, the Latvian DPs were able to organize an educational, cultural, social, and religious infrastructure, which helped to prevent the worst psychological effects of their status.

The Latvian DP population began to disperse starting in 1947, with some 17,000 emigrating to England, 20,000 to Australia, 19,000 to Canada, 45,000 to the United States, and 5,000 to South America. About 15,000 remained in Germany.

Some 4,000 remained in Sweden, which for many of the refugees had been their original refuge. The great dispersion was over by 1951. The "DP period" left its mark on the "western wing" of Latvian writing, because a large proportion of the DPs were of the Latvian prewar intelligentsia. Since 1991, when Latvia regained her independence, significant numbers of émigrés have helped with the transition to a market economy and parliamentary democracy. In the 1993 parliamentary elections the candidates' list of at least one political party--The Latvia's Way (*Latvijas Ceļš*) (q.v.)--contained a large number of émigré political leaders who were now competing for political office in the former homeland.

DUCHY OF COURLAND AND SEMIGALLIA. After the collapse of the medieval Livonian state (q.v.) by 1583 (the end of the Livonian War), its various component parts led a separate existence until they were all absorbed by the Russian Empire at the end of the eighteenth century. The last Master of the Livonian Order (q.v.), Gotthard Kettler, sought the protection of the Polish-Lithuanian state in 1561, even before the Livonian War (q.v.) was finished, and became the Duke of Courland and Semigallia. The Order was secularized and its various members became landholders and vassals of the ducal house. Kettler and his successors, in turn, became vassals of the Polish-Lithuanian monarchy. Until 1795, when Catherine the Great finally obtained full control over it, therefore, the duchy was nominally an independent state. In reality, its fate in the seventeenth century depended on the expansionist plans of the Polish-Lithuanian kings, and throughout the eighteenth, it came increasingly under the influence of Russia until the final absorption in 1795.

The duchy was governed from its capitals Jelgava (Ger. Mitau) (q.v.) and Kuldīga (Ger. Goldingen). Throughout the seventeenth century, the ducal house followed what appeared to be a mercantilist policy of economic development, with the best-known practitioner of this policy being Duke Jacob (1642-1682), grandson of Gotthard Kettler. Some historians, however, have argued that the policy of the ducal house was aimed more at its own enrichment than strengthening the state. The period of Duke Jacob's rule--involving economic development, acquisition of two small colonial holdings in West Africa (Gambia, q.v.) and the Caribbean (Tobago, q.v.), some improvement of the situation of the Latvian-speaking peasantry--was in retrospect the apex of Courland's separate history. His successors in the eighteenth century were wastrels and frequently lived outside the duchy for long periods of time, until the last duke, Peter Biron, turned the duchy over to the Russian Empire. In 1918, the territories of the duchy became component parts of the new Latvian state as Kurzeme (the northwestern section) and Zemgale (the southeastern section).

DUKE JACOB (Latv. **HERZOGS JĒKABS**). *See* **DUCHY OF COURLAND AND SEMIGALLIA**.

DUMA. The legislative body created in the Russian Empire by Tsar Nicholas II after the Revolution of 1905. This first experiment with parliamentarianism produced altogether four dumas in the 1906-1917 period. There were six Latvians in the first duma but that number became smaller in later ones. Though generally judged to have been a failed experiment because the Tsar both resented and mistrusted them, the dumas gave a handful of Latvian deputies the opportunity to participate in national-level politics, and such deputies as Jānis Goldmanis (q.v.), Jānis Zālitis, and Francis Trasuns (q.v.) continued to play a prominent role in Latvian politics after the founding of the independent Latvian state in 1918.

- E -

ECONOMY. Until the second half of the nineteenth century, the vast majority of Latvia's residents were farmers. The principal rural settlement pattern was the isolated farmstead (rather than the village), though there existed farmstead clusters as well. Most of the arable land (as well as forests and pastures) lay within large, private, and crown-owned estates, which depended for a labor force on peasant-serfs (to 1816-1819) and then on peasants who paid labor rents. Outright ownership by peasants of farmland started only in the 1860s and expanded quickly thereafter. Still, by 1914 just over 50 percent of farmland was still owned by estates, rather than individual peasant proprietors. Paralleling these changes, starting in the 1860s there was the growth of factory industry in urban areas, especially in Riga (q.v.), which triggered rural-to-urban migration of unprecedented size. By the start of World War I, Riga had become an important industrial center in the Russian Empire, and its port stood right behind St. Petersburg in the total volume of imported and exported goods.

Since the Latvian territory was directly on the eastern front, World War I (1914-1917) proved to be very destructive to the Latvian economy and the recovery from wartime disruption lasted until the early 1930s. Agrarian reform (q.v.) in the 1920s, confiscating large estates and redistributing their land, created a large class of smallholders and ensured that agriculture (q.v.) and agriculturally related small industry retained their central importance. By 1935, about 62 percent of the labor force was still employed in the agriculture sector, about 20 percent in non-agricultural industries, and about 18 percent in service occupations. World War II, when Latvia was again directly on the eastern front, was a reprise in terms of economic destructiveness of the World War I experience.

After 1945, in the Soviet period when economic priorities were determined by central planning from Moscow, the prewar patterns of economic growth changed substantially. Agriculture was collectivized, a series of five-year plans emphasized industrial development, and by 1959 the industrial sector of the labor force (37 percent) was nearly equal to the reduced agricultural sector (40 percent), with service occupations having expanded dramatically to 23 percent. By the early 1990s, only 16 percent of the labor force worked in agriculture, 30 percent in industry, and 54 percent in other occupations. Correspondingly, the proportion of the population residing in cities and towns in the Soviet period expanded rapidly, first surpassing the rural population in 1954 (50.6 percent versus 49.4 percent). Thereafter, population growth favored urban areas and by 1991 the proportions stood at 70 percent urban and 30 percent rural. By the early 1990s, the Baltic republics (Latvia included) had evolved into the most modernized and "western" economies in the Soviet Union.

The economic development of Latvia in the Soviet period, however, was predicated on a high degree of integration with the rest of the Soviet economy, with energy supplies (oil and gas) being imported from and manufactured products being exported to other Soviet republics as well as to the USSR's eastern European satellite countries. The collapse of the USSR in 1991 and the return of Latvian independence has meant, in the short run, considerable economic turmoil and a substantial transformation of economic relationships with other countries--characteristics Latvia now shares with other post-communist states. The transition to a market economy, beginning with legislation in 1990, has lasted longer than anticipated, especially with respect to state industrial plants; industrial and agricultural output has been reduced, and Latvia has remained heavily dependent on Russia for its basic energy supplies. In the early 1990s, indicators of growth tended to be negative, with the resulting increase in unemployment and underemployment. At the same time, Latvia had stabilized its currency (q.v.), removing itself from Russia's "ruble zone" and its staggeringly high inflation rates. Inflation rates in Latvia have been moderate. There has been substantial growth in the urban retail sector, as well as considerable progress in the dismantling of collective farms (q.v.) and in the creation of individual private farms. Having at least temporarily lost much of its eastern market (i.e., the countries of the former Soviet Union), Latvia has not yet found its economic niche in the new Europe.

The country's economy remains in transition, but, in comparative terms, prognoses about its long-term economic future by such lending agencies as the World Bank and International Monetary Fund are guardedly optimistic. Most of the labor force is skilled to highly skilled, the "work ethic" remains influential; and western, particularly the Nordic, European countries see the Baltic countries (including Latvia) as an area of investment. The basic structure of the labor force--with agricultural labor less than 20 percent of the total--is not likely to change, but the proportion of the labor force in heavy industry is likely to continue to fall and the proportion in commercial enterprise to increase.

EDUCATION. The history of formal educational institutions in the Latvian territory began in the early thirteenth century, when Albert, the third Bishop of Livonia (q.v.) and the founder of the city of Riga (q.v.), established a school in his Riga diocese to prepare young men for clerical careers. Since that time, schools of this type--though not numerous--were a normal part of Baltic urban life and, as everywhere else in Europe until well into the modern period, were established, sponsored, supervised, and funded by the Church, both Catholic and Protestant. Most evidence suggests, however, that only the Church and the urban mercantile classes really believed in the value of literacy skills.

The landed nobility, always on guard against possible sedition, thought that since peasant-serfs were meant for agricultural labor they did not need literacy skills not associated with religious worship, and therefore generally opposed peasant schooling. Peasant parents tended to think of schooling as a waste of time because literacy skills seldom led their children out of enserfment or the peasant estate (Germ. *Bauernstand*).

It was not until Swedish rule in Livonia in the seventeenth century that one can speak of a sustained interest among the political and clerical elite in the education of peasant children. The first serious efforts to establish rural schools appeared after 1694, when the Swedish monarch issued an order for estate owners to establish parish schools (Latv. *draudzes skolas*). Whatever was achieved, however, was destroyed by the destructive Great Northern War (q.v.), because by 1727 only 18 of Livonia's 54 parishes had schools and each of these was attended by only three or four pupils.

In the eighteenth century, the influence of the Moravian Brethren (q.v.) on peasant education was strongly felt, mostly in Livonia, where this pietistic movement encouraged school construction as well as widespread home instruction in reading and writing. Also, the Livonian Landtag (q.v.) (provincial parliament) in the 1760s directed its members--the Livonian titled nobility--to build schools on their estates, but by the end of the century only 134 of the 525 estates had such institutions. These events, as well as the general influence of Enlightenment thinking, had created a momentum, however, that carried into the nineteenth century and led the serf emancipation (q.v.) decrees of 1816-1819 to include provisions for the creation throughout the Baltic provinces (q.v.) of county schools (Latv. *pagasta skolas*).

Henceforth, the growth of primary and secondary schools in both urban and rural areas was continuous, resulting by the end of the century in literacy (q.v.) rates in the Russian Baltic provinces in the 80 to 85 percent range. The ideology of the Latvian "national awakening" (q.v.) gave pride of place to schooling, and most of its activists were, in fact, rural schoolteachers. Although the attendance at all levels of educational institutions was reduced somewhat by the Russification (q.v.) policies of the Imperial government during the 1885-1905 period, the general acceptance of the desirability of schooling remained nearly universal. The idea of education as the basis of social and economic upward mobility spread rapidly, as increasing numbers of young Latvians enrolled in the Riga Polytechnic Institute (q.v.)--the only institution of higher learning in the Latvian territory--or traveled to the universities in Dorpat (Tartu) in the Estonian part of Livland, or to the universities in St. Petersburg and Moscow.

In the twentieth century, the evolution of the educational system in Latvia followed the course of political developments, and reflected, regardless of the regime in power, the notions that compulsory public education was a normal aspect of a modern state and that the state had an obligation to fund educational institutions. The new independent Latvian state of the interwar period acted on these principles by requiring school attendance to age 16 and by funding a public school system that by the late 1930s enrolled from 80 to 100 percent of school-age children of each district. Paralleling the state-funded primary and secondary school systems was a state system of higher educational institutions and institutes at the center of which stood the University of Latvia (founded in 1919). Given the need to develop educational institutions quickly after 1918, the national and regional governments were the primary actors and private schools of all kinds remained relatively scarce.

This near-total state monopoly of educational institutions (and hence also of teacher training, curricular content, and educational standards) carried over into the post-1940 Soviet period, when the monopoly became total and operated in conjunction with the all-Union planning apparatus in Moscow. Education at all levels involved a heavy component of indoctrination in Marxist-Leninist ideology as well as steady expansion of the Russian language in most instructional areas (see RUSSIFICATION). At the same time, over the half-century of the Soviet period the Latvian educational system unflaggingly produced an increasingly more highly skilled labor force that fit the objectives of overall planning.

Since the 1991 reestablishment of Latvian independence, however, the idea of a totally state-funded and state-controlled educational system has been in retreat, as the Latvian government has had to wrestle with inadequate revenues and has therefore given educational funding substantially lower priority than it has ever had historically. Though created in part by economic necessity, this policy also has the intention of bringing into existence a private educational sector. The result--conceived of as a transition -- has indeed been a proliferation of private educational institutions of various kinds, but also a sharp reduction of the incomes of all professionals in institutions funded by the state budget and the beginning of something like a "brain drain" toward western countries.

EGLĪTIS, ANŠLĀVS (1906-1993). From 1915 to 1918, the Eglītis family were refugees in the interior of Russia, returning to Latvia after the proclamation of independence. His father, Viktors Eglītis (q.v.), by WorldWar I had already established a prominent position for himself in the Latvian literary world as a "decadent" writer, so that his son grew up in a literary household. Anšlāvs Eglītis began his literary career in the late 1920s, and by the time of World War II had achieved an excellent reputation as a novelist, playwright, and poet. Continuing his output during the war years as well as during the DP (q.v.) period in Germany from 1944 to 1950, Eglītis emigrated to the United States and finally established permanent residence in California. Because he was the most prolific and most popular author in the intellectual world of the Western Latvian émigrés, Eglītis's work was virtually unobtainable in Soviet Latvia except for literary specialists. After the mid-1980s, however, literary scholarship in Latvia has established widespread ties with Latvian writers throughout the world, and Eglītis's body of writings has assumed its rightful place in the history of Latvian literature (q.v.).

EGLĪTIS, VIKTORS (1877-1945). A poet and major Latvian literary figure before World War I and during the interior years, Eglītis developed his art in concert with the so-called "decadentism" of the early years of the twentieth century. In the interwar years, he worked as a teacher and lecturer of Latvian literature (q.v.) at the University of Latvia and continued to produce in all genres of writing, including literary history and literary criticism. In late 1944, he was arrested by the returned Soviet authorities and apparently died shortly thereafter.

EIDEMANIS, ROBERTS (1895-1937). A Latvian Bolshevik (q.v.) and officer in the Red Army, Eidemanis remained in the Soviet Union after the 1917-1920 period and continued to assume important posts in the USSR's military bureaucracy. He combined this work with publications in Latvian on various aspects of the military side of the 1917 Revolution and the later civil war in Russia, and from 1934 to 1937 was director of the Latvian Writers' Center in Leningrad. He was executed in 1937 in Stalin's purge of the Old Bolsheviks.

ELECTIONS. In Latvian history during the modern era, electing persons from among themselves to act on their behalf was an activity that became necessary for Latvians after the serf emancipation (q.v.) in the 1817-1819 period. The emancipation law had created local (*pagasts*) councils that required representation from the peasantry. Before this time, for centuries, Latvian peasants, as serfs and as residents on landed estates owned or rented by the nobility, were excluded from self-governance of any kind. During the rest of the nineteenth century, however, Latvians and most residents of the Baltic provinces (q.v.) were excluded from all but local (rural and urban) elections because there were no provincial parliaments outside of the periodic meetings (Landtage) of the Baltic German nobility. Latvians were first enabled to cast votes for (indirect) national-level representation only during the duma (q.v.) period from 1906 to 1917.

The creation of the independent Latvian state in 1918 and its new constitution provided for a national parliament (Saeima, q.v.), and there were altogether four free parliamentary elections during the interwar years until 1934, when Kārlis Ulmanis (q.v.) instituted his personal presidential rule. During the next 60 years (the Ulmanis authoritarian regime, the period of German occupation, and the longer Soviet period) free and uncoerced elections did not exist, although the last of these regimes did include electoral activity of various kinds in which candidates were invariably Communist Party members. The Communist monopoly over elected offices was broken in the spring 1990 elections of the Supreme Soviet (q.v.), when the Popular Front and the Latvian National Independence Movement ran candidates against the Latvian Communist Party (qq.v.) and obtained a governing majority. The first free and uncoerced parliamentary elections since the 1931 election of the fourth Saeima took place in 1993, when the fifth Saeima was elected. The renewed 1922 constitution also foresees local elections, which occurred in the fall of 1993.

EMIGRATION. Although statistical precision is impossible before the twentieth century, departure from the land of their birth has been a constant in Latvian history for many centuries. Before the nineteenth century, the flight of serfs (q.v.) from the estates to which they were attached was continuous, as was the service of Latvians in the armies of whatever external great power controlled the Latvian territories. Throughout the nineteenth century, when the Latvian territories were part of the Russian Empire, emigration in an eastern direction probably far outweighed emigration westward. Notable instances of large emigrations to other parts of the empire include the so-called "warm lands movement" (q.v.) in the 1840s, and the search for numerous professionally trained Latvians for employment outside the Baltic provinces (q.v.) throughout the second half of the century. Estimates at the turn of the twentieth century spoke of some 10 percent of all Latvians living in the Russian Empire outside the Baltic provinces. Political emigration expanded after 1897 with the government's crackdown on the political left and continued after the Revolution of 1905 for the same reasons. Centers of Latvian activity in this era were to be found in the United States (Boston, Philadelphia, New York), as well as in Switzerland and other western European countries.

A major emigration (est. 120,000) is associated with the establishment of the new Latvian state in 1918, when Latvian supporters of the Bolshevik (q.v.) movement left the Latvian territories to take up residence in the Soviet Union. The conclusion of World War II and the incorporation of Latvia into the Soviet Union resulted in the first significant westward move, as some 120,000 Latvians left to take up residence first in postwar Germany as DPs (q.v.) and then six or seven years later to depart from Germany as emigrants to North America, Sweden, Australia, and South America. As a result of emigration, wartime deaths, and the deportations (q.v.) carried out by the Soviet government, the proportion of Latvians in the Latvian territories is estimated to have dropped from about 75 percent in 1939 to about 63 percent in 1950. In the Soviet period after 1950, the number of emigrants from Latvia (mostly to other places in the Soviet Union) was far outdistanced by the numbers of immigrants--primarily Russians, Belorussians, and Ukrainians-- from other Soviet Republics.

ENDZELĪNS, JĀNIS (1873-1961). With an MA in comparative linguistics from Dorpat (Tartu) University (1905) and a doctorate from the University of St. Petersburg (1912), Endzelīns taught at Dorpat (Tartu) and Charkov Universities before World War I, but in 1920 became a professor at the University of Latvia. During the interwar period, he developed an international reputation as a scholar of the Latvian language as well as comparative linguistics, and played perhaps a greater role than anyone else in standardizing the principles of expression and writing in Latvian. Through his scientific work, Latvian became accessible for comparative purposes to scholars of linguistics. Endzelīns did not emigrate in 1944. After World War II, because of his international reputation, he was able to retain his high standing in Latvian academic life even while other scholars from the prewar period were attacked by the Latvian Communist Party (q.v.) and Soviet authorities as unreliable.

ESTATE (Fr. ÉTAT, Ger. STAND, Latv. KĀRTA). The term "estate" in one of its English meanings refers to a subpopulation the members of which have similar (or identical) rights and obligations recognized in law and custom. This manner of classifying elements of social structure was dominant in Europe before modern constitutions granted equal rights to all citizens, regardless of social standing or income. In the pre-modern period, inequality of rights and obligations of subpopulations was assumed to be natural.

In the Latvian territories before the twentieth century the highest and most important estate was the corporation of nobility (*Ritterschaft*), with Courland and Livonia (qq.v.) having separate nobilities. The nobility was believed to have the right of governance and shared that right only of its own volition. The lowest (though most numerous) estate was the peasant estate (*Bauernstand*), which until the nineteenth century had virtually no political rights and only those economic rights agreed to by the upper estates. Before the mid-nineteenth century, virtually all Latvian-speakers were in the peasant estate. Between these two stood the burghers (*Bürgerstand*, bourgeoisie, city dwellers) as well as, from the late eighteenth century onward and evidently only in Baltic society, a subgroup called the *Literatenstand*, which was composed of people in the liberal professions (law, journalism, teaching, etc.). Unlike the other groupings, the

Literaten did not have special privileges recognized by law. The estates were not classes because membership in them was not keyed to income. Though the legal system in the Baltic lost most of its estate base before the end of the nineteenth century, popular thought retained elements of it well into the twentieth century.

- F -

FASCISM. Strictly speaking, fascism was the philosophy of the political movement launched in 1922 by Benito Mussolini, but in subsequent decades the term was expanded to cover all manner of philosophies of the political right that incorporate racialist ideas, glorify the single-leader (*Führer*) principle and a mass-based political party that enacts his will, and rely on various forms of brutality to establish and maintain the social order.

In the specifically Latvian context, "fascism" has been used as the descriptive term for the authoritarian regime of Kārlis Ulmanis (q.v.) (1934-1940), most frequently by Latvian political historians working in the Soviet context who needed a concept for historical periodization and by Soviet-era propagandists who needed an effective single-word caricature of persons opposed to Communism and to the incorporation of Latvia into the Soviet Union. Where the Ulmanis regime belongs in a typology of political forms is an open question, because Ulmanis, though evidently an admirer of Italian corporatism and clearly disillusioned with parliamentarianism, suspended all political parties (including his own Agrarian Union, q.v.), enunciated a philosophy of national unity rather than one of racial purity, and did not use brutality as a means of governing. The one Latvian political movement--Pērkonkrusts (q.v.)--which did explicitly emulate Hitler's National Socialists (Nazis) was banned during the Ulmanis period (1934-1940) as well as during the period of the German occupation (1941-1944).

FÖLKERSAHM, HAMILKAR (1811-1856). Fölkersahm was a politically active member of the Livonian nobility (*Livländische Ritterschaft*) and represented its liberal wing in the Livonian Diet (Landtag). Recognizing that the labor-rent system introduced to rural Livonia (q.v.) after the serf emancipation (q.v.) of 1819 was not working very well, Fölkersahm argued for a new agrarian law that would create the possibility for peasants (most Latvians and Estonians) to buy the land that they worked. A provisional law of this nature was accepted by the Livonian Diet in 1849 and became the basis of additional laws that sparked the boom in peasant land purchases in the 1860-1890 period.

FRANCISCAN ORDER. A medieval monastic order named for St. Francis of Assisi. The Franciscans established a monastery in Riga (q.v.) in the 1230s and for the next 300 years played a significant role in the political and religious life of medieval Livonia (q.v.). By 1500 there were some seven Franciscan monasteries on Livonian territory, but by the 1560s all had been closed or demolished in the violence that accompanied the introduction of Lutheran (q.v.) Protestantism to the Baltic territories.

FÜRECKER, CHRISTOPHOR (c.1615-c.1685). One of the most prominent of those seventeenth-century Baltic German (q.v.) writers who concerned themselves with translating and producing religious texts into the Latvian language. Though he had received a theological education at Dorpat (Tartu) University, he did not become a clergyman and earned his living as a private tutor. Fürecker knew the Latvian language very well, and his Latvian renditions of church hymns not only became popular and were retained in Latvian Lutheran (q.v.) hymnals into the twentieth century but also played an important role in laying the groundwork for the later development of Latvian religious and secular poetry. Evidently, his work influenced both Georgius Mancelius and Ernst Glück (qq.v.), both of whom have similar standing in the history of the Latvian written word.

- G -

GAILIS, MĀRIS (1951-   ). Prime minister of Latvia in the Fifth Saeima (q.v.), from September 1994 to September 1995. Gailis was a member of the Fifth Saeima's dominant political party Latvia's Way (q.v.) and from 1990 onward had served in various capacities in the Ministry of Foreign Afairs under Prime ministers Ivars Godmanis (q.v.) and Valdis Birkavs (q.v.). He replaced Birkavs as prime minister when the latter's cabinet collapsed.

GAILĪTIS, KĀRLIS (1936-1992). Gailītis was a Lutheran theologian and clergyman who received his theological education and began his career during the Soviet period of Latvian history. From 1986 to 1989 he was the chancellor of the Consistory of the Evangelical Lutheran Church in Latvia, and archbishop of the Church from 1989 to 1992, when he was killed in an automobile accident. His predecessors in the archbishop's chair and Gailītis himself had to address the problems of Latvian Lutheranism (q.v.) arising from the existence of two parallel church organizations--one in the Latvian SSR and one in the Latvian émigré community in the West.

GAMBIA. One of the two small overseas colonies (the other was Tobago, q.v.) established by Duke Jacob of Courland (1610-1682). Influenced by mercantilist ideas, Jacob, who ruled Courland (q.v.) from 1642 onward, sought to expand the economic activities of his duchy through colonial acquisitions, and obtained several territories in Gambia in Western Africa from local African rulers. The colony was the object of raids by both the Dutch and the English but was only perfunctorily defended by Jacob's local forces. In 1664 Jacob was forced to cede the colony to England.

GERMAN ORDER (See **CRUSADING ORDERS***)*.

GERMANIZATION. A term with a very broad meaning, signifying in the Baltic context primarily a process through which an individual or a group changes, or is forced to change, its primary cultural identity to one associated with the German language. In Latvian cultural history, numerous variants of the process can be identified. Throughout the long centuries during which the political, economic, and cultural elites of the Baltic area were primarily German-speakers, small numbers of able and energetic Latvians always voluntarily assimilated to German-language culture as they ceased to be agriculturalists and took up other lines of work. The assumption was that German was the normal language of "higher culture," of administration, and of the law, while Latvian was the language of the peasantry. This dynamic was part of Baltic cultural life for so long that by the nineteenth century most residents--Baltic Germans and Latvians alike--understood it as a normal part of life, and the Baltic German (q.v.) literati in the first half of the century discussed how rural school systems could be used to make the process more deliberate and effective. Some of the Baltic German landed aristocracy opposed such plans, believing that peasant-Latvians should not be taught the language of the superior classes (Germans).

This seemingly "normal" aspect of Baltic life was cast in a different light by the Latvian cultural nationalists after the 1850s; for them Germanization was an unacceptable course of personal development for individual Latvians and a sociocultural injustice if transformed into policy by institutions. Individual Latvians who displayed a preference for the German language and German ways were now condemned and caricatured in literature as "osier Germans" (kārklu vācieši). In spite of such negative public attitudes, however, the incidence of assimilation among Latvians to German-language culture continued even into the early twentieth century, probably at a higher rate among educated than among uneducated Latvians but not in very large absolute numbers in either category. In the second half of the nineteenth century, some elements of Baltic German opinion--reacting to the Russification (q.v.) policies of the czarist government--again proposed deliberate and systematic Germanization of the Latvian population, but these plans remained empty talk. Germanization as deliberate state policy in the Baltic area surfaced again during both the First and Second World Wars, as policy-makers of the German Empire and the Third Reich drafted plans to extrude the indigenous Baltic populations from their historic territories and resettle the area with German farmers.

GLÜCK, ERNST (1651-1706). Glück was born in Saxony and studied Lutheran (q.v.) theology in Wittenberg and Leipzig Universities, where he developed pietistic leanings. He came to Livonia (q.v.) in 1673 and began to participate in the efforts the Swedish government--which controlled Livonia for most of the seventeenth century--was making in raising the educational level of the Latvian and Estonian-speaking peasantry. He served for three years as pastor in Daugavgrīva fort and, from 1683 to 1702, as pastor of the town of Alūksne and dean of the Koknese district in Livonia. From 1683 onward he was instrumental in founding the first Latvian (peasant) schools in Livonia, and then and later translated hymnals and catechisms from German into Latvian.

The reason Glück is a major figure in Latvian cultural history, however, is his translation of the Bible--both the Old and New Testaments--into Latvian, a task that lasted from 1685-1691. The "Glück bible" was fundamental for the later development of Latvian as a literary language since the new translation (there had been earlier translations of individual passages and chapters) demonstrated that all the biblical imagery and ideas could be rendered into Latvian, which was held to be an unpromising peasant language even by the Lutheran clergy who sympathized with the hard lot of their peasant congregations.   During the Great Northern War (q.v.) between Sweden and Russia, Glück and his family were transported in 1702 by Peter the Great's army from Alūksne to Moscow. Glück's foster daughter--a Latvian named Marta Skavronska--later became Peter's mistress, then his wife and, after his death, Empress Catherine I. Glück himself died in Moscow in 1705 and was buried in the German cemetery there.

GODMANIS, IVARS (1951-   ). A physicist and mathematician by training, Godmanis was a lecturer at the University of Latvia from 1986 to 1990, and also served as deputy chairman of the Latvian Popular Front (q.v.) from 1989 to 1990. After the spring 1990 elections of the Supreme Soviet (q.v.) brought to that body a majority of Popular Front deputies, Godmanis was chosen to preside over the Cabinet of ministers, which made him the "head of government" from spring 1990 to June 1993, when the first postwar Saeima (q.v.) (parliament) was elected. In effect, Godmanis headed a transition government, which came to power in what was still, in spring 1990, the Latvian SSR and left power two years after Latvia had become fully independent. His tenure was marked by much accomplishment, but also by an increasing loss of confidence in the transition government by the public at large. An indicator of how unpopular the Godmanis government had become by mid-1993 was the fact that in the June 1993 parliamentary elections, the Popular Front ticket (in which Godmanis was included) did not receive the minimum 4 percent of the vote that would have enabled the Front to have some deputies in the new Saeima. After leaving politics Godmanis became a sucessful businessman in Riga.

GOLDMANIS, JĀNIS (1875-1955). Goldmanis was among the Latvian political notables because of his service as a deputy in the Fourth Duma (1912-1917) and his work in organizing the Latvian Rifle Regiments (q.v.) in the czarist army. Later he also served in the Latvian Provisional Government, the Constitutional Convention, and as a deputy in the First and Second Saeima (q.v.). He fled Latvia in 1944 and emigrated to the United States in 1950.

GORBUNOVS, ANATOLIJS (1942-   ). Gorbunovs held a series of executive positions in the Latvian Communist Party (q.v.) from 1978 onward, including the post of ideological secretary of the Central Committee from 1988 to 1990. He joined the Latvian Popular Front (q.v.) at its founding and became increasingly a supporter of total reform, including the separation of the Latvian SSR from the Soviet Union. After the spring 1990 reforms, which brought to the Latvian Supreme Soviet (q.v.) a majority of Popular Front candidates, Gorbunovs served as chairman of the Supreme Soviet from spring 1990 to the June 1993 parliamentary elections, playing in this transition government the role of head of state.

   Having resigned from the Communist Party in 1989, Gorbunovs proved to be an effective political leader in the difficult transition years, as suggested by the high approval ratings he continued to have in public opinion polls even as the popularity of many of his colleagues in the Supreme Soviet and in the Cabinet of Ministers plummeted. Parting ways with the Popular Front for the June 1993 Saeima (q.v.) (parliament) elections, Gorbunovs was part of the ticket of Latvia's Way (q.v.), an electoral coalition that included many of the best-known deputies of the Supreme Soviet. Latvia's Way chose Gorbunovs as president of the Saeima, having received a plurality (though not a majority) of seats in July 1993. Now, however, he was no longer head of state, because the Saeima also chose a president (Guntis Ulmanis, q.v.) for the country as a whole. After the 1995 parliamentary election, Gorbunovs was replaced as president of the Saeima by Ilga Kreituse (q.v.), but he remained a deputy in the Latvia's Way Party.

GRĀMATU DRAUGS. *Grāmatu Draugs* (Friend of the Book) was a publishing house founded in 1926 in Riga (q.v.) by Helmārs

Rudzītis (q.v.) that brought about a coup in the history of Latvian book publishing by aiming inexpensive editions and widespread advertising at a mass book market. This strategy not only demonstrated the existence of a mass market for worthwhile but inexpensively produced books but also that such a market could be profitable. *Gramatu Draugs* remained one of the leading Latvian publishers throughout the interwar independence period and the period of German occupation (1941-1944), renewed its activities among the Latvian DPs (q.v.) in Germany after the war, and in 1949 transferred its operations to New York, where it continued to publish Latvian-language books as well as the principal Latvian émigré newspaper *Laiks (Time)*.

GREAT NORTHERN WAR (1700-1721). A series of military conflicts between Russia, Sweden, Denmark, and Poland-Lithuania over the question of who should control the eastern Baltic area and adjoining lands. Tsar Peter the Great was deeply unhappy about the control Sweden and Poland-Lithuania exercised over Baltic territory, because he believed that the Russian Empire--as the great power he wanted it to be--needed to be oriented toward the west and therefore should have western ports. He thus formed a military alliance with Denmark and Poland-Lithuania against Sweden, as a consequence of which the Polish King Augustus II (who was also the Count of Saxony) in 1700 invaded the Baltic with a Saxon army and attacked Riga (q.v.). The Swedish forces under the leadership of their new King Karl XII repulsed this attack after having already warded off a Russian attack on Narva in the north. Karl XII then invaded Poland-Lithuania and forced it to sue for peace. In the meantime Russian forces freely attacked, burned, and pillaged large sections of Livland (q.v.). Though the Swedes defeated the Russians at Murmuiža in 1705, the Russians triumphed over Swedish forces at Poltova in 1709. The Swedish defeat allowed Peter to lay siege to Riga, which surrendered in 1710.

With the fall of Riga the war was over for the inhabitants of the Baltic area, though hostilities continued elsewhere until 1721 when the Treaty of Nystad was signed between Sweden and Russia. As a result, Russia obtained Livland as well as a section of Finland. For the inhabitants of the eastern Baltic territories the war was disastrous not only because of the damage and loss of life associated with the fighting but also because of the plague epidemic (called in popular memory the Great Plague) that attacked the population in 1710-1711. The combination of warfare and plague devastated especially rural Livland, resulting in the virtual depopulation of many districts. Estimates place the number of Latvians immediately after 1710-1711 at 300,000, the lowest level Latvian population had ever reached or has reached since.

GRIGULIS, ARVĪDS (1906-1989). Grigulis began his career as a poet with his first publication in 1929, remained in the public's eye with occasional writings in the 1930s, but after 1945 during the Soviet period of Latvian history achieved high standing in the official literary establishment as a prose writer, poet, literary critic, and staunch defender of the literary values appropriate for a communist society. He died in 1989, shortly after the plenum of the Latvian Writers' Union (q.v.)--in a meeting that is said to have begun the "third national awakening" (q.v.)--roundly condemned those in the Soviet period who had placed Latvian literature (q.v.) at the service of the Communist Party, mentioning Grigulis by name.

GRĪNBERGS, TEODORS (1870-1962). Grīnbergs was a Lutheran theologian and clergyman who was awarded an honorary doctorate by the University of Latvia in 1929 and became archbishop of the Latvian Evangelical Lutheran Church in 1923. He held this post in Latvia until 1944 when he was deported to Germany before the reoccupation of Latvia by the Soviet army and continued his position as archbishop of the Latvian Lutheran Church in the émigré community. After 1945 Latvian Lutheranism (q.v.) had two parallel church organizations--one in Soviet Latvia and one in the west--each with its own church hierarchy and organized congregations.

GRĪNS, ALEKSANDRS (1895-1941). After finishing his secondary education in 1910, Grīns served in the Russian army, from 1916 onward in the Latvian Rifle Regiments (q.v.). He began his literary career in 1920 and during the next two decades became the most widely read historical novelist in Latvia. His novels frequently treated medieval themes, but several trilogies dealt with important periods in Latvian history such as the Great Northern War (q.v.) and the experiences of the Latvian Rifle Regiments. The writing in them tended to be a mix of historical accuracy and fantasy, and continued the tendency of the "national awakening" (q.v.) period to portray Latvian history in terms of heroic struggles against invading foreign enemies. He was deported in 1941 by the Soviet authorities and evidently executed.

GROSVALDS, FRIEDRICHS (1850-1924). After receiving his education in law at St. Petersburg University, Grosvalds worked as a lawyer in Riga (q.v.) and, from 1885 to 1919, was the head of the Riga Latvian Association (q.v.). During his tenure he also served in the post-1905 Imperial Russian Duma (q.v.), in the city council of Riga, and from 1919 to 1923 was the Latvian Ambassador to the Scandinavian countries.

GUERRILLAS (See PARTISANS).

- H -

HEINRICH OF LIVONIA (Latv. INDRIĶIS LATVIS) (c.1187- ?). The author of the *Chronicle of Heinrich of Livonia*, the oldest of the medieval chronicles (q.v.) that describe the twelfth- and thirteenth-century encounters between the German crusading orders (q.v.) and the inhabitants of the Latvian territories. Relatively little is known about his life. According to Latvian historians, Heinrich was among a group of boys chosen by Bishop Meinhard in the last decade of the twelfth century from the native population and sent to Germany (i.e., the German lands of the Holy Roman Empire) for an education in the monastery at Holstein. Returning to the Latvian region in 1203, Heinrich was appointed by Bishop Albert to be a lay religious leader (and possibly a clergyman) in what in Heinrich's chronicle is called the Imera district. His chronicle was written in the 1225-1227 period and is based on personal experience from his movements among the early crusaders and missionaries.

HERDER, JOHANN GOTTFRIED (1744-1803). Herder was a cultural philosopher in Germany during the second half of the Enlightenment period, when some of the leading figures of the "philosophical century" had begun to question its main tenets.

Though he believed in the idea of progress and the ideal of humanity (*Humanität*), he also assigned exceptional importance to human cultural diversity, believing that each people (*Volk*) had a unique culture and that all such cultures were of equal value. Even peasant peoples expressed their unique culture through their language, history, folkways, and traditions. Herder became part of Latvian history through his residence in Riga (q.v.) as a teacher in the school of the Riga Dome Church, through his interest in the Latvian folk songs (*dainas*, q.v.), a number of which appeared in German translation in his publications, and also through the fact that his cultural philosophy appeared to equalize the actual (and potential) cultural expressions of Europe's small peoples and those of the large national societies. Herder's thinking directly and indirectly was very influential among the leading figures of the Latvian "national awakening" (q.v.).

HERRNHUT (See **MORAVIAN BRETHREN**).

HISTORIOGRAPHY. Inclusively defined, historiography refers to the research and writing techniques used to establish and describe the past. The development of Latvian historiography is conventionally divided into: (1) a long period (roughly the nineteenth century) when research in and writing about the Latvian territories was accomplished largely by non-Latvians (Baltic Germans and Russians, qq.v.); (2) a shorter period (roughly the 1890s to World War I) during which the earlier descriptions were challenged by a small number (e.g., Jānis Krodznieks) of Latvian historians, some of them (e.g., Kārlis Landers) using the Marxist-Leninist interpretative scheme; (3) the interwar period of Latvian independence, which contained (mostly in the 1930s) the emergence of institutions and publications of a Latvian historical profession; (4) the period from 1945 to 1989, during which Latvian historical research and writing was accomplished, first, by historians in Latvia in the Academy of Sciences (q.v.) and universities using (in various ways and to differing extents) the Marxist-Leninist scheme of historical interpretation; and, second, historians in the West (mostly émigrés to the late 1950s), who followed the standard techniques of Western historiography and can be divided into those who were more interested in the Latvian population of the Baltic territories, those whose interest gravitated toward the history of the Baltic Germans, and those who were interested in the area as an aspect of general Russian, diplomatic, or economic history; and (5) the period that started in 1989 during which the institutional base for doing history in Latvia is being transformed, the Marxist-Leninist scheme of historical interpretation has been rejected, and the split between historians in and outside of Latvia has been virtually eliminated. Like all categorizations, this periodization of Latvian historiography is imperfect, and the revisionistic goals of the last period have yet to yield their first substantial results.

HUPEL, AUGUST WILHELM (1737-1819). Hupel was a well-known Baltic German (q.v.) writer and publisher in the Baltic provinces (q.v.) during the last decades of the eighteenth and early decades of the nineteenth century. His publishing efforts produced a series of descriptive works of Livland (q.v.) and Estland (1774-1782) when these provinces were not well known or understood.

- I -

INDEPENDENCE WARS (Latv. **ATBRĪVOŠANAS CĪŅAS, NEATKARĪBAS CĪŅAS**). A series of battles fought by the armed forces of the newly established Latvian government, headed by Kārlis Ulmanis (q.v.), from March 1919 to January 1920, as a result of which all the military units opposed to Latvian independence were driven from Latvian territory. In January 1919, the situation of the new Latvian government, formed after the November 18, 1918 proclamation of independence, looked hopeless. It had virtually no standing army. The hostilities of World War I had ended, and, although Germany had agreed to the armistice of November 11, 1918, its army still occupied Courland (q.v.) (Kurzeme). Moreover, by January 1919 the army of the Latvian Bolsheviks (q.v.) had taken power in Livland (Vidzeme), occupied Riga (qq.v.), and formed a government headed by Pēteris Stučka (q.v.).

In January 1919 the Latvian government, having fled to Liepāja (Ger. *Libau*) in Courland and now, in a sense, under the protection of the Germans, appointed Oskars Kalpaks (q.v.) to form a Latvian army. The volunteer Latvian army thus hastily created joined with the Germans in a temporary alliance against the Bolshevik forces. In March 1991, Kalpaks was killed and Jānis Balodis (q.v.) was named to command the Latvian forces. Political relationships deterioriated, however: the Germans expelled the Ulmanis government from Liepāja in April, and created a German-sponsored Latvian government headed by Andrievs Niedra (q.v.). Still, a combined German-Latvian army routed the Bolsheviks from Riga and Livland by the end of May 1919.

Having succeeded against the common enemy, the Latvian army under Balodis and the Germans now confronted each other. The German army units, commanded by Rüdiger von der Goltz, had in the meantime been joined by some units of the Russian "White" (anti-Bolshevik) army commanded by an adventurer named Pavel Bermont-Avalov. Von der Goltz and Bermont-Avalov formed an alliance against the Latvians and swept northward into Livland (Vidzeme). The Latvians in turn requested and received military help from the armed forces of the new Estonian government and a combined Latvian-Estonian army defeated the advancing German army near the Livland city of Cēsis (Ger. *Wenden*) (q.v.). The summer months brought a respite and allowed the Latvian army to expand and supply itself. Although the Versailles Peace Treaty was signed on June 28, and all armed forces of Germany were required to leave the territories they occupied, von der Goltz found various pretexts to delay his departure and continued his alliance with Bermont-Avalov.

The Niedra government, however, was dismissed in June and the Ulmanis government returned to Riga on July 8. In early November, the Latvian army, its ranks much enlarged and its infantry better trained and supplied, attacked the "bermontieši" (as the combined German-White Russian army had come to be called) near Riga, and continued to drive it south out of Latvian territory throughout November. By mid-December, von der Goltz's units, having also been defeated by the Lithuanian army, were on their way back to Germany. In January 1920, the Latvian national army, together with Polish units sent by Josef Piłsudski, defeated the remnants of the Latvian Bolshevik army, which by that time were still in control of the extreme southeastern corner of Latvian territory in Latgale (q.v.) (including the cities of Rēzekne and Daugavpils). This was the last military action of the "independence wars." Latvia signed peace treaties with Germany in July and with Soviet Russia in August 1920.

IRBE, KĀRLIS (1861-1934). Irbe was one of the more prominent Lutheran clergymen of Latvian birth before World War I, in a period when the Baltic German (q.v.) influence on Latvian Lutheranism (q.v.) remained strong. He helped organize the affairs of the Latvian Evangelical Lutheran Church in Russia as the president of its Consistory during the turmoil of World War I and the immediate postwar period and then served as its first Bishop of the Church in Latvia during the period from 1922 to 1931.

IRLAVA TEACHERS SEMINARY. Established in 1841 by the Courland Nobility (*Ritterschaft*), the Irlava seminary (teacher training institute) prepared some 835 youths to become primary- and secondary-school teachers, and from this number some 750 actually worked in that capacity in Courland (q.v.). In Latvian history, the Irlava seminary had the same intended role in Courland as the seminary headed by Jānis Cimze (q.v.) in Livland, namely, to educate young Latvians to become teachers primarily in rural areas in order to raise the cultural level of the Latvian peasantry. One unintended consequence was that after the 1850s many of these rural schoolteachers -- in Courland and Livland -- became the prime movers in the Latvian "national awakening" (q.v.), challenging Baltic German (q.v.) cultural, political and economic hegemony in the Latvian territories. The seminary was closed in 1900 when the Courland Nobility ceased its funding.

ISKOLAT. The word used to describe the short-lived government of soviets established at the end of 1917 in the small part of Vidzeme (q.v.) that had temporarily escaped occupation by the German army, which at that time controlled virtually all Latvian territory. The Iskolat "government" came into being as a byproduct of the October (November) Revolution in St. Petersburg, when the Bolsheviks overthrew the Russian provisional government. In the Latvian territories, the Bolshevik cause had made considerable headway, especially among the *strēlnieki* (q.v.), on whose help the Latvian Bolsheviks (q.v.) counted. From December 16 to 18 there took place in Valmiera (q.v.) the Second Congress of Latvian Workers, Soldiers, and Landless Persons with 297 delegates, who proclaimed the existence of a soviet government in the unoccupied part of

Vidzeme. Ultimate power was granted to a Latvian soviet consisting of 69 persons, which in turn elected an executive committee of 26 persons led by the Bolshevik Fricis Roziņš (q.v.). Roziņš had participated in the "new current" (q.v.) in the 1890s, worked on *Dienas Lapa* with Jānis Rainis and Pēteris Stučka (qq.v.), and had afterward become one of the leading Latvian Bolsheviks.

The Iskolat government, however, was unable to accomplish very much because, in February 1918, the German army occupied the rest of the Latvian territory, forcing the Bolsheviks and their supporters to flee. Moreover, since the Iskolat government's future plans (and those of the Latvian Bolsheviks in general) did not unambiguously call for an independent Latvia--which was being demanded by a now burgeoning national independence movement--Iskolat's appeal in broader circles was in any case limited. The Latvian Bolsheviks had to wait until 1919 for another try at establishing a Soviet Latvia.

IZGLĪTĪBAS MINISTRIJAS MĒNEŠRAKSTS (IMM). Published from 1920 to 1940, the IMM (Ministry of Education Monthly) was the official organ of the Education Ministry in the interwar period. But, in the elative absence of specialized scholarly journals in Latvia, the IMM also served as an outlet for numerous scholarly studies on history, linguistics, pedagogy, and biography.

- J -

JĀŅI. The Latvian festival marking the summer solstice and celebrated on June 23-24. Though this festival was probably very significant in the pre-Christian era in the Latvian territories, since the thirteenth century, June 24 was considered to be the birthday of John the Baptist and thus the pagan and Christian traditions were linked. In the Latvian church calendar, June 24 has been set as the name day for "John." In Latvian celebrations of Jāņi the Christian elements tend to be underemphasized, giving way to all manner of presumably non-Christian rites, decorations, activities, and songs (e.g., the wearing of oak-leaf wreaths). The high point of these events is the evening of June 23 and the night between June 23 and 24, and involves the lighting of bonfires, preparation of special foods and drinks, and the singing of special Jāņi songs, some of ancient vintage. In the Soviet period from 1959 to 1966, when Arvīds Pelše (q.v.) was the first secretary of the Communist Party, the Party's drive against "bourgeois nationalism" included for a time the prohibition of the Jāņi festival.

JANSONS-BRAUNS, JĀNIS (1872-1917). The son of a farmer in Vidzeme, Jansons-Brauns received his secondary education in Nicholas Gymnasium in Liepāja (q.v.), continued his education at Moscow University, but in 1895 switched to Dorpat (Tartu) University in order to study law. Having become preoccupied with politics, however, he did not finish his studies but after 1895 became a prominent figure in the "new current" (q.v.) and one of the leaders of the growing Latvian socialist movement. He broke into print with the 1893 publication in *Dienas Lapa* (q.v.) (the "new current's" newspaper) with a speech called "Thoughts on Contemporary Literature," in which he satirized Latvian writers and urged them to become literary realists so as to enter the mainstream of European literature. In subsequent writings he became increasingly critical of the "national" element in Latvian literature (q.v.) and increasingly insistent that it consciously pursue socially relevant themes, especially pertaining to the plight of the working classes.

Arrested together with many other "new current" figures in 1897 for revolutionary activities, he was exiled from the Baltic to Smolensk. After this his political career turned increasingly leftward. In 1904, he was elected to the Central Committee of the Latvian Social Democratic Party (q.v.) and, in 1905, he was one of the leaders of revolutionary activity in the Latvian region of the Baltic provinces (q.v.). During the last decade of his life, Jansons-Brauns led an unsettled existence, which alternated between short stays in Latvia and longer stays in various European countries where he was actively engaged in building the Latvian socialist movement. Throughout his political career, however, he retained an active interest in Latvian literature and remained as much a political writer as a literary critic. He died in 1917 in the North Sea on a voyage between England and Latvia when his ship was torpedoed by a German submarine.

JAUNĀ STRĀVA. See **NEW CURRENT.**

JAUNBEBRI PEASANT UPRISING (1841). Sometimes also known as the "Jaunbebri potato uprising," this incident followed a long series of bad harvests from 1835 to 1837 and in 1840. It was one of many disturbances of this kind in the Latvian territories during the 1830s and 1840s, as bad weather, harvest failures, and the labor rents of the post-emancipation combined to form in the peasantry a chronic but unsatisfied desire to improve their condition. Freedom of contract suggested to peasants freedom of movement as well, but the emancipation laws had left with the estate owners the right to control the movement of peasants across estate boundaries. Peasants flocked to Riga (q.v.) and other administrative centers for permission to emigrate to the "warm lands" (q.v.) of the Russian Empire. Estate owners requested detachments of soldiers to prevent such peasant wanderings.

In September 1841, in Jaunbebri in Vidzeme (q.v.) (Livland) there was a clash between a military contingent that had arrested some peasants and other peasants who had gathered for the potato harvest in Veselauska estate but now sought to free the prisoners. The confrontation grew in size and ultimately required some 10,000 soldiers and two cannon before the peasants were dispersed. About 113 peasants were tried and sentenced to run the gauntlets between soldiers to receive as many as 1,500 lashes. Among those who survived, many were imprisoned and later transported to Siberia.

JAUNLATVIEŠI. Meaning "Young Latvians" in English, this term appeared in Baltic German (q.v.) writings of the 1850s to describe the first generation of Latvians (such as Juris Alunāns and Krišjānis Valdemārs, qq.v.) who participated in the Latvian "national awakening" (q.v.). As used by Baltic German commentators, the term was clearly polemical and proposed that the authorities (including the czarist government) view the Latvian challenge to the Baltic German cultural hegemony as identical to the "Young Italy" and "Young Germany" (e.g., Heinrich Heine) nationalist movements in western Europe, many participants of which were outright revolutionaries. In Soviet-era Latvian historical writing, the term *jaunlatvieši* achieved wide usage again because it eliminated the need for the term "national" (as in "national awakening") and permitted "Young Latvians" to be portrayed more easily as the byproducts of economic change (i.e., as the development of a Latvian urban and professional "bourgeoisie" with its ideology of "bourgeois nationalism").

JAUNSUDRABIŅŠ, JĀNIS (1877-1962). Jaunsudrabiņš's first publication (a poem) appeared in 1896, and from that point onward his productivity never ceased. Already before World War I he had established a reputation as a poet, short story writer, and painter who drew his inspiration not only from the rural experiences of his youth but also from his wide travels. These characteristics of his creative work continued during the interwar period of independence, as well as after 1944 when he emigrated to Germany. His collected works were published (1981-1985) in 18 volumes.

JAUNVOLE'S PEASANT UPRISING (1841). One of the many peasant disturbances on the 1830s and 1840s in the Latvian territories. It was similar to the Jaunbebri uprising (q.v.), but differed from it in that Jaunvole estate was in Latgale (q.v.) and thus not in the Baltic provinces (q.v.) proper. In the latter, the earlier emancipation laws and the idea of "freedom of contract" fed peasant unrest, while in Latgale, where emancipation would not arrive until 1861, the principal causes seemed to have been a series of bad harvests and (to the peasants) unacceptable amounts of corveé (q.v.) labor.

In Jaunvole estate near Ludza some 1,000 armed peasants took over the estate, and actually engaged in combat with the Russian military contingents sent to disarm and disperse them. Some 21 peasants were killed and about 200 were tried for sedition. Those found guilty were forced to run a gauntlet of soldiers, with the most severe punishment being 8,000 lashes. Those who did not die were transported to Siberia.

JELGAVA (Ger. **MITAU**; Russ. **MITAVA**). The fourth largest Latvian city in 1989 (74,000 inhabitants), Jelgava was for centuries the principal city of the duchy of Courland (q.v.) and retained that role when the duchy became a Russian province. The present site of the city was already inhabited in the early thirteenth century, when the Swordbrothers (q.v.) decided to build a castle there in 1265 to assist with the further colonization of the indigenous population of this region and to aid in defense against the Lithuanians. Because of its central location, over the subsequent centuries control over Jelgava changed hands relatively frequently and several times it was almost completely destroyed, most recently during World War II.

JEWS. In the Latvian territories, the Jewish population was sparse until the nineteenth century. The 1834 soul revision (q.v.) listed some 500 in the Latvian districts of Livonia (Vidzeme) but a substantially greater number--some 23,000--in Courland (Kurzeme) (qq.v.). The Courland figures may be explained by the fact that this province adjoined the northern border of the so-called Pale of Settlement (i.e., the northern border of the Lithuanian lands), and there was apparently substantial south-to-north migration. During the rest of the nineteenth century and until the 1930s, the total number of Jews in the Latvian territories continued to grow, reaching a maximum of about 95,000 in 1925 with about half of this number living in the capital city of Riga (q.v.) where in the interwar years they constituted the largest ethnic minority (after the majority Latvian population). During the second half of the 1930s, the total number of Jews fell somewhat due to outmigration.

The nearly total destruction of the Jewish population in Latvia came in the first year of the German occupation of the country (1941-1942) with the application of the "final solution" policy. In the countryside, many Jews were executed in or near their places of residence, and the Riga ghetto was created for the rest. The Riga ghetto also contained Jews brought there from other parts of German-occupied eastern Europe. During the course of 1941-1942 a large proportion of this population was killed in several sites (Rumbula, Biķernieki) on the outskirts of Riga. The total number of Jews killed in Latvia in the 1941-1945 period is estimated at about 83,000. During the post-World War II decades, in-migration from other parts of the Soviet Union and natural growth expanded the Jewish population in Latvia to about 22,900 in 1989.

- K -

KALNBĒRZIŅŠ, JĀNIS (1893-1986). A dedicated Communist of the 1920s, Kalnbērziņš served as the First secretary of the Communist Party (q.v.) in Soviet Latvia from 1940 to 1959 and in addition held a number of high-ranking posts both in the Soviet Latvian government and the Communist Party of the USSR. He was a staunch supporter of all Stalinist measures, including those that resulted in the deportation (q.v.) of several hundreds of thousands of Latvians to Siberia and in the progressive Russification (q.v.) of the Latvian SSR.

KALNIŅŠ, BRUNO (1899-1990). Kalniņš was one of the leaders of the Latvian Social Democratic party (q.v.) during the interwar period and its best-known activist when the party reorganized itself in Sweden after the World War II. In the period of World War I, he was a member of the National Council as well as of the Constitutional Convention and was also elected to all four Saeimas (q.v.) (parliaments) on the Social Democratic ticket. Imprisoned briefly (as were all of the most prominent Social Democrats) after the Ulmanis (q.v.) coup in 1934, he was in emigration from 1937 to 1940, but returned to Latvia in 1940, becoming a political functionary of the reorganized army. From 1944 to 1945, he was imprisoned in the Stuthof concentration camp in Germany, from which he left for Sweden. Prominent in European Social-Democratic circles, he was from 1983 the honorary president of the Socialist International.

KALNIŅŠ, PAULS (1872-1945). An activist in the Latvian Social Democratic Party (q.v.) almost since its founding, Kalniņš was also a deputy to the Constitutional Convention as well as to all of the four Saeimas (q.v.) (parliaments). In spite of his attachment to the ideals of social democracy, Kalniņš had a reputation for fairness and was chosen as president of the Saeima from 1925 to 1934. Imprisoned briefly after the Ulmanis (q.v.) 1934 coup, he returned to private life during the next decade, but went into exile in Germany in 1944 as the Soviet army began to reoccupy Latvia.

KALPAKS, OSKARS (1882-1919). Kalpaks began to serve in the czarist army in 1908 and had achieved officer rank well before the First World War. In 1918, after the Communist coup in Russia, he changed his allegiance to the new Latvian Provisional Government after the Latvian declaration of independence and, in 1919, he was named commander of the Provisional Government's armed forces that he had played a major role in forming. In 1919, during a battle in which the Latvian army, now in a temporary alliance with German units still on Latvian territory, was fighting units of the newly formed Red Army, Kalpaks was killed by a German bullet in a crossfire. His contribution to the Latvian War of Independence (q.v.) has been commemorated with the declaration of a national holiday in February.

KANGARS. Originally one of the main figures in Andrejs Pumpurs' (q.v.) *Lāčplēsis*, the 1888 national epic, and Jānis Rainis (q.v.)

Uguns un nakts, a play based on the former. In both these works of fiction, Kangars is a political leader who plotted with the German crusaders and missionaries to help them conquer the Latvian territories. The term (written with a lowercase "k") has entered the Latvian language as a synonym for the terms "traitor" or "quisling," the latter of which has a similar derivation.

KĀRTA (*See* ESTATE).

KAUDZĪTE, MATĪSS (1848-1926) and **REINIS** (1839-1920). Two brothers whose position in the history of Latvian literature (q.v.) rests largely on their joint creation--the novel *Mērnieku laiki* (*Time of the Surveyors*), published in 1879. The novel was the first Latvian-written representative of this genre of literary creativity, and most Latvian literary historians rank it as one of the best, if not the best, novel ever written in the Latvian language. It is certainly unrivaled in terms of popularity and in terms of sharply drawn characterizations of personality types among rural Latvians. The novel was set in the second half of the nineteenth century, when surveying was a significant phenomenon in rural Latvian territories in connection with rapid changes in the ownership of farmland. Interweaving three plot lines--a romantic-sentimental, a satiric, and a criminal--the Kaudzītes' populated their novel with persons who quickly entered Latvian popular thought as types: the speechifying nationalist whose language is saturated with references to a grandiose "higher mission"; the crafty peasant, whose piety disguises a fervent materialism; the poseur, who pretends to have transcended his Latvian peasant background by filling his conversation with (ungrammatical) German phrases and expressions; the strong, silent, and honest young man who resists the pressure to conform. Both of the Kaudzīte brothers made other literacy contributions to the "national awakening" (q.v.) effort before 1879, and both continued to publish in various genres of Latvian writing afterward as well, especially in the area of pedagogical literature. But their fame rests on *Mērnieku laiki*.

KAUGURI PEASANT UPRISING (1802). The best-known of the peasant disturbances that punctuated the territory of present-day Latvia during the last decades of the eighteenth and the first half of the nineteenth century. In 1801, in Vidzeme (Livonia, Livland) the harvest was poor, and the provincial government was forced to suspend for a time the dues-in-kind that the peasantry was being asked to pay in lieu of the existing capitation tax. This extra labor was being used by estate owners to increase permanently corvée (q.v.) labor as such. Using the suspension period, many peasants--especially in the Valmiera (Wolmar) and Cēsis (Wenden) districts (qq.v.)--demanded the right to pay the capitation tax without intervention from estate owners and refused to deliver the extra corvee. Many demanded that the government free them from subordination to private estate owners and consider them instead crown peasants.

The resistance was particularly strong in Kauguri estate, where a crowd of about 3,000 peasants from Kauguri and surrounding estates gathered to express their opposition. The estate owner decided to call for help from the Russian military. On October 10, a clash killed 18 peasants and wounded eight. When additional military units arrived, the crowd dispersed. The leaders of the uprising were arrested, tried, and sentenced to Siberian exile for various lengths of time. Historians believe that this uprising and earlier ones of lesser severity led to the consideration of peasant reforms and eventually to the new Peasant Law of 1804, which in Livland sought, among other things, to fix by law the amount of corvée labor estate owners could require from peasant families.

ĶEMPS, FRANCIS (1876-?). After finishing his engineering education in St. Petersburg, Ķemps became from 1905 an active and important journalist in Latgale (q.v.) in the movement known as the "Lettgallian awakening." He was particularly concerned with refining the Lettgallian (q.v.) language. When he served as a deputy from Latgale in the Constitutional Convention and the first Saeima (q.v.) (parliament), he not only defended Letgallian cultural autonomy within an independent Latvia but also championed Lettgallian separatism.

ĶĒNIŅŠ, ATIS (1874-1961). After graduating from the Irlava Teachers Seminary (q.v.), Ķēniņš worked as a schoolteacher and, after 1900, directed several private high schools in Riga (q.v.), while at the same time establishing his reputation as a poet working in the romantic and symbolic style. He was also active in politics and, from 1919 to 1921, was the Latvian ambassador to Poland. In 1940, he actively opposed the single-list election carried out by the new Soviet Latvian government, for which action he was deported to Siberia. He later returned to Latvia where he worked in the Institute of Languages until his retirement.

KETTLER, GOTTHARD. *See* **CRUSADING ORDERS; DUCHY OF COURLAND AND SEMIGALLIA; LIVONIAN WAR**

KGB (*See* ČEKISTI).

KIRCHENŠTEINS, AUGUSTS (1872-1963). A microbiologist by profession and with sympathies for the political left, Kirchenšteins jumped to the front ranks of political leadership in 1940, when, after the occupation of Latvia by the Soviet Army, he was asked by the Moscow Communist leadership to form and head a government (a "People's Government") to replace that of Ulmanis (q.v.) As head of the new government in August 1940, he also headed the delegation that traveled to Moscow to formally request annexation of Latvia to the USSR. Kirchenšteins remained as chairman of the Latvian Supreme Soviet (q.v.) from 1940 to 1952 (having fled to the Soviet Union during the occupation of Latvia by the German forces from 1941 to 1945), while at the same time organizing and directing (from 1946 to 1962) the Microbiological Institute of the Latvian Academy of Sciences (q.v.).

KLĪVE, ĀDOLFS (1888-1874). Klīve finished his university studies in economics in Moscow in 1913 and thereafter worked as a teacher in Jelgava (q.v.). During the First World War he was deeply involved in organizations dealing with Latvian refugees and, in 1917, he became a cofounder of the Agrarian Union (q.v.) party on behalf of which he continued to work throughout the interwar years. He was a deputy to the first three Saeimas (q.v.) (parliaments) and held other offices such as president of the board of the Bank of Latvia (1931-1940). Emigrating to Germany in 1944 and to the United States in 1950, Klīve continued to work in émigré organizations for the rest of his life.

KNORIŅŠ, VILHELMS (1890-1938). An early adherent to the Bolshevik (q.v.) cause and a revolutionary activist, Knoriņš lived in Soviet Russia after the founding of the independent Latvian state and held a number of important party posts, including from 1927 to 1928 the position of secretary of the Central Committee of the Byelorussian Communist Party. He was also active in the apparatus of the Communist International. Having literary and historical interests, Knoriņš wrote works on party history and literary criticism, but was executed during Stalin's purge of "Old Bolsheviks". He was officially rehabilitated during the Khrushchev era.

ĶONIŅI (*See* **COURLAND KINGS**).

KONSUMS. The name of a union of cooperative organizations founded in 1907 and dissolved in 1937. Konsums was a good example of the strength and popularity of the cooperative movement in the Latvian territories before World War I and during the interwar period. By 1910, its membership consisted of some 74 cooperative organizations and 88 individual persons. In 1917 and again in 1918, rules of membership were changed so as to permit as members only organizations. By 1931, Konsums had among its members 337 cooperatives, 106 consumer organizations, 54 dairy producers' organizations, and 15 savings and loan associations. By 1937, Konsums was experiencing severe financial difficulties and had to be reorganized; its successor was a similar umbrella organization called Turība.

KREITUSE, ILGA (1952-   ). After the October 1995 election of the Sixth Saeima (q.v.), Kreituse, a member of the Democratic Party Saimnieks (q.v.) and a deputy in the Fifth Saeima, was elected to the presidency of the Saeimain November 1996, replacing Anatolijs Gorbunovs (q.v.). A historian by profession, she received her doctorate from Moscow State University in 1982 and returned to Latvia to teach in the University of Latvia and do research in the Latvian Institute of History and the Institute of Communist Party History.

KRIEVIŅI. Although literally the term is the diminutive form of the Latvian word *krievi* (Russians), it actually refers to a small population called Votes, brought as prisoners of war from Ingria to Courland (q.v.) by the master of the Livonian Order (q.v.) in the mid-fifteenth century. They were settled in the region of the city of Bauska. Speaking a Finno-Ugric language, they retained a distinct linguistic and cultural identity until the end of the nineteenth century (about 1,600 persons in 1820), when there was still one congregation in which services were conducted in the Vote language. By that time, however, their numbers had been reduced dramatically by intermarriage with and assimilation to the Latvian-speaking population of the region, so that the censuses of the twentieth-century did not list them as a separate "national" minority.

KRONVALDS, ATIS (1837-1875). From the late 1860s onward until his premature death, Kronvalds was the most outspoken and widely known participant of the Latvian "national awakening" (q.v.). He came to this position relatively late in comparison with other Latvian nationalists, perhaps because of the close personal ties he had developed with various members of the Baltic German (q.v.) intelligentsia. He grew up in meager rural circumstances, had to interrupt his secondary education because of a lack of resources, and depended upon Baltic German assistance to study for a semester at Berlin University. He made his living as a schoolteacher, but during the 1860s contributed increasingly to the Latvian-language press. By comparison with Krišjānis Valdemārs (q.v.), who argued for Latvian economic development, Kronvalds emphasized the need for Latvians not only to preserve but to develop and expand their language and culture. On this theme he engaged in polemical exchanges in the pages of the Baltic German-language press, with one of his lengthy defenses (1871) of Latvian culture--entitled *Nationale Bestrebungen*-- becoming one of the best-known documents of the Latvian "national awakening" (ironically, the work was not translated into Latvian until 1887).

In it, and in his other speeches and writings, Kronvalds adapted to Latvian circumstances the nationalistic ideas of Herder (q.v.) and Fichte, especially the former because Herder himself had lived and taught in Riga (q.v.) for a while. In Kronvalds's view, the Latvians were not simply a peasantry but a "nation." Their culture and language were of equal value to those of others, even though both the Latvian language and culture needed improvement and development. Working toward that goal,

Kronvalds created hundreds of neologisms for the language and ceaselessly argued that Latvian schoolteachers had as their primary responsibility the education of their pupils in their parental tongue. The sharpening of his attitudes on cultural matters led Kronvalds to publicly criticize even those Baltic Germans who were positively disposed toward Latvian cultural nationalism; the further development of Latvian culture, he argued, should be in the hands of Latvians themselves. Kronvalds died in 1875 at the age of 38, just when his viewpoint was gaining momentum within the Latvian intelligentsia.

KUNDZIŅŠ, KĀRLIS, SR. (1850-1937). Kundziņš, a Latvian, was the first prominent Lutheran (q.v.) clergyman and theologian in the pre-World War I period to emphasize the need for church reform in the Baltic in terms of the principle of nationality, illustrating in this attitude how the new forms of thinking created by the Latvian "national awakening" (q.v.) were eroding the traditional authority of the Baltic German (q.v.) population. In addition to his prominence in the Latvian Lutheran church after 1918, Kundziņš also established for himself an excellent reputation as a biographer of those Baltic German clergy--such as Ernst Glück and G. F. Stender (qq.v.)--who had played an important role in creating a Latvian literary language through their translations of sacred texts.

KUNDZIŅŠ, KĀRLIS, JR. (1883-1867). Son of Kārlis Kundziņš, Sr. (q.v.), the junior Kundziņš followed in his father's footsteps by becoming one of the most prominent figures of the Latvian Lutheran (q.v.) church in the interwar period through his theological writings and pedagogical work in the Theology Faculty of the University of Latvia. Emigrating to Germany in 1944 and to the United States in 1951, he continued to play a central role in helping to lay the organizational basis of a Latvian Lutheran Church outside of Latvia, becoming its Archbishop (i.e., chief official) in 1962.

KURELIS, JĀNIS (1882-1954). Kurelis served in the czarist army as well as in the army of the Republic of Latvia, in which he received the rank of general in 1925. During the Second World War and the period of German occupation of Latvia, Kurelis worked in the War Invalids' Association but later joined the Riga

Aizsargi (q.v.), in which in 1944 he organized a subunit that was known as "kurelieši" in order to help resist the advancing Soviet army in Kurzeme (Courland, q.v.). Initially supporting this action, the commanders of the German army in the Baltic area later came to believe that they were losing control over the formation and activities of the unit (which had grown to include some 1,000 soldiers and partisans) and evidently called for its dissolution. Some of the Latvian officers of the unit resisted the dissolution and were tried and executed for treason on the battlefield. Kurelis himself was believed by the Germans not to have been involved in the resistance and was released. Aspects of this episode have remained unexplained and mysterious to this day, since some of the German military leadership interpreted the "kurelieši" as a core of a nascent Latvian "national army" while historians tend to see the failure of the group to disband as the result of miscommunication, with resistance to German orders expressed by individual, lower-level Latvian officers.

KURLAND (*See* DUCHY OF COURLAND AND SEMIGALLIA)

KURS (*See* COURONIANS).

KURZEME (*See* COURONIANS ; DUCHY OF COURLAND AND SEMIGALLIA).

KVIESIS, ALBERTS (1881-1944). Kviesis was the third president of the interwar Republic of Latvia, serving for two terms from 1930 to 1936. A lawyer by profession, Kviesis was active in Latvian political affairs even before World War I and, during that conflict, worked in the Latvian Refugee Committee. A member of the Agrarian Union (q.v.) party, Kviesis served as a deputy in the National Council, the Constitutional Convention, and also from his party to the first three Saeimas (q.v.) (parliaments). When, in May 1934, Kārlis Ulmanis (q.v.)--the leader of Kviesis' own party--carried out his successful coup, Kviesis was allowed to remain as the elected president until the end of his term, when Ulmanis (q.v.) assumed the presidency himself. During the German occupation of Latvia (1941-1945), Kviesis worked for the Latvian "self-government" (q.v.), initially as a legal consultant and then as head of the Juridical Directorate.

- L -

LĀCIS, VILIS (1904-1966). Lācis was one of a number of prominent pre-World War II Latvian authors who did not flee Latvia to the west during the final years of World War II. His writings dealt with the everyday life of the working classes. Lācis's political sympathies had been with the Bolshevik (q.v.) movement for a long time, and he joined the illegal Latvian Communist Party (q.v.) in 1928. As a prominent leftist active in various workers' causes in the interwar years, Lācis was kept under surveillance especially during the Ulmanis (q.v.) period, but, in spite of this, his literary career flourished due to the popularity of his novels, especially *Zvejnieka dēls* (*The Fisherman's Son*) (1933). He served as minister of interior in the 1940 cabinet of Augusts Kirchenšteins (q.v.) that requested annexation of Latvia to the Soviet Union, fled to the interior of Russia during the German occupation from 1941 to 1944, and returned to the Latvian SSR after the war. There, he resumed his literary career (receiving several Orders of Lenin and the Stalin Prize) and held a number of largely symbolic but high party and government posts until his death in 1966.

LĀČPLĒSIS (See **ANDREJS PUMPURS**).

LĀČPLĒSIS, ORDER OF. The Latvian equivalent of the U.S. Congressional Medal of Honor, the Lāčplēsis Order was created in November 1919, and formalized by an act of parliament in 1920. Awarded for exceptional heroism, the Order used the name of the hero of Andrejs Pumpur's epic poem *Lāčplēsis*.

LAICĒNS, LINARDS (1883-1938). Although before World War I Laicēns was a nationalist and an active proponent of Latvian cultural autonomy within the Russian Empire, during the war he joined the Bolshevik (q.v.) cause. From 1928 to 1934 he was a deputy in the Saeima (q.v.) (parliament) from the left-wing Workers and Farmers Party, and in 1932 he emigrated from independent Latvia to the Soviet Union. A poet and literary figure of some note after 1909, he worked first in the social realism tradition but later produced works in which a class war ideology was dominant. He was evidently executed during Stalin's purge of the Old Bolsheviks.

LAIKS. Laiks (Time) is the name of several Latvian periodical publications, the most important of which have been the art and literature monthly published by Helmārs Rudzītis (q.v.) from 1946 to 1949, during the DP (q.v.) period in Esslingen in the American Zone of Germany, and the biweekly newspaper published by Rudzitiş publishing house *Grāmatu Draugs* (q.v.) in New York from 1949 onward. Over the decades the latter became the most important Latvian-language newspaper published outside Latvia, with its 4,500th issue appearing in October 1993. In July 1996, *Laiks* became a weekly newspaper, a change that reflected the gradual shrinkage of the Latvian émigré (q.v.) world after the reacquistion of Latvian independence in 1991.

LANDERS, KĀRLIS (1875-1937). After finishing his secondary education, Landers worked as a schoolteacher and from 1904 onward was an active member of the Latvian Social Democratic Party (q.v.). In 1912, he took up residence in Russia and became an increasingly ardent Bolshevik (q.v.), assuming important regional posts in the party hierarchy after 1917. In the history of Latvian-language historical writing, Landers stood out as the author of a very popular history of Latvia, published in three parts from 1908 to 1909. Written entirely from the historical materialist viewpoint, Landers's history was one of the first book-length expositions of Latvian history written by a Latvian.

LANDLESSNESS. Historically, the term is used for that segment of a society´s rural population that retains rural residence but does not own or have ready access to land. In Latvian history, the term could be applied, technically, to all peasants in the Latvian territories before the 1850s, because the peasants' "rights" to the land they worked had been very tenuous during the period of serfdom and became even more so after serf emancipation (q.v.) in the early nineteenth century. But the landless emerged as a "problem" needing a solution only during the second half of the nineteenth century, when population growth started to exert pressure on both the supply of rural land and against the estate system through which relatively few landowners (mainly the Baltic German nobility) owned a large proportion of all the farmland. Though, from the late 1850s onward, peasant land on estates was being sold to those who worked it, by 1897 there were some 600,000 persons (farmhands and their families) in the rural areas of the Latvian territories who worked as agricultural laborers with little opportunity to obtain farms of their own.

The peasantry itself was becoming stratified into the so-called gray barons (peasant landowners) and the landless. Historians attribute the popularity of socialist and eventually Bolshevik ideas among rural Latvians precisely to this large proportion of the landless, as evidenced by the demands of the March 1917 Congress of Landless Peasants (*Bezzemnieku kongress*) that met in Valmiera (q.v.), elected a council composed of Social Democrats and Bolsheviks (qq.v.), and issued a call for the confiscation of all landed estates and the redistribution of their land. The explosiveness of this problem in the Latvian context was substantially defused by the agrarian reform (q.v.) of the early 1920s in which the new Latvian government implemented just such measures of confiscation and redistribution.

LANDTAG. A quasi-parliamentary institution in the premodern period of the German-speaking lands of Europe, the *Landtag* assembled periodically to discuss the problems of the territories its deputies represented and to take appropriate action. In the Baltic area, meetings of various *Landtage* (pl.) took place from 1419 to 1918, making these assemblies the most important continuous political institutions of the region. Initially, to 1562, a *Landtag* existed for the Livonian (q.v.) state as a whole, but thereafter there were separate *Landtage* for each of the constituent provinces of the Baltic territories (Livonia, Courland, Estonia, Polish Livonia). Normally, these assemblies were dominated by the landed aristocracy (German-speaking for the most part in the Latvian territories), though other upper orders (burghers, for example) were occasionally represented in them as well.

Relations between the *Landtage* and the territorial sovereigns were frequently antagonistic, with monarchs (or dukes, as in Courland, q.v.) seeking to control the *Landtage* and the *Landtage* insisting on the preservation of their rights. In many European countries, these medieval assemblies evolved into truly representative parliamentary institutions, but this did not happen in the Baltic area. The Baltic *Landtage*, for example, permitted no representatives from the peasant order (*Bauernstand*), but created virtually all of the reform laws that from the early nineteenth century onward affected the lives of the members of that order.

The Baltic *Landtage* of the latter decades of the nineteenth century became at the same time centers of opposition to the rising Latvian demands for shared governance and to Russification (q.v.) efforts emanating from St. Petersburg, and therefore took on the appearance of being simply defenders of Baltic German privileges. These institutions in the Latvian territory were eliminated by the creation of the Latvian parliament, or Saeima (q.v.), in the new Latvian state after 1918.

LANGUAGE LAW. The Latvian Constitution of 1922 did not contain wording that made Latvian the language of the state. A decree giving Latvian that status was issued later during the personal rule of Kārlis Ulmanis (q.v.). The matter became moot, however, after the 1940 incorporation of Latvia into the Soviet Union and the return of Soviet power to Latvia in 1945. During the period from 1945 to 1989 language use in Latvia was determined more by the policy goals of the central Moscow government than by statutory laws or decrees, and the widely shared perception among Latvians was that Russian was being made the de facto official language of the state, of culture, and of education (*see* Russification).

One of the first laws of the so-called third awakening (q.v.) when Latvia was still part of the Soviet Union was the Language Law of 1989 (May 5) in which the Latvian Supreme Soviet (q.v.) proclaimed Latvian as the language of the Latvian state. The law was hardly enforced in the period preceding complete independence in August 1991, and then, during 1992, it was supplemented by strengthening laws and regulations in May, June, July, and November 1992. Summing up, the Language Law and accompanying regulations set out the meaning of the concept of "state language" as it applied to everyday use and created machinery for testing language competency among those of whom the law required knowledge of Latvian. Testing of Latvian competency began in 1992 and has continued since then in various areas of state and private employment. A degree of controversy has accompanied the implementation of the law, especially with respect to language requirements for naturalization and with respect to the accuracy and fairness of testing procedures.

LATGALE. In the interwar period of independence, Latgale was the second largest of the four main divisions of the country (Vidzeme, Latgale, Kurzeme, Zemgale), containing about 29 percent of the total population of Latvia. Its territory in modern times lay athwart the old pre-13th-century kingdoms of Talava and Jersika, although precise borders of the latter two are difficult to determine. While throughout the medieval centuries and until the seventeenth the inhabitants of the Latgale territory experienced a history similar to those of other Latvian lands, a separate history of Latgale began in the mid-seventeenth century, when western Latvian territories (including Courland, q.v.) were dominated by Protestant sovereigns (or dukes, in Courland), while Latgale remained under the direct rule of Catholic Poland. Furthermore, from the late eighteenth century onward, when Russian rule over all of the Baltic area became final, most of the territory of Latgale was included administratively in Vitebsk province, whereas the western Latvian territories lay in the Baltic provinces (q.v.) proper (i.e., Courland and Livland, q.v.).

In the nineteenth century, serf emancipation in the Baltic provinces was carried out in the 1816-1819 period, but in Latgale not until the general emancipation of Russian serfs in 1861. Latvian historians date the "national awakening" (q.v.) in the western Latvian territories as starting in the 1850s, but in Latgale not until the turn of the twentieth century. Though Latgale was a full-fledged constituent part of the Latvian state after 1918, it retained a distinct version of the Latvian language as well as some separatist sentiment among its intellectuals and political leaders. Because of geographical and occupational mobility, however, especially during the post-1945 Soviet period, the sharpness of regional differences in Latvia have tended to diminish. But the southeastern districts of Latgale still contain a greater Latvian, Russian, Polish, Belorussian, and Lithuanian cultural mix than any other area in present-day Latvia.

LATVIAN CENTRAL COUNCIL (Latv. **LATVIEŠU CENTRĀLĀ PADOME**). From 1945 to 1950, the council was the chief organization of Latvian emigrants in the immediate post-World War II period. Initially it concerned itself with refugees only in the Allied zones of Germany, but then included refugees in Austria and Denmark as well. Apolitical in intent, the council set itself the mission of improving the refugees' material and cultural conditions, freeing Latvian prisoners of war in Allied POW camps and protecting their rights, and providing material and medical assistance to invalids and the sick. When the council began its work in 1945, the Allied occupation zones in Germany alone contained some 120,000 Latvian refugees (citizens of Latvia); by 1951, due to further emigration, the number had dropped to about 12,500. The council was formed by representatives from all the Latvian DP (q.v.) camps (which became, as it were, electoral districts). In spite of internal divisions, the work of the council proved to be salutary for the Latvian DPs. In the first year of its existence, for example, the council helped the Latvian DPs organize 122 elementary schools with some 7,000 pupils, 57 high schools with some 600 pupils, and 45 kindergartens with some 1,700 children. It also sponsored and helped to organize the Baltic University (q.v.). After 1951, when the vast majority of Latvians had emigrated from Germany, the council ceased its activity and its functions passed on to émigré organizations in the new host countries.

LATVIAN COMMUNIST PARTY (Latv. **LATVIJAS KOMUNIS-TISKĀ PARTIJA, LKP**). The LKP dated its founding to 1904 and the congress that year of the various social democratic organizations of Latvia. This meeting also became the first congress of the Latvian Social Democratic Workers Party (q.v.), which during the revolutionary year 1905 and in the period after 1906 became increasingly more dominated by Latvian adherents of Lenin and the Bolshevik (q.v.) cause. The LKP manifested a significant presence in the events of Latvian history from about 1906 to 1920. The party was very influential among the *strēlnieki* (q.v.), the Latvian contingents of the czarist army, and twice (1917 and 1919) sought to establish a Bolshevik government in Latvia. After Latvian independence was consolidated by 1920, the Latvian Communists either took up residence in the USSR or in relatively small numbers continued to live in Latvia as an underground movement.

The party came into its own in 1940-1941 (when Latvia was occupied by the USSR) and again after 1945 (when the Germans retreated and the Soviet army returned). At the end of the war, the Latvian Communist Party numbered around 8,000 persons in Latvia and during the next 40 years by the mid-1980s the membership had grown to about 17,000. As a constituent part of the CPSU (Communist Party of the Soviet Union), the Latvian Communist Party was, of course, the dominant political force in the Latvian SSR, with its "leading and guiding role" guaranteed by the Soviet Constitution. In time, party membership was required for virtually all important positions in Latvia, and therefore for intelligent and ambitious young Latvians such membership became almost inevitable. Members were frequently recruited from the ranks of the party's youth organization Komsmol, which in the 1980s numbered around 300,000 members in the age group from 14 to 28. The LKP began to lose members in Latvia from about 1989 onward, and particularly rapidly after May 1990, when the Latvian Supreme Soviet (q.v.) declared Latvian independence. The LKP was declared an illegal organization by the Latvian government after the August 1991 coup in Moscow.

LATVIAN LEGION. The name given to the Latvian military units formed in Latvia during the German occupation of the country from June 1941 until the end of World War II. The German occupation came after a year of Soviet rule during which Latvia had been occupied by the Soviet army (June 1940), annexed to the Soviet Union (August 1940), and subjected to socio-economic sovietization and deportation (q.v.) actions (June 1941). By 1941, therefore, the Germans were able to exploit Latvian anger about the preceding year to form volunteer auxiliary guard battalions (about 3,000 persons initially) to protect military objects such as bridges and railroads. Many Latvians continued to believe (in spite of all direct indications to the contrary and in spite of what was known about German plans to colonize eastern Europe) that service in the German military efforts would be repaid by the reestablishment of an independent Latvia. During the next three years approximately 41 such auxiliary battalions were formed. In the period from 1941 to 1942, these battalions were used by the German army for a wide variety of purposes, including direct military engagements on the eastern front and in battles with Soviet partisans.

When the German military effort had ground to a halt by January 1943, however, military leaders decided that the scattered Latvian battalions would be better used if united into a single unit (Legion). The start of the conversion of the Latvian guard battalions into battalions of a "Latvian Legion" generally under Latvian command began on February 8, 1943. By early 1944, there had come into being a Latvian Legion with two divisions (the 15th and the 19th), both attached to the Waffen SS. Only the highest commanders of both were German; the rest of the officers where Latvian. In order to bring these divisions to full strength, the German occupying government conscripted additional men into them, in violation of the Hague Convention of 1907 prohibiting the conscription of soldiers in occupied territories. Conscription of Latvians into the Latvian Legion and into the German war effort generally continued until the end of the war, with the age of conscripts becoming increasingly younger. When the war ended, some 140,000 to 148,000 Latvian soldiers had participated in the German war against the Soviet Union in various kinds of units. Another 35,000 to 60,000 Latvians were transported to Germany as a foreign labor force.

LATVIAN NATIONAL INDEPENDENCE MOVEMENT (Latv. **LATVIJAS NACIONĀLĀS NEATKARĪBAS KUSTĪBA, LNNK).** The LNNK was one of several Latvian "informal organizations" formed in 1988, when Mikhail Gorbachev's new policies of glasnost and perestroika permitted the registration and activities of such groups. Its first congress took place in Ogre on February 18-19, 1989, and Edvārds Berklavs (q.v.) was elected chairman. The LNNK was unapologetically nationalistic, calling for the reestablishment of an independent Latvia on the basis of the 1922 Constitution. With the formation of the more centrist (and therefore more inclusive) Popular Front (q.v.), the LNNK repositioned itself in the right wing of the Latvian political spectrum, but cooperated with the Popular Front in the Supreme Soviet (q.v.) elections of spring 1990, and therefore had representation in the Supreme Soviet that governed Latvia from 1990 to 1993 as a transition government.

The LNNK had its own slate of candidates for the parliamentary elections of June 1993, and, in contrast with the fate of the Popular Front, received representation in the Fifth Saeima (q.v.). It chose, however, not to enter into a coalitions government with Latvia's Way (q.v.), thus remaining in the parliamentary opposition.

LATVIAN RIFLE REGIMENTS (See **STRĒLNIEKI).**

LATVIAN SOCIAL DEMOCRATIC WORKERS PARTY(See **SOCIAL DEMOCRATIC PARTY).**

LATVIAN-SOVIET TREATY OF 1920. Signed in August 1920, the treaty ended hostilities between Soviet Russia and the Republic of Latvia and drew the eastern boundaries of Latvia so that they now included within Latvian territory the districts of Daugavpils,

Rēzekne, and Ludza, which heretofore had been part of the province of Vitebsk, as well as the Abrene (q.v.) district. In the treaty Soviet Russia also renounced all claims to Latvian territory and recognized Latvia's sovereignty and independence "for all time."

LATVIAN WRITERS' UNION. The principal organization of Latvian writers during the Soviet period, founded in 1940 when Latvia was incorporated into the Soviet Union. It was one of the so-called "creating" (*radošās*) organizations (others being the Architects' Union, the Journalists' Union, etc.) in which membership was mandatory for a successful career in one's chosen occupation. The Writers' Union had an ambiguous role during the Soviet period of Latvian history. It was, on the one hand, an organization through which the Soviet state and the Communist Party could control literary intellectuals and impose on them various orthodoxies; on the other, as individual stories have shown, it could also function as a protective organization when efforts at free expression ran counter to the wishes of state and party functionaries. With its budget coming from the Latvian state, the Union could afford to fund periodical publications (the journals *Karogs, Avots, Daugava;* the literary newspaper *Literatūra un Māksla*), award prizes, and sometimes see to the extraordinary welfare needs of its members. The Union's members met in a general congress every five years, and in the intervening years its affairs were conducted by a board. In recent Latvian history, the Writers' Union played an important role in initiating the so-called "third national awakening" (q.v.) when, on June 1-2, 1988, it held a meeting together with other "creating" unions and provided a forum for a wide-ranging critique of Communist political and literary orthodoxy.

LATVIA'S WAY, LW (Latv. LATVIJAS CEĻŠ). Latvia's Way is an electoral coalition formed in the months preceding the June 1993 Saeima (q.v.) (parliamentary) elections with the purpose of bringing together on one ticket the most popular politicians of the 1990-1993 transition government (e.g., Anatolijs Gorbunovs, q.v.), well-known émigré Latvian leaders (e.g., Gunārs Meierovics, q.v.), and others who had not previously held public office. In the developing spectrum of Latvian politics, the LW held a centrist position, promising continued efforts to bring free-market principles to Latvia's economy, to draft a new citizenship law that would protect the cultural and linguistic interests of the nation, and to integrate Latvia into existing European transnational political structures. It thus stood between such electoral groupings on the right as the Latvian National Independence Movement (q.v.), which argued for a set of more openly nationalistic policies; and the Harmony for Latvia party on the left, which highlighted the needs of the Russian-speaking minority of the country.

LW ran a slate in every electoral district of the country, receiving the plurality of seats (36) in the Fifth Saeima but not a majority. From July 1993 to July 1994, LW governed in coalition with the Agrarian Union (q.v.), which gave the coalition 48 parliamentary votes. The Cabinet, comprised of LW and Agrarian Union ministers, was headed by Valdis Birkavs (q.v.) from the LW as prime minister. In July 1994, the coalition foundered, in part because of the Agrarian Union's position on the question of agricultural tariffs, and Birkavs's government resigned. Having formally incorporated itself as a political party in 1993, however, the LW continued to be an important political force in the Saeima. But in the fall 1995 parliamentary election, LW lost more than half its seats (falling from 36 to 17) and thus also its commanding role. The LW entered the coalition government of Andris Šķēle (q.v.) in December 1995, now sharing the spotlight with the newly popular Democratic Party Saimnieks (q.v.).

LATVIEŠU AVĪZES. Latviešu Avīzes (Latvian Newspaper) was the first continuous periodical publication in Latvian, starting in 1822. The newspaper was founded and edited by K. F. Watson, one of the Baltic German (q.v.) *Literaten* who were interested in increasing literacy among the peasantry (i.e., Latvians) and therefore worked hard to create publications in that language. Initially, the newspaper's materials were written in an apolitical, didactic, and humanistic vein. However, after 1857, when it became the property of the Lettisch-literärische Gesellschaft (q.v.), it took on an increasingly militant tone in opposition to the activities of the Latvian "national awakening" (q.v.). In the second half of the nineteenth century, the paper became mostly a defender of Baltic German privileges and positions and retained this viewpoint until it stopped publication in 1915. Its 87-year existence made it the longest continuously appearing Latvian-language periodical until World War I, a longevity record that in the twentieth century was matched only by the newspaper *Cīņa* (q.v.).

LATVIEŠU DRAUGU BIEDRĪBA (See **LETTISCH-LITERĀ-RISCHE GESELLSCHAFT**).

LAW. The history of law in the Latvian territories generally followed the political history of the area, but the two were never completely synchronized. The transformation of the political system nearly always occurred more rapidly than the transformation of the legal system. In the nineteenth century, the inhabitants of the Latvian territories were governed by laws, codified in the 1845-1864 period, unique to the Baltic provinces (q.v.) as well as by the general laws of the Russian Empire codified in the *Svod zakonov Rossijskoj Imperii.* When political independence arrived in 1918, these bodies of law had to be adjusted to the new political circumstances, and the process lasted well into the late 1930s. In many, though not all respects, the laws of the Russian Empire continued as the laws of independent Latvia. After the incorporation of Latvia into the USSR in 1940, Soviet authorities were quick to introduce into the Latvian SSR the general legal code of the Soviet Union. After the first redeclaration of independence in May 1990, the Latvian Supreme council (q.v.) (Parliament) began to dismantle the Soviet-period legal structures but found that the process was far more complicated and time-consuming than was anticipated. Thus, from 1990 to August 1991, Latvia's laws continued to be in large part those of the late Soviet period, and this situation continued even after independence was fully reacquired and the Soviet Union had disintegrated. Though the 1922 Constitution is now once again the basic law of the country and the 1937 Civil Code has been revived, a final modernized Latvian Code of Laws has not yet been produced.

LEAGUE OF WOMEN OF LATVIA. A grassroots movement started in Latvia in early 1989 by mothers of draft-age men who were concerned about the reported abuse of their sons in the Soviet Army. The movement grew rapidly as cases of mistreatment increased and as the Soviet Army itself began to experience disciplinary and organizational problems, in part because of Mikhail Gorbachev's policies of glasnost and perestroika. The Army encountered increasing difficulties in meeting its recruitment quotas in the Baltic region, as many young men simply refused to show up for induction, and some went AWOL.

The League of Women sought official approval for alternatives to military service and also created a kind of underground railroad for young men. The problem of draft resistance in the Baltic remained from 1989 an important strand in the increasingly strained relations between these borderland republics and Moscow, with the latter unable to devise ways (beyond sheer force) to increase compliance.

LEITĀNS, ANSIS (1815-1874). Leitāns was a prominent figure among the Latvian literary activists in the pre-"national awakening" (q.v.) period. He was self-educated and worked from 1947 to 1967 as the secretary of the local council in the Pinkenhof (*Piņki*) estate. From 1856 to 1874, he was cofounder and editor of the very popular periodical publication *Mājas Viesis* (*The Home Visitor*), which provided its Latvian-language readers with translations of the literature of other countries, and original writings that featured didactic, sentimental, and noncontroversial themes. Retrospectively, literary historians have placed Leitans in the nineteenth-century *veclatvieši* (q.v.) generation, which sought means of raising the educational level of Latvians especially in rural areas without provoking confrontations with the Baltic German (q.v.) and czarist authorities.

LETTGALLIANS. The people of one of the tribal societies that in the period from the sixth to the thirteenth centuries populated the area of present-day Latvia. The Lettgallians lived in the eastern regions and may have been numerically the largest of these pre-Christian Baltic peoples. Archaeological evidence suggests social and political stratification, rulers (kings), but no political unity. Thirteenth-century written sources mentioned two major Lettgallian "kingdoms"-- Tālava and Jersika. In their effort to subjugate the indigenous populations, the German crusading orders (q.v.) saw the latter -- Jersika -- as especially tempting because it controlled water traffic on the Daugava River (q.v.) and also had already been Christianized by Orthodox missionaries from the east. Jersika was overrun in 1209, and its population converted to Christianity. To the Lettgallians in Tālava, the German threat seemed less important than the traditional enmity toward Estonians to the north with whom the Lettgallians fought continually throughout the thirteenth century, sometimes joining forces with the Germans. An important rising by the Lettgallians against German control took place in the Salasele castle, but was put down quickly. By 1214, the Lettgallians in the north were also subjugated. A number of warriors from Lettgallia fled to Lithuanian territories where the struggle against the crusading orders continued.

The later history of Lettgallian territory (eastern Latvia) differs substantially from lands to the east, because the latter became part of the German-influenced and German-controlled Livonian Confederation while Lettgallia did not, remaining under the influence of Poland. The distinctiveness of the Lettgallian dialect of the Latvian language has remained strong until the end of the twentieth century. The presence of the Lettgallians in Latvian history is memorialized in the name "Latgale" (q.v.) -- one of the four traditional divisions of Latvian territory.

LETTISCH-LITERÄRISCHE GESELLSCHAFT. Known in Latvian as the "Association of Latvian Friends" (Latviešu Draugu Biedrība), the LLG was founded in 1824 by 14 Lutheran (q.v.) clergymen from Livland and Courland (qq.v.) with a common interest in Latvian language and folklore. The organization signified the appearance among the Baltic Germans (q.v.) of a more scholarly interest in Latvian culture and remained active in Baltic cultural affairs for the next century. In the course of time the LLG published the collected papers from its meetings in a 20-volume series entitled *Schriften des Lettisch-literärischen Gesellschaft*, which contained some of the most searching scholarly and semi-scholarly papers on Latvian culture that had appeared to date.

The relationship between LLG and Latvians remained troubled throughout the nineteenth century. Though numerous Latvians belonged to it, the LLG attacked the Latvian "national awakening" (q.v.) and in the 1870s expelled those of the leaders of the Riga Latvian Association (q.v.) who had joined the LLG. It continued to have in its ranks numerous first-rate Baltic German scholars (e.g., August Bielenstein, q.v.), but during World War I the leadership of the LLG welcomed the idea of annexing the Latvian territories to Germany proper. After the founding of the Latvian state in 1918, the LLG renewed its statutes but its activities gradually faded from view.

LIEPĀJA (Ger. **LIBAU**). After Riga (q.v.), the most important port city in the Latvian territories, and conceivably the second most important city according to other standards (size, cultural significance) as well. In the thirteenth century when the acquired Baltic territories were being subdivided between the Livonian Order (q.v.) and Church lands, the district that contained the village from which Liepaja developed was first allocated to the Church, but a century later the territory had been acquired by the Order. In the course of time, Liepaja shared with Jelgava (Ger. *Mitau*) (q.v.) the rank of the most important urban centers of the Duchy of Courland (q.v.), and in 1625 Liepāja acquired a city charter. It was not until the seventeenth century also that Liepāja's significance as a port city began to grow because of the inadequacy of waterways leading to it. When in the nineteenth century other forms of transportation gained in importance, so did the city´s role in Baltic and Russian Imperial trade as well as in the Empire's naval defense system. Liepāja retained and expanded its commercial and military significance in the interwar independence as well as throughout the Soviet period, reaching a population of about 100,000 in the year 1979.

LITERACY. Although Lutheran (q.v.) clergymen in the Latvian territories agreed with the general Protestant policy of requiring literacy skills of their parishioners, financial support for school systems remained meager until the end of the eighteenth century. There was considerable opposition among the Baltic German (q.v.) landowning nobility to the idea of peasant education (q.v.), and the clergy, in whose appointments the landed nobles frequently had veto power, had to be very circumspect when--as many of them did--they sought to improve peasant schooling. Though peasant schools began to grow in number after the 1760s, most historians suggest that peasant literacy was improved as much by self-learning at home, as literate parents taught these skills to their children. Already by the early nineteenth century, peasant (i.e., Latvian) literacy statistics showed impressive proportions of peasants being able to read and write, and by the end of the century, in the Imperial census of 1897, literacy levels in the Baltic provinces (q.v.) were among the highest in the Russian Empire (upward of 85 percent for both men and women).

LITERATURE. Using the most inclusive definition--all writing in the Latvian language--Latvian literature can be said to have begun in the sixteenth century with translations into Latvian of sacred texts by both Protestant and Roman Catholic (q.v.) clergy for whom

Latvian was a second or third language. A somewhat less inclusive definition--writing in Latvian for purposes other than religious instruction--would place the beginnings of secular Latvian literature in the mid-eighteenth century, though then it was still written by persons (primarily Baltic Germans, q.v.) for whom Latvian was not the first language of their childhood. The most restrictive definition--writing in Latvian by persons for whom Latvian was the first language of their childhood--would place the start of Latvian literature in the 1850s in the Latvian "national awakening" (q.v.).

Thereafter, during a developmental period of about four decades Latvian literature (defined restrictively) expanded into all genres of literary creativity and witnessed the appearance of works generally regarded as "classic." The brothers Kaudzīte (q.v.) published the first Latvian novel, *Mērnieku laiki*, in 1879; Andrejs Pumpurs (q.v.) wrote the national epic *Lāčplēsis* (q.v.) in 1888; and in the 1890s a new generation of writers such as Jānis Rainis, Aspāzija, Jēkabs Apsītis, Rudolfs Blaumanis (qq.v.), Jānis Poruks, and Anna Brigadere began writing careers that in most cases lasted well into the twentieth century. Before the 1890s, Latvian writing was characterized by realistic descriptions of Latvian--largely rural--life, or, alternately, as in the case of Andrejs Pumpurs, drew inspiration from the Latvian oral tradition. During the 1890s and thereafter, Latvian literature became more "European," as writers were directly inspired by more general stylistic trends and by themes outside the Baltic world. By the beginning of the First World War Latvian literature had become a significant domain of general Latvian culture.

The writers of the independence period (1918-1940), therefore, had a solid base to build upon and, unlike the pre-World War II authors, did not have to submit their work to censorship by officials of the imperial government. Consequently there was an explosion of literary activity, expressed in the widest possible diversity of styles and genres. Realistic description remained important, however, and life in the countryside a favorite subject in both poetry and prose. Because of the sharp breaks in Latvian history represented by the two world wars, few important writers started and finished their productive careers entirely within the 20-year independence period. Those who were at the peak of their careers in the 1920s had begun to write in the pre-World War I years, and those who began in the 1930s had to continue writing in very straitened circumstances after 1945.

The Second World War split Latvian literature into two parts, because a large proportion of the 1930s writers emigrated to the west when it became clear that after 1945 Latvia would once again become a Soviet Republic. Until the late 1980s, then, Latvian literature was being written in Latvia under the relatively strict controls imposed by the Communist Party (q.v.) and the Latvian Writers Union (q.v.); and in the western countries--Sweden, Germany, England, Canada, the United States, and Australia--to which most refugee Latvian writers emigrated after a six- to seven-year period in DP (q.v.) camps in postwar Germany. Both contexts placed constraints on literary creativity--the Soviet Latvian through official literary orthodoxy (especially socialist realism) and the émigré through separation from the culture of the Latvian homeland. In both contexts, however, creative efforts continued, so that after 1990, when Latvian independence was re-proclaimed, the two branches of Latvian literature could begin the difficult task of reintegration.

LIVLAND (See **LIVONIA**).

LIVONIA. The English rendition of the German term "Livland," designating both the late medieval state in the Baltic area and the province when the Baltic area became part of the Russian Empire in the course of the eighteenth century. The Latvian language distinguishes between these two entities, calling the medieval state *Livonija* and the later province *Vidzeme.* The land included in the two entities was decidedly different. Medieval Livonia appeared by the end of the thirteenth century, after subjugation of the indigenous Baltic peoples by the German crusading orders (q.v.), and consisted of four ecclesiastical states (the archbishopric of Riga and the bishoprics of Kurland, Dorpat, and Ösel) and the lands of the Livonian Order. These five entities covered most of the territory of present-day Latvia and Estonia. Medieval Livonia disappeared from the maps as the result of the Livonian Wars (q.v.) (1558-1583), when Denmark, Sweden, and Poland-Lithuania claimed and received segments of Livonian territory.

Until the eighteenth century, sections of the old Livonian lands were alternately under Polish-Lithuanian, Danish, Swedish, and Russian control. When, as a result of the Great Northern War (q.v.) (1700-1721), Russia expelled Sweden from the eastern

Baltic regions, most of the old Livonian lands came under Russian control, with a section of them now becoming the "Province of Livonia" (Ger. *Livland*)--one of the three Baltic provinces (q.v.) of the Empire (the others were Courland, q.v. [Ger. *Kurland*], and Estonia [Ger. *Estland*]). The province of Livland consisted of a northern section in which the peasantry was Estonian-speaking and a southern section in which it was Latvian-speaking. After 1918, when both Latvia and Estonia became independent states, the ethnographic boundary was used for the national boundary between them and the province of Livonia was divided between the two new states. Within Latvia, the term "Vidzeme" replaced "Livonia."

LIVONIAN ORDER (See CRUSADING ORDERS, DUCHY OF COURLAND AND SEMIGALLIA, LIVONIAN WAR).

LIVONIAN WAR (1558-1583). By the end of the fifteenth century, the inability of the Livonian states to get along with one another made Livonia (q.v.) a tempting target for territorial expansion by larger neighbors, notably Russia, which was also seeking an outlet to the Baltic Sea. In 1476 and then again in 1501 and 1502, Russian forces invaded the eastern sector of Livonia, annexed territory, and deported some of the peasantry to the interior of Russia. Worse losses by the Livonian side were prevented by the energetic leadership of Walter von Plettenberg, who was Master of the Livonian Order from 1494 to 1535. In 1558, Ivan the Terrible began a more serious effort against Livonia, thus launching a quarter century of almost uninterrupted warfare that eventually drew in Denmark, Poland-Lithuania, and Sweden.

Anticipating Livonian defeat at the hands of the Russians, the bishop of Ösel offered his territory to Denmark; the landowners and urban patriciates of the Estonian regions in northern Livonia sought protection from Sweden; and the elites of the southern parts of Livonia gained similar protection from Poland-Lithuania. In the latter transaction, the last Master of the Livonian Order, Gotthard Kettler, became duke of the territory of Courland and Semigallia (q.v.), and a vassal of the Polish-Lithuanian crown. The new territorial interests of these powers naturally prolonged the conflict, especially when Sweden and Poland-Lithuania found it expedient to become temporary allies against the Russian invader. No side was powerful enough to overwhelm the other, and in 1583 all sides agreed to peace. Russia agreed to withdraw its forces, though it kept a small slice of Livonian territory in the east and Denmark assented to cede to Poland-Lithuania and Sweden most of the territory over which she had gained control. The new masters of the eastern Baltic--exercising their power directly and indirectly--were Poland-Lithuania and Sweden. The medieval Livonian state that had coalesced into a regional power at the end of the thirteenth century had ceased to exist.

LIVONIANS (also LIVS). Though they were among the peoples who resided in the territory of present-day Latvia from the sixth century onward, the Livonians differed from the rest in that they spoke (and continue to speak) a Finno-Ugric rather than a Baltic language. They inhabited territory extending around the Gulf of Riga and stretching inland for several dozens of kilometers. They were evidently the first of the Baltic-area residents to deal continuously with the German monks, merchants, and crusading orders (q.v.) when these arrived in the Baltic area at the end of the twelfth century and founded the city of Riga (q.v.) in 1201. The Livonians were subjugated by the Germans relatively early, certainly by the end of the second decade of the thirteenth century. They were also the first of the area's peoples to be converted to Christianity, though their attachment to the new religion proved tenuous during the succeeding centuries.

Before the coming of the Germans, the Livonians were socially differentiated and had political leaders, though no political unity. Thirteenth-century written sources distinguish four politically distinct districts in their territory. After the crusading orders finally established their dominance, the Livonians continued to be mentioned in sources as a linguistically separate subpopulation, though their numbers diminished over the centuries as they intermarried with Latvians. By the end of the twentieth century, only several hundred Livonian-speakers remained, but Latvian censuses continued to record them as a separate ethnic group. Their presence in Latvian history is memorialized in the terms "Livonia," "Livland," and their derivatives. Some confusion has resulted from the conventional use of these terms for a succession of late-medieval and post-medieval political states and provinces in the Baltic area but these were the creations of the new political upper orders and not of their diminishing numbers of Livonian-speaking residents.

LIVS (*See* **LIVONIANS**).

LKP (**LATVIJAS KOMUNISTISKĀ PARTIJA**). (*See* **LATVIAN COMMUNIST PARTY**).

LNNK (**LATVIJAS NACIONĀLĀS NEATKARĪBAS KUSTĪBA**). (*See* **LATVIAN NATIONAL INDEPENDENCE MOVEMENT**).

LUTHERANISM. Lutheranism arrived in the territory of present-day Latvia soon after Martin Luther's challenge to the Church in 1517. Territorially speaking, these dates still fall within the history of the Livonian Confederation, of which the Latvian lands had been part since the end of the thirteenth century. By the first half of the sixteenth century, however, Livonia (q.v.) had become internally decentralized and externally weak as the result of the continuing power conflicts between the Livonian Order (q.v.) and the leaders of the ecclesiastical states in Livonia, as well as between both of these powers and well-organized merchants in such relatively wealthy cities as Riga (q.v.). The situation in Livonia resembled in many respects that of the Holy Roman Empire, where decentralization and internal conflict had also created a welcome context for a powerful reform movement within the Church. Followers of Luther's reforms began to arrive in Livonia already in the 1520s, where they were welcomed by the city of Riga. The Master of the German Order (q.v.) adopted Lutheranism in 1525, which meant that the Livonian Order had to take at least a permissive attitude toward the new teaching.

Freedom of religious belief in Livonia was proclaimed in 1554 over the opposition of the officials of the ecclesiastical states, but they were in no position to resist the new situation. The complete secularization of the Livonian Order and the ecclesiastical states followed later during the course of the Livonian War (q.v.), which began in 1558. By the beginning of the seventeenth century, Lutheranism had become the dominant form of Christianity in most of the lands of present-day Latvia. The important exception was Latgale (q.v.) (the eastern region), which remained under Polish-Lithuanian influence and control and hence retained Roman Catholicism (q.v.) until modern times. From 1561 to 1629, the Polish-Lithuanian rulers, having gained control of other sections (Courland and territory north of the Daugava River, qq.v.) of the now-collapsed Livonian state introduced there a certain amount of Counter-Reformation activity, but this was insufficient to change the central place of Lutheranism among the elites. During the period of Latvian independence from 1918 to 1940, some 75 percent of the Latvian population was of the Lutheran faith.

- M -

MĀJAS VIESIS. *Mājas Viesis* (The Home Visitor) was a weekly publication in Latvian dealing with literature (q.v.) and politics published from 1856 onward. During the first decades of its existence it was a significant outlet for the writings of the first generation of Latvian writers of the "national awakening" (q.v.) period. In the 1880s, the publication became much less confrontational with respect to Baltic authorities, but revived its "progressive" tone in the 1890s when it became an important outlet for the writers of the "new current" (q.v.). It ceased publication in 1910 for economic reasons.

MALĒNIEŠI. Derived from Latv. *mala*--border or edge; English equivalent--rubes, hicks). A word that first appeared in Latvian writing in the 1860s to signify those Latvians who lived far away from the urban centers of burgeoning Latvian cultural activity and probably did not understand or actually opposed the programs of the urban activists. Though initially used in a translation of German stories, the Latvian word took on a polemical meaning relatively quickly and symbolized, among others things, a growing urban-rural break in the Latvian-language cultural world.

MANASEIN REVISION. An inspection tour in 1881-1883 of the Baltic provinces of Livonia and Courland (qq.v.) by the Russian Senator Nicholas Manasein, this "revision" became a major turning point in the political history of the Latvian territories. As a result of his findings--which were to a great extent based on some 20,000 grievance petitions sent to Manasein from Latvian rural areas--the senator concluded that Baltic German (q.v.) hegemony was widely unpopular and recommended to the czar that the Imperial government introduce various measures to Russify the Baltic area. Latvian nationalist activists who had assisted Manasein had not expected this conclusion, and the ensuing Russification (q.v.) period of Latvian history (lasting formally until World War I) enhanced the feeling among Latvian activists that the Imperial government could not be trusted.

MANCELIUS, GEORGIUS (Latvianized as **JURIS MANCELIS**) (1593-1654). Mancelius was a Baltic German (q.v.) clergyman and writer born in the Baltic area. Throughout his clerical career, he dedicated himself to the improvement of the Latvian language and the creation of at least a religious literature (q.v.) in it. He occupied a series of important positions in the Lutheran (q.v.) church in Livonia (q.v.), as well as the prorectorship and rectorship of the Dorpat University from 1632 to 1638. Beginning in the 1640s, he wrote, translated, and compiled a variety of works in Latvian, some of which remained in widespread use as devotional literature for the next 200 years. With the publication of his book of sermons in 1654, Mancelius is considered by literary historians to have begun a new phase of development for Latvian as a literary language, which lasted until the mid-nineteenth century when writing in Latvian began to be produced largely by authors for whom Latvian was their first language.

MĀTERS, JURIS (1845-1885). An activist of the "national awakening" (q.v.) period, Māters was largely self-educated but nonetheless became widely known, first, as an author of popular fiction (especially his novel *Sadzīves viļņi* [*Waves of Social Life*], published in 1879), and, second, as a champion of the Latvian peasants, particularly smallholders. He engaged in polemics with the Riga Latvian Association (q.v.), which he accused of exploiting rural national sentiments to enhance its own standing in Riga (q.v.), and published extensive advice (in the newspaper *Tiesu vēstnesis*, which he edited) to rural leaders on how to take advantage of the 1860s law and rural reforms. Māters's viewpoint represented the first division in the ranks of the Latvian national movement.

MAURIŅA, ZENTA (1897-1978). Perhaps the most accomplished and popular essayist in the history of Latvian writing, Mauriņa finished the University of Latvia in 1927 and earned her living as a teacher. Her first publication--a translation into German of a Latvian poem--appeared in 1919, and since that time her productivity was continuous, lasting throughout the interwar period as well as after 1944 when she emigrated to and continued to reside in Germany and Sweden. Her nonfictional writing consisted of literary and philosophical essays that frequently revolved around the theme of human suffering (to some extent a reflection of the fact that Mauriņa was struck by polio at the age of five and spent the rest of her life in a wheelchair). In the post-World War II period, she frequently published in German and thus became one of the few Latvian writers to have a continental readership.

MEIEROVICS, GUNĀRS (1920-). Having received his primary and secondary education in Latvia, Meierovics left Latvia in 1944, lived in post-World War II Germany as a refugee, and emigrated to the United States in 1950. There he worked as a researcher for the U.S. Department of Defense and became very active in Latvian émigré organizations, especially the American Latvian Association. In 1988-1989, when the perestroika period in Latvia began, Meierovics was heading the World Federation of Free Latvians (q.v.), which somewhat later established a bureau in Riga (q.v.) in order to forge links between western Latvian organizations and the various reform movements gaining strength in Latvia. In the parliamentary election of June 1993, Meierovics ran as a candidate of the Latvia's Way (q.v.) coalition and was selected as a deputy. Briefly, in July 1993, he was a strong candidate for the presidency of Latvia, a position that was to be filled through election by the Saeima (q.v.) (parliament) rather than by popular vote, but he withdrew in favor of Guntis Ulmanis (q.v.). During the 1993 election, Meierovics enjoyed a very high level of name recognition, especially among the older generations of Latvians who remembered his father, Zigfrīds Anna Meierovics (q.v.), the very popular first foreign minister of the interwar Latvian Republic.

MEIEROVICS, ZIGFRĪDS ANNA (1887-1925). Though he received a degree in the commercial sciences from the Riga Polytechnical Institute (q.v.) in 1911, Meierovics's career in the Baltic business world was relatively short. The First World War and the occupation of the Baltic area by the German army engaged him in refugee relief work, and unfolding developments drew him increasingly deeper into the politics of establishing a Latvian national state. After the March 1917 Revolution in Russia, he was in Riga (q.v.), having cast his lot with those who were working to form a viable provisional government for Latvia. After the declaration of independence on November 18, 1918, having been appointed foreign minister in the new Latvian government, he took on a series of assignments that brought him to Europe as part of a Latvian delegation that pleaded the case of Latvian independence with the governments of the Allies, at the international conferences following the war, and at the League of Nations. In these forums, he argued for international recognition of Latvia's sovereignty over the skepticism of the great Western powers and outright opposition by the USSR and the Baltic German (q.v.) representatives. After Latvia became a League member, Meierovics ended his appointment as Foreign Minister, but in the early 1920s took on a series of assignments dealing with Latvia's international economic relations. By that time, he had become one of the best-known and most popular of the political leaders of the new Latvian state. His career was cut short when he was killed in an automobile accident in Latvia in 1925.

MENDERS, FRICIS (1885-1971). Menders was an active member of the Latvian Social Democratic (q.v.) movement from 1904 onward and, as many of the pre-World War I Latvian Social Democrats, lived in western Europe in exile until 1917. There, in 1914, he received a doctorate in law from the University of Bern. After Latvian independence, he remained active in parliamentary politics and was elected to all four of the interwar parliaments on the Social Democratic ticket. In the Latvian Saeima (q.v.), he represented the Social Democratic Party's left wing and defended close cooperation with the USSR. He remained in Latvia after the conclusion of World War II, and in 1948 he was deported to the interior of the USSR. He returned to Latvia in 1955, but until his death in 1971 continued to have run-ins with the authorities, some of which resulted in imprisonment and internal exile in Latvia for short periods of time. A prolific and opinionated writer, Menders published in the Latvian periodical press during most of his life in Latvian, German, and Russian.

MERKEL, GARLIEB (1769-1850). Merkel was one of a handful of Baltic German (q.v.) writers and journalists who toward the end of the eighteenth century brought to the Russian Baltic provinces (q.v.) the critical spirit of the French Enlightenment. Born in Livonia (q.v.) of parents who were themselves Baltic Germans, Merkel spent most of his student years in Prussia at the

Universities of Jena, Leipzig, and Frankfurt on the Oder, until in 1801 he received a Ph.D. from the latter. He was a versatile writer and by the end of his life had acquired a reputation in the German-speaking cultural world as an able literary critic, counting among his friends and correspondents such figures as Schiller, Goethe, Herder, and Wieland.

Though he never wrote in Latvian, Merkel holds an extremely important place in the development of Latvian self-consciousness because of his book *Die Letten, vorzüglich in Liefland am Ende des philosophischen Jahrhunderts* (1796), published when he was 27. In *Die Letten* Merkel castigated the Baltic landowning nobilities for maintaining and defending the institution of serfdom (q.v.) and pointed to its deleterious effects among the Latvian-speaking peasants. In the spirit of J. G. Herder (q.v.), he seemed to be making a case for the Latvians not simply as an oppressed *peasantry* but as an oppressed *nation*, which had been mistreated for centuries by the Baltic Germans and was now reaching the end of its patience. Understandably the book aroused a storm in Baltic German landowning circles. *Die Letten* was not translated into Latvian until 1905, but in the second half of the nineteenth century the writers of the Latvian "national awakening" (q.v.), having received German-language educations, knew the work well and used it to guide their own ideas. Merkel published several more works about Latvians and Estonians, but none were as controversial as the 1796 treatise. His later descriptions of the Baltic peoples were often quite fanciful and he invented heroic traditions and entire mythologies for them. In 1869, the Riga Latvian Association (q.v.) placed over his grave a memorial stone engraved with the words "In memory from the grateful Latvians."

MORAVIAN BRETHREN (also **HERRNHUT MOVEMENT; Latv. BRĀĻU DRAUDZE**). During the 1720s and 1730s, the provinces of Estland and Livland (q.v.) were visited by missionaries from the German pietistic movement headed by Count Ludwig Zinzendorf in Herrnhut in Saxony. These "Moravian Brethren" preached a radical equality among Christian believers and a simplification of worship and life in general. Among both the Estonian and Latvian peasantry these views found resonance, and the Moravian meetinghouses increasingly drew worshipers away from their Lutheran congregations. At Valmiera (*Wolmar*) (q.v.) the Moravians founded a school to train congregation leaders. By the end of the eighteenth century, an an estimated 5,000 peasants, mosly in Livland had drifted away from Lutheranism (q.v.) and were actively engaged in Moravian congregations. Understandably, this was not acceptable to the Baltic Lutheran Church, which pressed the czarist government for, and in 1743 obtained, an order closing the Moravian congregations. This did not destroy Herrnhutism, however, because the movement continued surreptitiously until in the nineteenth century, due to its continuing popularity, the Lutheran church authorities were forced to permit it again. One estimate gives the number 30,000 as the maximum size of all the Herrnhut congregations in the Baltic in the nineteenth century. Latvian historians credit the Herrnhut movement with having had a positive effect on the Latvian peasantry, insofar as it underlined the need for literacy (q.v.) in the Latvian language, self-reliance, the choice of religious leaders from among the peasants themselves, and a sober and industrious way of life. Some interpreters see the Herrnhut congregations as the first "national" movement in Latvian history.

MUNTERS, VILHELMS (1898-1967). Though he had a degree in chemical engineering, Munters began working for the Latvian Foreign Ministry as early as 1920, and during the next decade and a half held a series of increasingly more responsible positions in that institution. In 1936, after the authoritarian regime of Kārlis Ulmanis (q.v.) was well established, Munters was appointed foreign minister and held that post until 1940 when he was deported to Siberia by the new Soviet Latvian government. In 1941, while in exile, he was arrested and sentenced to a 25-year prison term, of which he served 13 years, returning to Latvia in 1958. Here he worked at various editorial posts and in 1962 began to publish widely on topics relating to pre-Soviet Latvian life, expressing views that were generally consistent with the Communist Party line about the Latvian past and with the party's thinking about contemporary policy matters. From the time he emerged into the limelight in the Ulmanis (q.v.) regime, Munters was a controversial figure among Latvian political leaders, frequently being accused of opportunism, lack of fervor in defending Latvian foreign policy interests, and a hidden admiration of the Soviet Union.

- N -

NATIONAL AWAKENING. In the narrowest sense, the Latvian "national awakening" was the cluster of social and cultural changes that from the 1850s to the 1880s created in the Russian Baltic provinces (q.v.) a generation of nationalistically inclined Latvian cultural activists. In a more inclusive sense, the phrase has been applied as well to the Latvian cultural flowering of the 1920s, immediately after the acquisition of political independence; and to the Latvian collective efforts that in the period from 1988 to 1991 led the country out of the Soviet Union and restored it as an independent and sovereign state. The last of these "awakenings" is sometimes also referred to among contemporary Latvians as the "third awakening," a concept that was given wide currency in the voluminous writings of the physicist and cultural journalist Jānis Stradiņš (b. 1933) (q.v.) during the perestroika period in Latvia.

The "first" awakening, however, has remained the prototype for the series. In the 1850s and 1860s, university-educated Latvians--sometimes referred to as the "Young Latvians" (*jaunlatvieši*, q.v.)--began to resist the Germanization and Russification (qq.v.) that seemed always to accompany educational and social upward mobility among Latvians, and to insist that a Latvian-language culture, supported by Latvian institutions, was not only possible but desirable. Inspired by the writings of the German cultural philosopher J. G. Herder (q.v.) and such German nationalists as J. G. Fichte, the Latvian activists challenged German-language cultural hegemony in the Baltic area and saw as one of their main tasks the "awakening" of other Latvians to these new truths. Writers, schoolteachers, and journalists such as Juris Alunāns, Atis Kronvalds, Krišjānis Barons, and Krišjānis Valdemārs (qq.v.) sought to establish a Latvian press (e.g., the newspaper *Peterburgas Avīzes,* q.v.) critical of Baltic German control, improve the Latvian language so that it could be used to express the ideas of the modern world, and popularize the idea that regardless of where they lived all Latvians were members of one nation (Latv. *tauta*). Other, more practical-minded activists founded in 1868 the Riga Latvian Association (q.v.) to give Latvians in the main city of the Baltic provinces a center of their own.

The relentless efforts of this first generation of "awakeners" were successful in all these spheres, and by the end of the 1880s the institutional groundwork for a Latvian-language national culture had been laid: the *tauta* had "awakened." In these decades, however, the activists called for no more than Latvian *cultural* autonomy, believing that Latvians could continue to live in their ancestral territory as a component of the Russian Empire. The cultural nationalism of this first period did not transform itself into a political nationalism (calling for political independence) until the Revolution of 1905 in the Baltic provinces.

NEW CURRENT (Latv. JAUNĀ STRĀVA). The term used by historians of the Latvian intelligentsia to designate a generation of writers in the mid-1890s whose ideas constituted a sharp break with the nationalist thinking of the "national awakening" (q.v.) period. The "new current" was not a movement or party in the strict sense and who did or did not belong to it is a matter of debate. Its beginnings are associated with the poet Eduārds Veidenbaums (1867-1892) and a group of Latvian students at Dorpat (Tartu) University in Livonia (q.v.), who in 1891 published the first volume of a multivolume series of writings called *Pūrs* (*The Dowry*). Each volume contained a collection of essays on "radical" topics such as historical materialism, Darwinism, and workers' rights, intending with these to introduce into public debate controversial subjects from contemporary western European thought. This radicalism had to be tempered, of course, because of censorship and possible imprisonment.

Though the "new current" did not have a socialist core, socialism, including its Marxist variant, was a philosophy in which many of its activists (such as Jānis Rainis, q.v.) were deeply interested. Correspondingly, the "new current" was severely critical of contemporary Latvian nationalism, claiming that the "national awakening" impulse was spent and nationalism had become a facade for profit-making among the business classes. Many of the writers identified with the "new current" became the core of the Latvian socialist movement at the end of the 1890s, while others remained parliamentary liberals in their politics and attached themselves to the idea of a Latvian national state. The radical impulse the "new current" represented found its culmination in the 1905 revolutionary events in Latvia, after which the political configuration changed entirely.

NIEDRA, ANDRIEVS (1871-1942).   Although he had studied theology at Dorpat (Tartu) University and taught religious studies in Riga (q.v.) from 1898 on, at the turn of the twentieth century Niedra was first and foremost a very popular writer of novels and poetry. His searching and philosophical novels about the everyday conflicts of Latvian--especially rural--life, explored among other things the psychology of Latvian-Baltic German relationships. Politically, he was a conservative, which in the pre-World War Latvian context meant opposition to all manner of revolutionary activities. He attacked the 1905 revolutionaries, opposed any dealings with Social Democrats, and urged cooperation with Baltic Germans (q.v.). During the period of World War I, he stood apart from the Latvian mainstream efforts to establish a new government and, in fact, for about three months in 1919 headed a cabinet that was assembled with German support as an alternative to the struggling government headed by Kārlis Ulmanis (q.v.). Niedra's efforts received very little support in the Latvian population, and at the end of 1919 he emigrated. In 1924, he returned to Latvia and was tried for treason and was exiled. From 1924 he worked as minister of a German congregation in East Prussia. He returned to Latvia during the German occupation as of 1941, and died in 1942.

NONRECOGNITION POLICY. Under the nonrecognition policy maintained by the United States and some 30 other countries from 1940 onward, these states did not recognize the incorporation of Latvia (as well as Estonia and Lithuania) into the Soviet Union. The consequence was that from 1940, in the eyes of the U.S. government (and other governments), Latvia continued to have a de jure existence but not a de facto one. Thus, Latvia (and Estonia and Lithuania) continued to have legations, in Washington, D.C., and other Western capitals, with Latvian diplomats having nearly the same rights and privileges as other diplomats and the legation having the right to deal with U.S. residents who had not given up their Latvian citizenship. In dealing with the Soviet Union, the U.S. did not permit its diplomats to travel in an official capacity in the Baltic republics, judging that official trips could be read as formal recognition of incorporation. Many maps of Europe published in the U.S. and showing the Baltic states as constituent parts of the USSR carried a special statement that the U.S. did not officially recognize this inclusion. The policy continued in force until 1991, when, in

September, the U.S., USSR, and other states reaffirmed the independence of the Baltic countries and the three became members of the United Nations as sovereign and independent states.

- O -

OSTLAND. The administrative region devised by the German authorities for the three Baltic states and Belorussia during the German occupation of the region in the 1941-1944 period. Ostland and the other administrative regions of eastern territories conquered by the Third Reich were subdivided into districts, and the entire structure was governed through a hierarchy of commissars at the head of which was the minister of state in Berlin Alfred Rosenberg. The *Reichskommissar* for Ostland was Heinrich Lohse and the *Generalkommissar* for Latvia was Otto Drechsler. The occupation government published in Riga (q.v.) a semiofficial newspaper for the entire Ostland territory, called *Deutsche Zeitung für Ostland.*

- P -

PARTISANS (Latv. **PARTIZĀNI, also MEŽA BRĀĻI [FOREST BROTHERS]**). In the sense of loosely organized guerrilla units fighting behind enemy lines or in enemy territory, the term "partisans" plays a role in historical descriptions of Latvia during the periods of the First and Second World Wars. But the term is not neutral, because one historian's "partisans" are likely to be another historian's "bandits" or "terrorists." Anti-Bolshevik guerrilla units numbering in total perhaps 400 to 500 persons harassed the armed forces of the Communist government of Peteris Stučka (q.v.) when it was in power in Latvia during the first four months of 1919. These partisans were fighting on behalf of the national government of Kārlis Ulmanis (q.v.). During the Second World War, anticommunist partisans, numbering perhaps 6,000 persons, harassed the Soviet Army in June-July 1941, as it retreated in face of the advancing German Army. In the years 1941 to 1943, numerous units of "red" partisans were infiltrated into German-occupied Latvia, and during 1943-1944 harassed the

German *Wehrmacht* as its position weakened on the northeastern front. They and their supporters are estimated to have numbered around 20,000 persons.

The most sustained partisan activity in Latvia, however, was carried out in the decade from 1945 to 1955 as the Soviet Union reestablished its control over Latvian territory. Units of the defeated Latvian Legion (q.v.) and other opponents of the Communist regime, numbering an estimated 10,000 to 15,000 persons over the entire period, withdrew into forests (hence "forest brothers") and continued the fight, which sometimes took the form of pitched battles of partisans units against units of the Soviet Army or the special military forces of the NKVD (later KGB). Though the partisan movement had a degree of structure, there was no unified leadership and their success depended largely on how long the general population was willing to support the struggle. The partisan ranks were replenished by the deportations (q.v.) of 1949. An estimated 2,000 representatives of Soviet power are estimated as having been killed over the 1945-1955 period. By the early 1950s, however, the ranks of the partisans were thinning rapidly, and support for them in the general population was waning. The last members of the movement had surrendered to the authorities by 1955.

PAŠPĀRVALDE **(Ger. LANDESEIGENE VERWALTUNG; Engl. NATIVE SELF-GOVERNMENT).** The generic name for the Latvian governmental apparatus during the German occupation of Latvia from 1941 to 1945 in the World War II period. After the German invasion in July 1941, and the flight to the Soviet Union of many administrative personnel who had worked for the Communist government of the previous 12 months, continuity was provided by the revival of some of the governmental, judicial, and administrative institutions and personnel of the pre-Soviet period (i.e., the Ulmanis [q.v.] period before June 1940). But the work of these persons immediately ran counter to the German plans to administer Latvia according to a much larger scheme that included all three Baltic states as well as Byelorussia (*see* OSTLAND). For another year, until mid-1942, there was a considerable amount of confusion, as the German occupation authorities and Latvian political leaders tried to delineate spheres of administrative authority.

Eventually, a directorate system was introduced, which located decision making pertaining to Latvia's internal affairs in such directorates as education, judiciary, social welfare, etc. which were headed by Latvians. Insofar as appointments to all official positions had to be approved by the German occupying authorities and insofar as large areas of everyday life (e.g., those pertaining to Jews, German nationals, the economic interests of the German Reich, etc.) were entirely removed from the directorates, the scope of their authority was relatively limited. The directorate system, not very stable to begin with, began to erode seriously in 1943 because of the high turnover of competent personnel and by mid-year 1944 it had become chaotic. In the fall of 1944, the German occupying authorities eliminated the whole structure.

PĒKŠĒNA, MARIJA (1845-1903). Pēkšēna was the first woman writer of note to write and publish in the Latvian language, with one of her plays receiving first prize in a competition organized by the Riga Latvian Association (q.v.) in 1870. The play was performed several times in the later 1870s, but, possibly because of its lack of success, Pēkšēna did not pursue her literary career any further.

PELŠE, ARVĪDS (1899-1983). Born in Livonia (q.v.), Pelše joined the Communist Party in 1915 and moved to Russia in 1918 when the independence of Latvia was declared. From that date until 1940, Pelše lived in the Soviet Union, holding a series of positions in the CPSU and in governmental and academic institutions. In 1940, after the occupation of Latvia by the Soviet army, he was sent to Latvia to assist with the integration of the country into the Soviet framework. He fled to the Soviet Union in the German occupation period (1941-1945), returned to Latvia in the fall of 1944, and for the next decade and a half worked in high party positions and dedicated himself to the fight against "bourgeois nationalism" and the bourgeoisie as a class. In 1959, after that year's purge (*see* EDUĀRDS BERKLAVS) of the Latvian Communist Party, Pelše became first secretary and held that position until 1966, when he left for Moscow to become a member of the CPSU Politburo. Pelše's work in Latvia was marked by a virulent hatred of any thought or action, especially in the intelligentsia, that could be interpreted as approval of Latvian national interests and by his active support of all measures expanding Russian influence and presence in the Latvian SSR.

PĒRKONKRUSTS (Engl. THUNDERCROSS). The Latvian political organization that from 1930 to 1934 emulated in Latvia the fascist organizations of western Europe, adapting fascist ideology to fit Latvian circumstances. The intent of Pērkonkrusts was to ensure that Latvian society was in every respect controlled by Latvians; consequently, it was anti-Semitic and opposed those provisions of the 1922 Latvian Constitution that guaranteed cultural autonomy to national minorities. Pērkonkrusts is estimated to have had about 5,000-6,000 members, though it claimed more, and its most prominent leader during the 1930s and the early part of the 1940s was Gustavs Celmiņš (q.v.). After his 1934 coup, President Kārlis Ulmanis (q.v.) dissolved all organizations, including Pērkonkrusts, deemed to threaten the stability of the state; Celmiņš himself was imprisoned for three years and then exiled from Latvia.

Although the organization as such did not exist from 1934 onward, many of its former members and leaders continued to act with a degree of solidarity, especially after the invasion of Latvia by the German army in July 1941. During the German occupation, Pērkonkrusts sought briefly to revive itself as a functioning political organization, but the German authorities were as suspicious of the organization's motives as Ulmanis had been and formally dissolved it about a month after the invasion. While many of its members became collaborators of the German occupation authorities, others, acting from nationalistic motives, joined the "underground" opposition to the German occupation.

PĒTERBUGAS AVĪZES (See NATIONAL AWAKENING).

PETERS, JĀNIS (1939-   ). Having established an excellent reputation as an insightful poet from the early 1960s onward, Peters became a member of the Communist Party in 1973 and chair of the Council of the Latvian Writers Union (q.v.) in 1985 and served in that capacity until 1989. He was therefore a prime mover in the events that with 1988 and the founding of the Latvian Popular Front (q.v.) began the process that led the Latvian SSR into an increasingly independent stance toward Moscow, resulting in the independence declaration of May 1990 and actual independence by the end of August 1991. From 1990, Peters represented the Latvian government in Moscow and from the fall of 1991, became the Latvian Ambassador to Russia. Peters's creative work and political opinions have been marked by a deep concern for the maintenance of Latvian national uniqueness, and also with the cross-fertilization of national cultural traditions.

***PLETTENBERG, WOLTER* VON** (c.1450-1535). Master of the Livonian Order (q.v.) from 1494 to 1535, von Plettenberg was probably the most clear-sighted of the Order's leaders in the final century of its existence. The Order was wealthy and possessed numerous territories in medieval Livonia (q.v.), but its effectiveness was threatened by internal conflict, continuous struggles against other territorial rulers of the Livonian state, and the expansionism of the Russian state under Ivan the Terrible. During his tenure, von Plettenberg's wise diplomacy maintained the Order's influence on events in the Baltic area, but after his death the internal corruption of the Order continued. The Order was officially secularized and in effect disbanded in 1562.

POLISH-SWEDISH WAR (1600-1629). The settlement of the Livonian War (q.v.) in 1583 left Poland-Lithuania in control of most of the Baltic territory to the north, while Sweden gained only a section of present-day Estonia. This outcome was unsatisfactory to the Swedish Vasa dynasty, which dreamed of an empire that included all of the eastern Baltic territories and that could resist Russian moves westward. Moreover, the German-speaking estate owners and burghers of the Baltic territories after 1583 grew increasingly resentful of Polish-Lithuanian rule, and especially, since they were Lutherans (q.v.), of the Polish Counterreformation efforts. In the last decades of the sixteenth century, therefore, the Baltic political elites made it known that they would favor being released from "the Polish yoke" by the Swedish Protestant rulers.

The Polish-Swedish War began in 1600 with a Swedish invasion of the Baltic territory and continued intermittently for the next three decades until the Peace of Altmark in 1629. Most of the battles took place in the territories north of the Daugava River (q.v.) (in present-day Estonia and Vidzeme, q.v.), and devastated these territories. Though Poland-Lithuania won some notable battles, Sweden emerged victorious in the end. The Treaty of Altmark left Sweden in control of all of the territory north of the Daugava; Poland retained nominal control of the Duchy of Courland and Semigallia (q.v.), the dukes of which, however, were more autonomous than subservient. Direct control by Poland-Lithuania was exercised over the eastern Latgale (q.v.) region, which starting with this period came to be increasingly referred to as "Polish Livland" (*Inflanty Polskie*). This territorial configuration remained in force until the end of the seventeenth century, when the Great Northern War (q.v.) once again introduced Russia into the regional competition.

POPULAR FRONT (Latv. **TAUTAS FRONTE**). Founded on October 8-9, 1988, the Popular Front in Latvia emerged as the leading so-called "informal organization" supporting the perestroika and glasnost policies of Mikhail Gorbachev, and, as a mass-based organization, quickly eclipsed even the Latvian Communist Party (q.v.) in terms of membership. It was more centrist and therefore more inclusive than the Latvian National Independence Movement (LNNK) (q.v.), which had been established earlier in 1988, and thus attracted a larger number of people dissatisfied with their Communist Party membership and Communist rule in general. Chaired by Dainis Īvāns, a journalist, the Popular Front rapidly shifted its goals and rhetoric from support of Moscow's new policies to demands for autonomy and independence for Latvia, and over the next 14 months organized a series of mass meetings on the days marking especially memorable events in twentieth-century Latvian history (June 13-14, the deportations of 1940; August 23, the anniversary of the Molotov-Ribbentrop Pact; November 18, the proclamation of Latvian independence in 1918). The commemoration of these events had been forbidden in the Soviet period and any demonstrative activity on them had been condemned as "bourgeois nationalism."

In the spring 1990 elections for the Latvian Supreme Soviet (q.v.), the Popular Front and the LNNK fielded candidates in opposition to the Communist Party, and in the resulting Soviet there was a majority of deputies from these noncommunist organizations. Thus, in May 1990, the Soviet declared its intention to work for the eventual renewal of Latvian independence, which finally came after the unsuccessful August coup in 1991. During the two and a half years after renewed independence, however, the Popular Front, now under the leadership of Romualds Ražuks appeared to be losing its relevance to the state-building tasks at hand. In the parliamentary elections of June 1993, the Front--though fielding its own list of candidates as one of 23 parties and electoral coalitions--did not even receive the minimum 4 percent of the vote needed for parliamentary representation. Many of the most prominent Popular Front politicians had shifted their loyalties to other groups, such as Latvia's Way (q.v.), the electoral coalition that received a plurality of the vote.

POPULATION. Because the first modern (though incomplete) census of Latvian territories took place only in 1881 (a census of the Baltic provinces [q.v.] only) and the second in 1897 (the first Russian Imperial Census), aggregate population statistics for earlier periods have to be estimated. Estimates for the late eighteenth and the nineteenth centuries can employ the soul revisions (q.v.), but for earlier periods they must be based on calculations using estimated population density and estimated territorial size. In the twentieth century, the government of the independence period carried out general censuses in 1920, 1925, 1930, and 1935; in the Soviet period there were censuses in 1959, 1970, 1979, and 1989. Using these sources, the aggregate population of present-day Latvian territories over the centuries and the proportion of Latvians in the aggregate population can be estimated as the following:

Year	Total population	Percent Latvians
Early 13th century	est. 250,000-350,000	
Mid-18th century	est. 500,000	
1800	est. 720,000	est. 89.8
1863	1,240,988	
1897	1,930,000	
1914	est. 2,552,000	
1920	1,596,000	72.7
1925	1,845,000	73.4
1930	1,900,000	73.4
1935	1,950,000	75.5
1959	2,093,000	62.0
1970	2,364,000	56.8
1979	2,503,000	53.7
1989	2,666,000	52.0
1993	2,606,000	53.5
1996	2,501,000	55.2

PUGO, BORISS (1937-1991). Born in Russia, Pugo received his university education at the Riga Polytechnical Institute (q.v.), and from the early 1960s onward worked in the Latvian SSR as an engineer and in a series of increasingly responsible positions in the Communist Party organization and government institutions, including from 1980 in the KGB. He became first secretary of the Latvian Communist Party (q.v.) in 1984 and held that position until 1990 when he moved to Moscow to become interior minister in the USSR government. From this position, Pugo participated in the organization of the August 19, 1991 coup against Mikhail Gorbachev and, when that failed, committed suicide.

PUMPURS, ANDREJS (1841-1902). Pumpurs grew up in a district of Livonia (q.v.) that was especially noted for the preservation of the Latvian oral tradition, which became an important source for his creative work later in life. Born into a rural family of modest means, he received a grade school education after which he embarked on a checkered but adventurous career as an agricultural laborer, raftsman, surveyor, forester, volunteer topographer during the Russo-Turkish War, and officer in the Russian army. Familiarity with Slavic culture, especially Serbian history, convinced him that the Latvians too deserved at least cultural autonomy, and this belief, evidently developed during the 1870s, brought him into the Latvian nationalists' camp of that decade.

Pumpurs had already published incidental writings in the Latvian press, but now he began seriously to exploit his knowledge of the Latvian oral tradition in order to acquaint Latvians with their cultural heritage. Undoubtedly his most memorable accomplishment is the epic poem *Lāčplēsis* (*The Bearslayer*) (1888), which he wrote after discovering that the Latvian oral tradition contained no epic poetry. While Lāčplēsis was a relatively minor figure in Latvian folklore, Pumpurs' imaginative rendering of Lācplēsis's adventures turned him into a national symbol of heroism. The Lāčplēsis theme--the figure of Lačplēsis standing for the Latvian nation challenged and subdued by external evil forces--was used repeatedly by later writers at dramatic turning points in Latvian history (e.g., Jānis Rainis in his play *Uguns un Nakts* [1905]), with its most recent incarnation being a 1988 rock opera called *Lāčplēsis* (music by Z. Liepiņš, libretto by Mārā Zālīte). In 1920, the Lāčplēsis Order was created by the Latvian Saeima (q.v.) (parliament) as the nation's highest military honor.

PURVĪTIS, VILHELMS (1872-1945). A preeminent Latvian painter of the pre-World War I and interwar periods, Purvītis finished the St. Petersburg Art Academy in 1897 and then traveled widely in Western Europe, entering his works in many exhibits and winning several prizes. He lived in Riga (q.v.) after 1900, was elected to membership in the Russian Academy of Art in 1917, and, after Latvian independence, founded the Latvian Academy of Art and was rector and professor of it until 1934. He supervised virtually all the exhibits of Latvian art that were held abroad in the interwar period. Shortly before emigrating to Germany in 1944, he gathered all his paintings in Jelgava (q.v.) where they were destroyed in bombing raids on the city. Through his pedagogical work, Purvītis left an indelible impression on several generations of artists and teachers of art. Though he experimented with virtually all the styles that were current during his lifetime, the subject matter of his work was almost entirely the natural scenery of Latvia and its various aspects.

- R -

RAINIS, JĀNIS (1865-1929). Pseudonym of Jānis Pliekšāns. During his adulthood, Rainis was recognized as the best playwright and poet Latvian literature had produced to date, a status he has never lost. The son of a relatively well-to-do farmer, he received his primary and secondary education in Latvia, and in 1884 enrolled in the law faculty of St. Petersburg University. After finishing his legal education in 1889, Rainis worked as a clerk in the Vilnius (Lithuania) district court, but by that time his journalistic activities had already begun to overwhelm his interests in a career in law. As a student he had begun to publish political commentary in the periodical press, and in 1891 he assumed the editorship of *Dienas Lapa* (q.v.), a newspaper that became the principal outlet of the ideas of the so-called new current (q.v.) in Latvian thinking. Rainis and his generation of the Latvian intelligentsia were influenced by Western, especially German, Marxism and sought to transplant it to the Baltic provinces.

Encountering the expected resistance of czarist authorities, Rainis and his wife, Aspāzija (q.v.), chose Swiss exile in 1905, remaining there until 1920. Upon their return to now-independent Latvia, they were greeted as national heroes. Rainis was an active member of the Latvian Social Democratic Party (q.v.), its deputy in the Saeima (q.v.) (parliament), and minister of education from 1926 to 1928 during a Social Democratic government. Though he died a disappointed politician, Rainis's standing as one of the "classic" authors of Latvian literature grew after his death to the extent that even the authorities of the Soviet period were reluctant to tinker with it. Rainis's art combined a dialectical view of individual development with a profound belief in the principle of nationality, both of which, in his view, interacted to raise consciousness to a higher level of humanity. His poetry and drama, as well as his translations of Western classics (e.g., Goethe's *Faust*, 1897-1898), stretched the expressive capabilities of the Latvian language far beyond the limits it had reached before Rainis began to write.

RANCĀNS, JEZUPS (1886-1969). Born in Latgale (q.v.), Rancāns was one of the most distinguished Roman Catholic (q.v.) churchmen-politicians of the interwar period in Latvia. He received his theological education in St. Petersburg before World War I, where he remained to teach until the start of the war. In 1917, he participated actively in Lettgallian (q.v.) political life, and after the declaration of Latvian independence was a frequent emissary from the new Latvian government to the Holy See. He served as a delegate to the National Council and was elected to all four Saeimas (q.v.) (parliaments) on the ticket of the Lettgallian Christian Farmers and Catholics. Fleeing from Latvia to Germany in 1944, he resumed his religious and political work among the Latvian DPs (q.v.), and in 1951 emigrated to the U.S. and worked in the Grand Rapids, Michigan, diocese. He was a delegate to the Second Vatican Council from 1962 to 1965. Throughout his political career, Rancāns was a firm defender of Latvian sovereignty, but also of the cultural and religious traditions of his native Lettgallian region.

REDUCTION (REVERSION) OF ESTATES (Latv. MUIŽU REDUKCIJA). An absolutist policy introduced during the rule of Charles XI of Sweden (1660-1687), as a result of which the landowning aristocracies (Ger. *Ritterschaften*) of Livland (Livonia, q.v.) and Estland (Estonia)--the section of the Baltic controlled by Sweden--were forced to either prove their claim to their estates or revert control of them to the Swedish crown. The policy was grounded in the feudal theory that ultimately all land is "held" from the monarch. During the earlier part of the seventeenth century, Swedish monarchs had granted estates (including the Baltic estates) to aristocrats for all manner of real and imagined services. Some crown properties had been sold to pay for royal debts. Whether the new policy was basically economic (to increase royal revenues) or political (to reduce the power of the aristocracies) or a mixture of both is a debatable question.

With respect to Livland the "reduction" policy was initiated in April 1681, with the creation of a royal commission for "reduction," By 1687, over the strong and continuous opposition of the Baltic German (q.v.) landowning aristocracies, some five-sixths of the Livonian estates had been reverted to the crown. Simultaneously with the reversion, royal agents and commissions worked out new regulations for the treatment of serfs (q.v.) on royal domains when administered by the crown directly or when leased from the crown by private individuals. A number of Latvian and Estonian historians--painting a picture of the "good Swedish times" in contrast to the "bad Russian times" that were to arrive in the eighteenth century--have argued strongly that these reversion reforms improved the lot of the enserfed peasants by creating regulations for corvée (q.v.) labor and restricting other heretofore unlimited serf-owner rights. Restrictions placed on estate treatment of serfs by the reversion policy disappeared toward the end of the century and particularly after Sweden lost Livonia to Russia as a result of the Great Northern War (q.v.).

REITERS, TEODORS (1884-1956). Reiters was an eminent figure in the Latvian musical world in the pre-World War I period as well as during the interwar years, particularly in his specialty, which was choral music and its conducting. He finished his musical education in the St. Petersburg Conservatory in the period from 1907 to 1917 and, after 1918 and the declaration of Latvian independence, worked to lay an institutional groundwork for the continuation of the strong indigenous Latvian choral tradition. In 1920, he founded the Reiters Choir, which by 1940 had presented some 485 concerts, about 56 of those outside of Latvia. In 1944, he emigrated to Sweden, continuing his musical work there until his death in 1956.

RELIGION. The first of the Baltic littoral peoples to encounter Christianity (in its Eastern Orthodox version) were probably the Lettgallians (q.v.), who from the ninth century onward were in contact with the peoples of Kievan Rus. Western Christianity arrived with the German crusading orders (q.v.) in the late twelfth century and sought actively to extirpate the pre-Christian faiths of the native Balts. Though by the fourteenth century the institutions of the western Church were well established in medieval Livonia (q.v.) and all the Balts had been Christianized (at least nominally), "pagan" beliefs remained alive at least until the seventeenth century, judging by the complaints of the clergy. In the sixteenth century, the Livonian church reformed itself in line with Lutheran (q.v.) beliefs, but the Livonian Wars (q.v.) and Poland's acquisition of considerable amounts of Baltic territory meant that among eastern Latvians (and in pockets of the western territories) Roman Catholicism remained a living faith.

In the mid-eighteenth century, in what had become the Russian province of Livland (q.v.) the pietism of the Moravian Brethren (q.v.) (the so-called Herrnhut movement) seized the imagination of thousands of peasants for whom the Lutheran Church had become too closely linked with the Baltic German (q.v.) governing classes, and left a strong pietistic tradition in Latvian religiosity. Also, in the nineteenth century, the fragility of Lutheranism among Latvians was demonstrated by the voluntary conversion, in the 1840s, of thousands of peasants to Russian Orthodoxy, when rumor had it that joining the "Czar's church" would bring grants of land in the Russian interior.

Nonetheless, by the end of the nineteenth century, Lutheranism remained the faith of the majority of the Latvians, even though by that time Roman Catholicism, Russian Orthodoxy, and Protestant Baptism were strongly represented in the population. The migration of many Jews (q.v.) from the Pale of Settlement northward also meant the expansion of the adherents of Judaism, especially in Riga (q.v.), Kurland province, and southeastern Livland. In the 1920s, after the establishment of the independent Latvian state, Lutherans made up 57.2 percent of the population, Roman Catholics 22.6 percent, Orthodox 14.0 percent, Jews 5.2 percent, and other faiths about 2 percent. The interwar situation was more complex than these figures indicate, because some 300,000 registered Lutherans did not belong to a Lutheran congregation, only 55 percent of those registered in a congregation seldom if ever took communion, and among Latvian intellectuals (for the most part) there was a popular movement to restore pre-Christian Latvian religious forms, based on folklore material (*see* DIEVTURĪBA).

Lutheran and other forms of religious worship became increasingly difficult in the Soviet period after 1945, when churches were severely taxed, the training of clergy hindered, the printing of religious literature restricted and sometimes denied, and the Soviet Latvian government enunciated atheism as its official creed and taught it as such in primary and secondary schools. In spite of, or perhaps because of, these government-sponsored attacks on organized religion, many of the dissidents (q.v.) in Latvia were strongly religious and expressed their challenge to Communist orthodoxy on that basis.

Since 1991, when Latvia reestablished its independence, religion and religious organizations, as other aspects of life, have been in a state of flux. The University of Latvia has reestablished the Faculty of Theology (closed in 1940) and religious life in general has experienced a revival. The same faiths that were strongly represented in the Latvian population before World War II remain dominant, with the exception of Judaism, the adherents of which were almost completely exterminated during the German occupation of Latvia in the 1941-1945 period. Reliable statistics about religious life in Latvia are not currently available.

RIGA. From its founding in 1201, Riga has been the largest and most important urban center of the eastern Baltic littoral. Initially, the city was meant to be the principal center for the Christianization of the Baltic area, but benefiting from its location on the Daugava River (q.v.) and the Gulf of Riga, it quickly emerged during the thirteenth century as a significant commercial center, especially for entrepôt trade between western Europe and the Russian states east of the Baltic area. Joining the Hanseatic League in 1282 enhanced the city's economic wealth and importance during the late medieval centuries. From the beginning the Riga patriciate was German-speaking, even though the total population of the city--particularly support occupations such as teamsters and builders--contained substantial numbers of non-Germans, especially Latvians. The Riga merchant elite always had an uneasy relationship with the religious and secular authorities governing the Baltic area and frequently perceived itself as an independent force, dealing on the basis of equality with the Catholic Church, the Livonian Order (qq.v.), and, later, various occupying powers such as the Poles, Swedes, and Russians. This sense of autonomy did not diminish until the second half of the 19th century, when the city, together with the rest of the Baltic provinces (q.v.), became increasingly subject to Imperial law.

Riga's population at the start of the eighteenth century is estimated at 11,000 and by the end of the century, at 29,500. But the period of most rapid population growth came in the decades between 1863 and 1914, when the population grew from 77,500 to 517,500 persons. By the time of World War I the city's population was about 40 percent Latvian-speaking and, in addition to its traditional roles as a Baltic German (q.v.) commercial and Russian administrative center, it had also taken on the role of the principal center of Latvian cultural and organizational life in the Baltic provinces.

Not surprisingly, when the Latvian state came into being in 1918, Riga became the capital and retained that status from 1918 until the present. Its population continued to grow during the interwar period of Latvian independence (about 350,000 by 1940 [63 percent Latvians]) and the post-1945 Soviet period (about 843,000 by 1979). After 1945, however, the composition of Riga's population began to change substantially. The city became the headquarters of the Baltic Military District of the USSR and therefore a place of residence for large numbers of military personnel. Also, because of Soviet-period population policies, which deliberately recruited large numbers of Russians and other eastern Slavs to Latvia, the proportion of Latvians in Riga by 1979 had been reduced to about 33 percent. In 1991, when the USSR disintegrated and Latvia regained its sovereignty as an independent state, Riga--still the capital--contained about one-third of the country's entire population, but only about one-third of the city's inhabitants listed themselves as being of Latvian nationality.

RIGA LATVIAN ASSOCIATION, RLA (Latv. **RĪGAS LATVIEŠU BIEDRĪBA**). The Riga Latvian Association was one of the by-products of the socioeconomic transformations experienced by the Latvians during the second half of the nineteenth century. From mid-century on, rural-to-urban migration in the Latvian territories increased rapidly, as did the national and political consciousness of Latvians. Political power in the Baltic provinces (q.v.) and their main cities--such as Riga (q.v.)--was in the hands of the Baltic German (q.v.) urban patriciate, and the czarist government in St. Petersburg controlled carefully the number and types of organizations it allowed to be formed in the western borderlands of the Empire. The first attempts (1860-1961) by the Latvians in Riga to establish an association came to naught, but in 1868 permission was obtained. On paper, the RLA was an association to raise humanitarian assistance for famine-stricken Estonians. In reality, the association quickly became the most significant organization the Latvians had in Riga or anywhere else. By the end of its first years, the RLA had some 230 members, and by the end of its first decade some 1,000.

From the outset the RLA established a series of committees to pursue a varied cultural program--lectures, theater performances, concerts, publications. Its organizational and creative impulses linked up with the broadly experienced "national awakening" (q.v.) in the cities and countryside, and therefore in due course the RLA was popularly referred to as "mother" (*māmuļa*). Inevitably, there was dissension in its ranks as to whether scarce resources should be directed toward practical improvements in Latvian life or cultural improvements. In the 1890s, a new generation of Latvians--largely at universities-- perceived the RLA as having become the captive of the increasingly wealthier Latvian business families of Riga and accused them of disguising the profit motive with nationalist rhetoric. The RLA continued its existence until 1940, when it-- and most private organizations--were closed by the new Latvian Soviet government. In 1990, the RLA was reestablished as the power of the Communist Party in Latvia diminished and the perestroika policy of Michael Gorbachev came to permit private organizations in the Soviet Union. After a 50-year interruption, the RLA has resumed its activities amid controversies about which of several groups should be considered the true heir to the spirit of the original organization.

RIGA POLYTECHNIC INSTITUTE (RPI). In 1862, leaders of the free professions in Riga received permission to establish an institution of higher learning in the city that would train its students in technical subjects, especially engineering. Starting with 16 students, after a decade the "Polytechnikum," as the institute was popularly known, had an enrollment of about 130 and offered programs in engineering, chemistry, agriculture, mechanics, architecture, and commerce. Founded as a private university with students covering a high proportion of their tuition fees, the Polytechnikum eventually came under the supervision of the St. Petersburg government's Ministry of Finance and afterward the Ministry of Education.

It was reorganized in 1896 as the Riga Polytechnic Institute (RPI), a move that consolidated its resources and gave it greater visibility in the Empire. In 1896, in the Russification (q.v.)

period, the RPI was forced to change its language of instruction from German to Russian. By the turn of the century, certainly in some of the exact sciences and in the technical fields, the RPI was the preferred educational institution over the older and more famous Baltic university at Dorpat (Tartu). The buildings and organization of the RPI became the basis in 1919 of the University of Latvia, the national university of the newly established republic. After World War II, when Latvia had been incorporated into the USSR, a number of engineering and technical sectors were separated from the University of Latvia and became the basis of the Riga Technical University which, in a sense, continued the tradition of the RPI.

ROMAN CATHOLICISM. Although after the Protestant Reformation of the sixteenth century the majority of Latvians were Lutheran (q.v.), Roman Catholicism continued to play a major role in Latvian history. This was partly because the Lutheran territories always continued to have a scattering of Roman Catholic congregations and, partly because the eastern districts--Latgale (q.v.)--of the Latvian territories that were not part of the Baltic provinces (q.v.) proper remained predominantly Roman Catholic due to their inclusion in the Polish Lithuanian Commonwealth and their continuing association with Polish and Lithuanian cultural influences even during the Russian Imperial period. When Latvia became independent in 1918, Latgale entered the new state with a predominantly Roman Catholic population. In the last (1935) census of the interwar period, Catholics were approximately 14.5 percent of the total Latvian population.

ROZIŅŠ, FRICIS (1870-1919). From the 1890s onward, Roziņš was a social-democratic activist and participant in the "new current" (q.v.) movement. Arrested by the authorities in 1897 and subjected for a while to internal exile, Roziņš emigrated to England in 1899 where he became an active organizer, writer, and publisher on behalf of Latvian social democracy. He returned periodically to Latvia after the 1905 Revolution, but he was arrested and deported to Siberia in 1908. From 1912 to 1917, having escaped from Siberia, he emigrated to the United States, publishing a Latvian social-democratic newspaper there. After 1917, Roziņš was fully supportive of the Bolshevik (q.v.) wing of Latvian social democracy, and in 1919 served as minister of agriculture in the short-lived Latvian Bolshevik government of Pēteris Stučka (q.v.).

RUDĒVICS, ANSIS (1890-1974). Rudēvics was a Latvian Social Democratic (q.v.) activist from 1907 onward and retained his standing as a leader of the Social Democratic Party throughout the interwar independence period. He was a deputy to the Constitutional Convention as well as to all four Saeimas (q.v.) (parliaments). During the period of Ulmanis's (q.v.) authoritarian rule, Rudēvics remained active in underground left-wing party activity, urging closer cooperation with the communists. Exiled from Latvia in 1938, he returned in 1940, joined the Communist Party, fled to the USSR during the German occupation, and returned to Soviet Latvia after World War II to work in various jobs in the state publishing houses.

RUDZĪTIS, HELMĀRS (1903-   ). Rudzītis was an innovative publisher in interwar Latvia who in 1926 established the firm *Grāmatu Draugs* (Friend of Books) with the intention of providing the reading public with inexpensive editions of world literature and the writings of Latvian authors. Instead of printing runs of about 2,000--the normal average for the time--Rudzītis printed around 18,000 copies. The idea caught on with readers, and by 1944 the firm had published some 1,500 titles in Latvian. Emigrating to Germany in 1944, Rudzītis renewed his firm in Esslingen and continued to publish for the Latvian DP (q.v.) community, until emigrating to the United States in 1949. There *Grāmatu Draugs* was reopened in New York, where in the period 1949 to 1985 it had published some 740 titles. In addition, the firm also published from 1949 onward the Latvian-language biweekly newspaper *Laiks* (*Time*) (q.v.), which with its editions of approximately 10,000 quickly became the principal newspaper for the Latvian émigrés in the Western world. In the history of the Latvian printed word, Rudzītis's role has been unique, in part because of his conviction (in independent Latvia) that Latvian-language publications had a mass market in Latvia and in part because of his efforts (in the post-World War II period) to establish an outlet for Latvian-language writings in the West.

RUDZUTAKS, JĀNIS (1887-1938). From 1905 onward, Rudzutaks was an active member of the Latvian Social Democratic Party (q.v.), but spent most of his time in the pre-World War I period in jail because of illegal activities. In 1917, he joined the Bolshevik (q.v.) movement and, after the 1918 declaration of Latvian independence, took up residence in Soviet Russia, working at a series of mid-level Communist Party posts in Moscow and elsewhere. He was executed in 1938 in Stalin's purge of the "Old Bolsheviks" but rehabilitated during the Khruschev era.

RUSSIANS. In Latvian portrayals of their own history, Russians and Baltic Germans (q.v.) play equally ambivalent roles. On the one hand, because of their location, the Latvian territories served as a magnet for Russian westward expansionism from the time of Ivan the Terrible (1530-1584), a process that was finally completed by the end of the eighteenth century when Catherine the Great acquired the Duchy of Courland (q.v.). Periodic Russian military incursions that were immensely destructive to the civilian population were then replaced by a permanent Russian military and administrative presence that lasted until World War I, was broken by the interwar independence, and returned, in the guise of the USSR as it is thought, after World War II. From the mid-nineteenth century to the present, the Russian presence has always been expected to be accompanied by efforts at Russification (q.v.)--administrative, cultural, and demographic. The current ethnic (nationality) composition of Latvia (about 52 percent Latvian, about 48 percent non-Latvian [about 34 percent Russian]) is perceived to be the result of precisely such Russification policies during the Soviet period.

On the other hand, the modern period of Latvian history contains many examples of Latvian readiness to adapt to the Russian presence, broadly interpreted. During the "national awakening" (q.v.) period, at least one prominent Latvian nationalist--Krišjānis Valdemārs (q.v.)--sought to play his connections in the Russian government against the Baltic German political and economic hegemony in the Baltic provinces (q.v.). Numerous Latvians in the second half of the century sought and found employment in the major Russian cities of St. Petersburg and Moscow. And an equally large component of Latvian political, economic and cultural leaders received their education in Russian institutions and remained working in Russia until the advent of the independent Latvian state in 1918. The ambivalence of Latvian-Russian relations can be summed up as involving, on the Latvian side, extreme suspicion of Russian political and military intentions, combined with a receptivity to and enjoyment of Russian high culture, especially the literary culture of the pre-Soviet period of Russian history.

RUSSIFICATION. In Latvian history, the term signifies (1) the process through which individuals and groups changed their primary cultural identity to one associated with the Russian language and culture; and (2) state policy designed to accomplish such a goal. Historically, Russification and Germanization (q.v.) were the two processes of assimilation that appeared to Latvians themselves to be the greatest threats to the survival of a Latvian-language population and a Latvian-language culture. Germanization seemed threatening because German for centuries had been the language of the Baltic elites and therefore a necessity for socially and economically upwardly mobile Latvians. Russification, on the other hand, when it became systematic, had behind it the power of the central government-- the czarist government in the nineteenth century and the government of the USSR in the twentieth.

Russification policy in the nineteenth century was promulgated in the period after 1885, as the conservative government of Czar Alexander III decided to obtain greater control over the non-Russian western borderlands of the Empire. In a series of measures after the mid-1880s, the government required the use of Russian at virtually all levels of the education system and in the court system, and decreed also that children of "mixed" marriages should be brought up in the Russian Orthodox faith. Since before the 1880s, the Latvian "national awakening" (q.v.) movement had frequently looked to the czarist government for assistance in the Latvian cultural struggle against the Baltic German (q.v.) elites, the Russification policy by the central government was both a disappointment and a new threat. Formally, Russifying laws and edicts remained in force until World War I, but in reality they were counterproductive because the Latvian national consciousness continued to grow and expand even while the Russification policy was in effect.

A second wave of policies with Russification as their goal is seen by Latvians to have started with the incorporation of Latvia into the USSR in 1940 and lasted until the beginning of the perestroika period in 1985. These policies are interpreted as having been disguised in (1) efforts to promote industrialization in Latvia by expanding hugely the non-Latvian labor force through recruiting Russian-speaking emigrants to the area; and in (2) expansion of the role of the Russian language in the educational system on the basis of the argument that Russian would be the language of *homo sovieticus*--the new Soviet citizen who would appear when the national identities of constituent peoples diminished in importance and eventually merged. Though the proportion of Latvians in Latvia did indeed decrease substantially in the postwar decades (falling to 52 percent in the 1989 census), the Russian-language policy proved once again (as in the late nineteenth century) to be counterproductive in that it intensified both the protectiveness among Latvians for their national culture and resentment toward Russians in general and the Russian-dominated central government in particular. These resentments played a major role in building the momentum that resulted in Latvia's regaining its status as an independent sovereign national state in 1992.

- S -

SAEIMA. The official name for the Latvian parliament, created by the 1922 constitution, which was the basic law of independent Latvia during the interwar years. In the period from 1922 to 1934 there were altogether four 100-deputy Saeimas, elected in 1922, 1925, 1928, and 1931. In 1934, as a result of his successful coup, Kārlis Ulmanis (q.v.) suspended the activities of the Saeima and governed by personal rule until 1940, when all of the interwar political institutions were replaced by the structures of Soviet government. In the period from 1945 to 1993, the structural analogue to the old Saeima was the Supreme Soviet (q.v.) (Latv. *Augstākā Padome*), which, however, was a Communist single-party organ. In June 1993, after the 1991 renewal of Latvian independence, a parliamentary election was held on the basis of the renewed 1922 Constitution for a fifth Saeima, which began its work in July 1993. The Saeima had (and now has) its own officers, including a president, and a series of legislative committees. Since the electoral system permitted multi-party competition for the Saeima, elections involved large numbers of parties (up to 100 in the interwar period) but the majority of these never obtained representation. Still, in the interwar period numerous parties did gain the right to have deputies, so that cabinets normally consisted of coalitions. This interwar tradition continued in the Fifth Saeima (1993-1995) in which eight political parties were represented, two of which formed the first coalition cabinet. The Sixth Saeima, elected in the fall of 1995, had nine parties represented in it, which failed to form a cabinet and required the president of the country to call upon a non-partisan businessman--Andris Šķēle--to become prime minister and create a viable coalition cabinet.

SALASPILS. A settlement near Riga (q.v.), Salaspils was the site of an important battle during the Polish-Swedish War (q.v.) in 1605 and, more recently during the period of German occupation (1941-1945), the location of the largest concentration camp in the Baltic area. In the period from 1942 to 1943, according to Soviet-period sources, an estimated 53,000 civilians were killed there.

SALNAIS, VOLDEMĀRS (1886-1948). A Social Democratic activist in the pre-World War I period, Salnais was imprisoned for illegal activities in 1905, served out his sentence, but in 1913 emigrated to the United Sates and returned to Russia in 1917 after the March Revolution. There he worked for a while in the Latvian National Council in Vladivostok and returned to Latvia after the independence declaration of 1918. From 1921, he served in a series of high-level posts in the Latvian government, including that of foreign minister from 1933 to 1934. He was a deputy to the Saeima (q.v.) from 1923 to 1925 in the party headed by Mārģeris Skujenieks (q.v.). From 1937 to 1940, he was Latvian Ambassador to the Scandinavian countries. During the whole period of his governmental and diplomatic activities, Salnais continued to edit and publish collections of official economic and demographic statistics. Emigrating to Sweden in 1944, he worked on behalf of Latvian organizations there until his death in 1948.

SELF-GOVERNMENT (See PAŠPĀRVALDE).

SELONIANS. The people comprising one of the tribal societies living on the territory of present-day Latvia from about the sixth to the fourteenth centuries. Their language is presumed to have been Baltic and their settlements were bordered on the south by Lithuanian lands, on the north by the Daugava River (q.v.), and on the west by Semigallians and Livonians (qq.v.). The northern borderlands of Lithuanian territory contained a considerable mixture of Lithuanian and Selonian settlements as well. Archaeological evidence suggests that the Selonians were socially and politically stratified and had regional rulers (kings), but no political unity. They evidently were not able to offer much resistance to the German crusading orders (q.v.), which subjugated them relatively early, in the first decades of the thirteenth century, by defeating their forces in the main Selonian center in Selpils. The Selonians did not play a major role in the continuing thirteenth- and fourteenth-century struggles by the

Baltic tribal societies against the ever-growing power of the German crusading orders. Toward the end of the medieval centuries the Selonians merged with other Baltic peoples to form the Latvians. Their presence in Latvian history is not memorialized in the surviving names of major Latvian administrative divisions, as is the case of the Couronians (Kurzeme), Semigallians (Zemgale), and Lettgallians (Latgale) (qq.v.).

SEMIGALLIANS. The people comprising one of the tribal societies living on the territory of present-day Latvia from about the sixth to the fourteenth centuries. Their language is presumed to have been Baltic and their settlements extended in a fanlike pattern southward from the Gulf of Riga into the northern region of present-day Lithuania. Archaeological findings suggest that the Semigallians were socially stratified, had political leaders (kings), but were not politically unified. Some seven subdivisions of Semigallian territory have been identified, each with a fortified castle, and at least two political leaders (Viestarts, Nameisis) are mentioned by name in thirteenth-century written sources.

The Semigallians were engaged in almost continual warfare against the German crusading orders (q.v.), participating in an attack on Riga (q.v.) in 1228, and in the battle at Saule in 1236, which almost destroyed the Swordbrothers'(q.v.) contingents and forced them to unite with the German Order. In the second half of the thirteenth century, Nameisis appears to have tried to unify the Semigallians against the crusading orders and, in 1279 and 1287, led his soldiers in major battles against the Germans. These efforts had come to naught by the end of the thirteenth century, however, and a significant portion of the Semigallians migrated southward into Lithuania where the struggle against the crusading orders was continuing. The Semigallians who remained in their ancestral territory were eventually all Christianized and merged with other Baltic peoples to form the Latvians. The presence of the Semigallians in Latvian history is memorialized in the name "Zemgale"--one of the four traditional divisions of present-day Latvian territory.

SERF EMANCIPATION (1816-1819). In the Baltic provinces (q.v.) of Estland, Livland (q.v.), and Kurland, serf emancipation took place some 40 years before the general emancipation of serfs in the Russian Empire in 1861. These reforms came after a decade and a half of lesser peasant reform laws in 1804 and 1809 and reflected the conclusion among Baltic estate owners that personal emancipation of the peasants was an idea whose time had come. To protect themselves, however, they proposed--and Czar Alexander I agreed--that personal freedom for the peasantry be granted in exchange for absolute rights of ownership by landowners of all land that had earlier been allocated for peasant use. The relevant decrees were announced on May 23, 1816, for Estland; August 25, 1817, for Kurland; and March 26, 1819, for Livland. The decrees envisaged emancipation as a process, however, so that it was not until around 1832 that all peasants in the Baltic had had their status changed from serfs to free persons.

The laws said that the peasantry had the right to acquire land, but did not require landowners to sell it. Restriction on free movement across administrative boundaries remained in force. The relationship between peasant and lord was henceforth governed by free contracts, which, given the restrictions on movement, disadvantaged the peasantry. For the next 40 years peasants "rented" the land they worked largely on the basis of labor rents, and outright ownership by peasants of rural land remained rare. Estate owners retained the right of corporal punishment, but everyday peasant life gradually became governed more by the local county (*pagasts*) authorities who increasingly came from the ranks of the peasantry itself. Estate owners were allowed to withdraw from responsibilities they had had earlier as part of their "patriarchal" role vis-à-vis "their" peasant-serfs. Given the obstacles to peasant landownership, the reforms in popular rural parlance were said to have given the peasants "the freedom of birds" (*putnu brīvība*). On the other hand, they did create local rural institutions in which peasants were able to acquire some of the skills of self-government. It should be noted that these reforms did not affect the Latvian-speakers in Latgale (q.v.)--now the eastern districts of Vitebsk province--where serf emancipation came only in 1861.

SERFDOM. The term serfdom refers to the legal status of many peasants during the medieval centuries in Western Europe and from about the sixteenth to the nineteenth century in the European east. Though having numerous variations, serf status meant at its core that the peasant-farmer held (rather than owned) the land he or she worked, was in a legal sense forbidden to leave, had to deliver unpaid labor (corvée, q.v.) and other payments to "his" lord, and was virtually in all respects under the lord's jurisdiction. In the Latvian territories, the enserfment process of rural people began in the late fifteenth to early sixteenth centuries and lasted until the nineteenth century's serf emancipation (q.v.) laws. In those centuries, because upward of 90 percent of all Latvians in the Baltic territories were rural, virtually the same proportion of the Latvian population was enserfed, so that the period of serfdom, emancipation, and the post-emancipation decades form a very long stretch of Latvian history. Since agriculture in the Latvian territories took place on landed estates, the typical Latvian serf was a resident of private or crown estates, lived in an isolated farmstead settlement pattern (occasionally in hamlets), and dealt on a daily basis with local authorities such as the estate bailiff and other estate functionaries and the local clergyman. Because of the fact that the elites in the Latvian territories in these centuries were non-Latvian (Baltic German [q.v.], Polish, Swedish, Russian), the history of Latvian serfdom inescapably had an ethnic (or nationality) component that became an important part of the portrayals of Latvian history by writers of the "national awakening" (q.v.) period.

ŠĶĒLE, ANDRIS (1958-   ). In late December 1995, Šķēle was asked by President Guntis Ulmanis (q.v.) to try to form a cabinet, when it became obvious that the elections for the Sixth Saeima (q.v.) had produced a deadlocked parliament in which neither the parties of left nor the right could produce a cabinet acceptable to the other side. Not a deputy himself nor a member of any party, Šķēle formed a coalition cabinet that received 70 votes, a substantial majority. Before becoming prime minister, Šķēle had worked in the Ministry of Agriculture as deputy minister and in the Latvian Privatization Agency as acting director general, but since 1993 had become a successful businessman and entrepeneur in Riga.

SKUJENIEKS, MĀRĢERIS (1876-1941). Skujenieks participated in the 1905 Revolution in Latvia as an active member of the Latvian Social Democratic Party (q.v.) but afterward resumed his studies of commerce and statistics in Moscow. After the start of World War I, he continued to work in Russia, but gradually moved into activities important to Latvians, such as refugee relief. From 1919 onward, he returned to Latvia to help create the basic institutions of the new state, and served as a deputy in all four Saeimas (q.v.) (parliaments) as member of a social-democratically oriented splinter party. In the early 1930s, he served briefly as prime minister, minister of interior, and minister of finance. A supporter of the Ulmanis (q.v.) coup in 1934, Skujenieks remained part of Ulmanis' cabinet until 1938, when he resigned as a result of fundamental disagreements. Virtually for the whole interwar period, he directed the National Statistical Office and published a series of works dealing with the fundamental economic and demographic statistics of the country. In 1940, after the establishment of Soviet power, Skujenieks was imprisoned, transported to Moscow, and in 1941 executed in Ljubjanka prison.

SOCIAL DEMOCRATIC PARTY, **SDP** (Latv. **LATVIEŠU SOCIALDEMOKRĀTISKĀ STRĀDNIEKU PARTIJA**) . The Social Democratic Party, the official name of which was the "Latvian Social Democratic Workers Party," was founded in June 1904 and was therefore the oldest organized Latvian political party. The larger historical context of the SDP was the "new current" (q.v.) movement, many adherents to which became convinced Marxists, drawing their inspiration primarily from the philosophies of German and Austrian social democracy. More immediately, the SDP was the logical organizational conclusion of many the legal and illegal social-democratic "cells" that proliferated in the Baltic territories and among Latvian left-wing exiles in Western Europe and the United States after the arrests, trials, and expulsion from Latvia of social-democratic activists in 1897. In 1905 the SDP played a leading role in organizing and conducting the strikes and antigovernment demonstrations of that year and, as a consequence, witnessed after that year the flight from Russia of even larger numbers of its leaders.

The period between 1905 and 1917 in the history of the SDP was one of rivalry within the party between those socialists who remained true to its original *democratic* principles and those who became supporters of Lenin's belief in the need for violent revolution and a proletarian dictatorship. Permanent division in the party's ranks on this score came at the 5th Party Congress in September 1917. The Bolshevik (q.v.) wing, now linked to the Russian Bolsheviks, continued to make efforts, especially after November 1917, to establish a Bolshevik government in Latvia, and opposed the separation of the Latvian territories from what they expected to become a Bolshevik-governed Russia. The democratic wing cooperated with "bourgeois" parties in advancing the idea of an independent Latvian state and participated in the declaration of Latvian independence on November 18, 1918. After the end of the five-month Bolshevik government of Peteris Stučka (q.v.) in Latvia, most Latvian Bolsheviks took up residence in Soviet Russia, whereas the Latvian Social Democrats participated in independent Latvia's provisional government, Constitutional Convention, and all four Saeimas (q.v.) (parliaments) of the 1922-1934 period.

During the parliamentary period the SDP was the largest Latvian political party in parliamentary seats and membership, thus becoming the principal rival of the somewhat smaller Agrarian Union (q.v.), which, however, headed more cabinets and supplied three of the four Latvian presidents of the interwar years. In large part because of its relatively inflexible ideological stance, the SDP remained out of cabinet coalitions almost all of the time in the 1922-1934 years, preferring the freedom that came with being the principal opposition party. After the 1934 coup of Kārlis Ulmanis (q.v.), the SDP was dissolved but most of its leading members remained in Latvia. During the first year (1940-1941) of Soviet government in Latvia, many of them were deported to Siberia along with leaders of the "bourgeois" parties. In 1944, most of the surviving SDP activists emigrated and, in 1949, in Sweden renewed the SDP as an exile Latvian political organization, which listed among its goals the freeing of Latvia from Soviet occupation. In the 1990-1993 period, the SDP renewed itself in Latvia as well and competed in the 1993 Saeima (parliamentary) election, but did not receive a sufficiently large proportion of votes cast to have Saeima representation.

SONG FESTIVALS. During the first period of "national awakening" (q.v.) there was a strong emphasis among Latvians on the need to develop group activities of various kinds. Among other obstacles to a healthy Latvian national consciousness was the fact that the contiguous Latvian-speaking populations lived in separate provinces (Livland, Kurland, Vitebsk) and did not think in terms of common Latvian interests. The czarist authorities as well as the Baltic German (q.v.) authorities, however, were wary of giving permission to even non-political large gatherings, fearing political consequences. Singing societies (Ger. *Gesängvereine*) tended to fall into an uncertain category; they had already become a staple of German-language culture in the nineteenth century and they also seemed to be an aspect of peasant self-betterment, which the authorities encouraged. In the Latvian territories, the first regional song festival was held in Dikļi in 1864, with the participation of a choir of about 1,000 persons.

The most notable event of this kind, however, was the First General Song Festival in Riga (q.v.) in 1873, which was the largest peaceful gathering the Latvians had planned and had been permitted to have since becoming part of the Russian Empire. Though not overtly political, the First Song Festival could not help but be a significant step in the development of a Latvian national consciousness. The first festival established a tradition, that, by agreement, was to continue with a general festival to be held quadrennially. This tradition has in fact been upheld with the timing being interrupted by two world wars. After 1944, with the development of a large émigré Latvian community in the West, parallel general song festivals were held in North America and in the Latvian SSR. The future of the North American festivals is probably in doubt because of the return of Latvian independence in 1991. The twenty-first general song festival in Latvia was held in Riga in July 1993.

SOUL REVISIONS. In the Latvian territories, the first soul revisions, introduced for the Russian Empire by Peter the Great in 1718 as a tax census, were carried out in Livonia (Livland) in 1782 and in Courland (qq.v.) in 1797. In principle, the revisions were to be carried out every 15 years on an empire-wide basis, but their frequency in the Baltic provinces (q.v.) differed because of peculiar provincial historical conditions. After the first revisions, the next ones were carried out in 1795 (Livonia), 1811 (both provinces), 1816 (both), 1826 (both), 1833 (both), 1850 (both), and 1857 (both). The 1816, 1826, and 1833 revisions were done in connection with the emancipation of serfs (q.v.), and the 1857 Imperial revision was the last of the whole series.

SPĀĢIS, ANDREJS (1820-1871). Spāģis was an activist during the "national awakening" (q.v.) period in the nineteenth century. As a result of an unsuccessful legal battle against a Baltic German (q.v.) landowner over local authority, Spāģis was forced to spend much of his life from the early 1850s onward outside the Latvian territories: in Germany, where he studied agricultural sciences;

and in Russia, where he worked as supervisor of a landed estate and at other jobs in Moscow and St. Petersburg. His principal publications, in German, harshly criticized the conditions in which the emancipated peasantry of the Baltic area, especially Courland (q.v.), were living in the 1850s, and attacked the Baltic German monopoly over landholding.

STATE FARMS (See **COLLECTIVE FARMS).**

STENDER, GOTHARD FRIEDRICH (Latvianized as **VECAIS STENDERS**) (1714-1796). Stender was among the best-known Baltic German (q.v.) clergymen and writers in the eighteenth century who worked assiduously at developing the Latvian language into a literary vehicle. His philosophical starting point was the Enlightenment proposition that education (q.v.) was desirable for all, including peasants; politically, however, he backed away from any "enlightened" criticism of the distribution of power in the Baltic provinces (q.v.). In his voluminous writings--which included grammars, sermon books, hymnals, secular songbooks, natural histories, geographical descriptions, and various kinds of didactic literature--he urged Latvian peasants to accept the socioeconomic upper orders as their natural superiors. But his literary products played a major role in expanding the consciousness of his Latvian readers of their immediate Baltic world as well as of the world outside the Baltic region. Stender's publications continued to be reprinted well after his death into the nineteenth century and remained at the core of the Baltic German effort to raise the cultural level of the Latvian peasantry until the beginnings of the Latvian "national awakening" (q.v.).

STRADIŅŠ, JĀNIS (1933-   ). An accomplished specialist in physical chemistry by education and training but with a strong interest in the history of science, Stradiņš wrote frequently and extensively on cultural and political matters for the periodical press during the glasnost and perestroika period in Latvia and was granted a kind of mentor like role in the process that led to the reestablishment of Latvian independence in 1991. He popularized the idea that the events of 1988 and later--especially during the period of the Popular Front (q.v.)--were a "third national awakening" (q.v.), analogous to the self-assertive national activism in the nineteenth century (the first awakening) and the interwar independence period (the second). His writings on the meaning of Latvian national symbols--the flag and coat of arms-- and on street and place-names played a role in guiding restoration decisions in these domains. Stradiņš was also influential in the reforms that converted the Latvian Academy of Sciences (q.v.) from a Soviet-style research institution to an organization that awarded honors in the form of membership for personal accomplishment in research, writing, and other fields.

STRAUBERGS, JĀNIS (1886-1952). After finishing his primary and secondary education in Livonia (q.v.) (Vidzeme), Straubergs spent most of the pre-World War I years as a schoolteacher in various parts of the Russian Empire and returned to Latvia only after the declaration of independence in 1918. Thereafter, during the interwar years, he became one of the most widely read popularizers of Latvian history, particularly of the history of Riga (q.v.) and a number of rural localities (Sīpele, Bērzmuiža, etc.). Though not having received a professional education as a historian, Straubergs was skilled in archival use and, given the fact that professionally trained Latvian historians were scarce, filled a niche at a time when the hunger of Latvians for history written by Latvians was at its peak. In the Soviet period after 1945, he worked as an instructor at the University of Latvia and in the governing board of the Latvian National Archives.

STRAUBERGS, KĀRLIS (1890-1962). A philologist specializing in classical languages and a folklorist, Straubergs received his education at the University of Moscow and the Archaeological Institute in Moscow in the pre-World War I years, and during the war fought in the Latvian Rifle Regiments (see STRĒLNIEKI). After 1918, he held a variety of high-level posts in the educational and cultural institutions of the Latvian state, including that of minister of education in 1924 and director of the Folklore Archive from 1929 to 1944. Immensely prolific, Straubergs published widely in all his specialties, but his most lasting studies were probably in the Latvian folklore field, about which he continued to write even after emigration to Sweden in 1944.

STRĒLNIEKI (Russ. STRELTSI). Narrowly defined, the Latvian term *strēlnieki* refers to the eight battalions (1,200 soldiers each) of Latvian soldiers formed in the czarist army in 1915 during the

First World War. In a broader sense, the term is used by Latvians to refer to all the Latvian soldiers who fought in both of the world wars, regardless of which side they were fighting on. In some ways the history of these military units symbolizes the complex history in which their geographic location involved the Latvians during the twentieth century.

In the first years of World War I, the czarist army refused to allow the formation of nationality-based military units, but manpower needs forced the issue. The Latvian *strēlnieki* fought against the German army mostly in the Baltic region. By the end of 1916, however, an inept higher (Russian) command, high casualties, and a seeming stalemate on the front had created among the Latvian troops substantial resentment. During the period from 1917 to 1918, the *strēlnieki* gradually divided--one segment growing more supportive of the Bolshevik (q.v.) movement, another of the newly proclaimed Latvian republic and its beleaguered and virtually powerless new government. This division persisted into 1919-1920, when the Baltic--and especially Latvian--area continued to be a battlefield among military units led by postwar German adventurers, supporters of the Whites in the Russian Civil War, units of the new Latvian national Army, and the Latvian units of the newly formed Red Army. Fighting on Latvian soil did not cease until mid-year 1920, but the *strēlnieki* who had remained in the Red Army continued in the battles against the Whites elsewhere in Russia.

A similar bifurcation of Latvian army units occurred in World War II, when Latvian units--estimated at some 100,000 members --recruited into the Soviet Army (which had occupied Latvia in 1940 but had withdrawn in 1941 as the German *Wehrmacht* advanced into the Baltic), fought in 1944-1945 in Latvia against the Latvian units of the German army--the so-called Latvian Legion (q.v.). In the post-World War II period, Western émigré Latvians celebrated largely the exploits of the *strēlnieki* who had defended the new Latvian state in the 1918-1920 period, while official ceremonies in the Latvian SSR commemorated only those *strēlnieki* who had supported the Bolsheviks and the Lenin government. Current popular attitudes in Latvia appear to be interested in celebrating the exploits of both simultaneously.

STUČKA, PĒTERIS (1865-1932). Stučka was born in Livonia (q.v.) (Vidzeme) of relatively well-to-do farming parents and in 1888 finished his education in law and jurisprudence in St. Petersburg, subsequently becoming a lawyer in Riga (q.v.). He participated in the "new current" (q.v.) movement and was arrested in 1897 and exiled to Siberia until 1903, by which time he was a convinced social democrat. In 1907, he moved to St. Petersburg, joined the Bolshevik (q.v.) wing of Russian social democracy, and from that point onward remained dedicated to the Bolshevik cause. The venue of his organizational and conspiratorial work remained Russia, but after the March Revolution of 1917 and the Latvian declaration of independence in 1918, Stučka became involved in trying to establish a Soviet Latvia and succeeded in doing so for a period of five months in 1919. He chaired the Council of Commissars that governed that part of the Latvian territory that was not occupied by the German army, but the Bolshevik government, its civilian supporters, and its armed force were driven out of Latvian territory by the end of summer 1919, by the army of the new Latvian national government. Subsequently Stučka returned to Russia and continued to work in high positions in the Communist Party and the Soviet government and to concern himself with the codification of Soviet law.

In the post-1945 period in Latvia, Stučka was an officially revered figure, with his name being used for a new city built at the end of the 1960s and also for a while in the formal designation of the University of Latvia. In the 1989-1991 period, his name was dropped from all the designations in which it had figured for decades and his statue was removed from the square in front of the Presidential Palace in Riga.

SUDRABKALNS, JĀNIS (1894-1975). Sudrabkalns was a very prolific writer whose literary career began before the First World War, spanned the entire interwar period of Latvian independence, and lasted well into the Soviet period during which he placed his considerable talents increasingly at the service of the propaganda apparatus of the Soviet Latvian state and of Marxist-Leninist ideology. Mixing romanticism with realism, Sudrabkalns's literary work covered virtually all genres of writing, including literary criticism.

SUPREME SOVIET (Latv. AUGSTĀKĀ PADOME, AP). Until the June 1993 election of the fifth Saeima (q.v.) (parliament), the AP was in principle the highest law-making body in Latvia. It was a single-chamber legislature consisting of deputies representing districts and institutions and dominated by members of the Latvia Communist Party (q.v.). The last AP, elected in the spring of 1990, became in effect the transition government because structurally the AP was a holdover from the Soviet period, but with a majority of deputies from the Popular Front and the LNNK (qq.v.). By voting in 1990 to renew the 1922 interwar constitution, the AP was actually participating in its own demise as an institution, because that document called for a multiparty election in the near future. Approximately one-third of the deputies elected to the 1993 Saeima from various parties and electoral coalitions had also served in the last AP.

ŠVĀBE, ARVĒDS (1888-1959). Though he received his university training in history in Moscow, Švābe made his debut in Latvian intellectual history as a poet in the pre-World War I years. After 1918, his earlier literary efforts were eclipsed by his stature as a historian, which he developed as an instructor and then professor at the University of Latvia and as a leading participant in a wide variety of Latvian cultural institutions in the interwar years. From 1936-1941 he chaired the Department of Latvian History at the University of Latvia. His 50 published books included fundamental studies in Latvian agrarian history, legal history, medieval history, and a well-known basic survey of Latvian history in the nineteenth century. During the latter part of the interwar independence period, Švābe was chief editor of the 21-volume *Latviešu Konversācijas Vārdnīca* (*Latvian Encyclopedia*), the foremost general reference work on things Latvian produced during that period. After emigration to Sweden in 1944, he also edited a shorter three-volume *Latvian Encyclopedia*.

SWORDBROTHERS (*See* **CRUSADING ORDERS**).

- T -

TAUTAS FRONTE (*See* **POPULAR FRONT**).

TOBAGO. An island near the northern coast of Venezuela, directly north of the larger island of Trinidad. In 1640, Tobago was purchased from the Duke of Warwick by Duke Jacob of Courland, who was determined to have overseas colonies (cf. Gambia, q.v.). Though economically beneficial to Courland in the early decades, this colonization effort in the New World came to an end in 1890, by which time the Duchy of Courland (q.v.) had demonstrated that it was incapable of governing, protecting, and further exploiting the colony over such long distances. By the end of the seventeenth century European activities on the island had almost ceased, but it did remain a bone of contention between England and France during the eighteenth century.

TRASUNS, FRANCIS (1864-1926). Trasuns was one of the leading political activists and journalists in the pre-World War I period in Latgale (q.v.), those districts which before the formation of the Latvian state were administratively part of Vitebsk province and not of the Baltic provinces (Livland, Estland) where most Latvians lived. He received his theological education in St. Petersburg, but after 1891 the Russian authorities kept him under surveillance and in 1896 exiled him to the interior of Russia. Trasuns argued for cooperation of all Latvians regardless of where they were living, and through his publications became one of the leaders of the so-called "Letgallian awakening." After 1905, he was an elected representative to the Russian duma (q.v.) from Vitebsk. After 1918, he lived in Riga (q.v.) and participated in the work of the National Council, the Constitutional Convention, and the first two Saeimas (q.v.) (parliaments). He also worked for a while as a minister for Letgallian Affairs in a cabinet headed by Kārlis Ulmanis (q.v.).

- U -

ULMANIS, GUNTIS (1939-   ). On July 7, 1993, Guntis Ulmanis was chosen by the newly elected Fifth Saeima (q.v.) (parliament) to be president of Latvia, which renewed the institution of the national presidency that had been discontinued with the beginning of the Soviet period in 1940. The last occupant of the presidency had been Guntis Ulmanis' paternal grandfather's brother Kārlis Ulmanis (q.v.). Guntis Ulmanis had been deported to Siberia in 1941, but returned to Latvia in 1946, finished his primary and secondary education and graduated from the Economics

Faculty of the University of Latvia in 1964. From 1965 to 1989, he was a member of the Latvian Communist Party (q.v.), from which several efforts were made to expel him because of his kinship with the last president of the independent interwar state. Before election to the presidency, Guntis Ulmanis worked as the director of social services in the Riga district and was on the board of the Latvian State Bank. He is a member of the (renewed) Agrarian Union (q.v.), which received the second highest plurality of deputies in the Fifth Saeima. In June 1996, Ulmanis was reelected to the presidency for his second term, receiving 53 votes in the parliament.

ULMANIS, KĀRLIS (1877-1942). Ulmanis was the most prominent and controversial political leader of the first period of Latvian independence (1918-1940). Born into a farm family and completing his secondary education in 1896, he then pursued more specialized training in agricultural, especially dairy, sciences in Germany and Switzerland. During this time he continued to write for the Latvian press, and in 1905 was arrested by the czarist police for an article thought to be threatening to public order. Ulmanis was freed in 1906, but in 1907, fearing further harassment, chose exile in the United States. In 1909 he graduated with a degree in dairy science from the University of Nebraska and in 1913 returned to Latvia.

Ulmanis continued his work as an agricultural journalist, becoming active as well in various quasi-political agriculturalist organizations. In 1917, he was instrumental in forming the Agrarian Union (q.v.), which was to become one of the principal political parties during the first independence period. Together with other Latvian political parties, the Union joined in proclaiming an independent Republic of Latvia on November 18, 1918. From that date until the end of the parliamentary era in 1934, Ulmanis served in leadership positions--mostly as prime minister--in virtually every government. On May 14-15, 1934, Ulmanis and a small group of trusted friends carried out a coup, suspending parliament and all political parties (including the Agrarian Union) and introducing his personal rule at the head of a cabinet of ministers appointed by him. He justified his step by arguing that Latvian political life had become virtually paralyzed because of parliamentary inactivity and corruption.

From 1936 to 1940, Ulmanis was both head of government (prime minister) and chief of state (president). Though continuing to promise a new reformed constitution, he instead reorganized the Latvian economy along corporatist lines and introduced hundreds of other reforms stressing national unity and emphasizing the agrarian sector above others. In 1939, Ulmanis's government agreed to the stationing of Soviet troops on Latvian soil and, in 1940, he remained in office for about a month after the Soviet Army in June occupied the country and Soviet officials engineered the election of a pro-Soviet government that was to request annexation of Latvia to the USSR in August. Before annexation, however, Ulmanis had been deported to Russia where he died, apparently in 1942, at the age of 65.

UPĪTS, ANDREJS (1877-1970). Upīts was possibly the most prolific Latvian author in the twentieth century, since his literary career as a journalist began before the First World War and ended well into the Soviet period of Latvian history. Always an exponent of literary realism and deeply sympathetic to various left-wing political causes before World War II, Upīts had little trouble fitting into the post-1945 Latvian literary establishment in which he quickly became the most lionized figure. In his literary criticism he was a staunch defender of socialist realism, and viewed the history of Latvian literature in terms of authors' contributions to the "progressive" movement of history. In the later decades of his life, Upīts participated in the Latvian Communist Party's (q.v.) frequent attacks on Latvian émigré authors and the cultural world they had created outside of Latvia after the Second World War.

- V -

VĀCIETIS, JUKUMS (1873-1938). Vācietis was born in Courland (q.v.) and in 1909 graduated from the Military Academy in St. Petersburg. He commanded one of the regiments of the Latvian Rifles (q.v.) during the First World War but, after the March 1917 Revolution, joined the Bolsheviks (q.v.). After the Bolshevik coup, he achieved high rank in the Red Army, serving as its commander in chief in the period from 1918 to 1919 and organizing the Red Army's invasion of the Baltic area in support of the short-lived Soviet Latvian government in 1919. Removed from his post in 1919, Vācietis became an instructor of the Red Army's Military Academy, and was executed in 1938 in Stalin's purge of the "Old Bolsheviks." He was rehabilitated posthumously in the Khrushchev era.

VĀCIETIS, OJĀRS (1933-1983). Vācietis finished his higher education at the University of Latvia in 1957, worked thereafter for a series of newspapers, and starting in the late 1950s began to emerge as a leading poet of his generation. Though published widely during his lifetime, Vācietis was nonetheless straining against the limits of the permissible and many of his poems, which could not be published during his lifetime because of censorship, appeared posthumously. Vācietis also translated numerous Russian authors into Latvian.

VAGRIS, JĀNIS (1930-). Vagris was a functionary in the Latvian Communist Party (q.v.) until 1988, when he was chosen for the position of first secretary. He thus presided over the party during the period when it had started to dissolve rapidly and when its role in the governing of Latvia during the Soviet period was starting to receive virtually total public condemnation.

VALDEMĀRS, KRIŠJĀNIS (1825-1891). Valdemārs was one of the principal activists of the nineteenth-century Latvian "national awakening" (q.v.) having decided in his youth that he would seek to maintain his ethnic identity instead of assimilating either to the German- or Russian-language communities as was still being done by many talented Latvians of his generation. He was born into a family of well-to-do farmers in Livonia (q.v.) (his father was a farmstead head) and received his primary and secondary education in the Baltic area. In 1854, however, Valdemars began to study economics at Dorpat (Tartu) University and there, together with Krišjānis Barons and Juris Alunāns (qq.v.), he began to develop what was to become the ideology of the Latvian nationalist movement. Even before Dorpat, he had started to publish (in Latvian and German) on a wide variety of subjects, and this activity now became increasingly confrontational (aimed at Baltic German cultural hegemony) and didactic (intending to instruct Latvians on how to improve their economic lot).

Valdemārs caught the attention and earned the goodwill of the czarist government with a series of writings on maritime affairs in the Baltic provinces (q.v.), and this helped to prevent serious difficulties arising from his defense of Latvians as a nation oppressed by Baltic Germans (q.v.). He helped to found the *Pēterburgas Avīzes* (q.v.), and by the late 1860s, had become well-known in the Baltic area as an uncompromising defender of Latvian national aspirations. Valdemārs then moved to Moscow and developed connections with the Slavophile movement there, while at the same time urging Latvian students living in Moscow to write and work in the interests of their conationals in the

Baltic provinces. He remained in Moscow for the rest of his life, continuing his journalistic and organizational activities on behalf of Latvian causes. His closeness to the Slavophiles, however, forced him to take an ambivalent stance on the Russification (q.v.) policies the central government began to direct against the nationalities of the western borderlands after the mid-1880s. As a Latvian nationalist, Valdemārs emphasized economic development as the principal Latvian concern, in contrast to other members of the Latvian national movement such as Atis Kronvalds (q.v.), who emphasized the preservation of the Latvian language and the expansion of Latvian cultural endeavors.

VALDMANIS, ALFRĒDS (1908-1970). Valdmanis was a notable economist and politician in the interwar period of Latvian independence, who during the 1930s worked largely within the Ministry of Finance, becoming minister in 1938-1939 during the Ulmanis (q.v.) regime. Afterward, he held a variety of posts in state enterprises and, from 1941 to 1943, during the German occupation of the country worked as the head of the Directorate of Legal Affairs in the Latvian civilian government (*see* PAŠ-PĀRVALDE). He emigrated to Germany in 1944, and after 1945 he worked in various jobs in the administration of refugee affairs (including the International Refugee Organization from 1947 to 1948). In 1948, Valdmanis emigrated to Canada where he ultimately worked as consultant for economic development in the province of Newfoundland.

VALMIERA (Ger. WOLMAR). Valmiera, located in the center of Livonia (q.v.) (Vidzeme), is Latvia's eighth largest city, with a 1989 population of 29,500 persons. It was first mentioned in medieval chronicles in 1213 and a castle was built there by the Swordbrothers (q.v.) in 1224. Like many of the cities of central Livonia, Valmiera was destroyed completely several times over the centuries because it lay in the path of armies moving from east to west (toward Riga).

VALTERS, MIĶELIS (1874-1968). Valters received his primary education in Liepāja (Libau), and then moved to Riga (qq.v.), where he became active in the "new current" (q.v.) movement. Like many among these activists, he was arrested in 1897 and sentenced to internal exile in Daugavpils (q.v.). But he chose to emigrate instead, and lived abroad--mostly in Switzerland--for the next 15 years, becoming during this time a well-known author of prose, poetry, and political commentary. Valters returned to Latvia in 1915, and from that time onward worked actively in Latvian politics, occupying a centrist (democratic bloc) position. In 1918-1919, he served as minister of interior, and afterward filled a series of diplomatic posts, including that of Latvian Ambassador to Rome, Paris, Warsaw, and Brussels. Being in Belgium in 1940 when the Soviet Union occupied Latvia, he remained there and for the next three decades continued to write and publish on questions of Latvian politics and loss of independence. Many historians of Latvian political thought credit Valters with the first systematic defense (in the pre-World War I period) of the idea of total separation of Latvia from the Russian Empire.

VECLATVIEŠI. Meaning "old Latvians" in English, this term was used in two specific historical contexts to juxtapose earlier and later adjacent Latvian generational groups and their typical attitudes and behaviors. First, in the mid-nineteenth century, *veclatvieši* was used to describe those Latvians who had received their professional training before the "national awakening" (q.v.) (i.e., before the 1850s) and therefore shied away from confrontations with Baltic German (q.v.) and czarist authorities, in contrast with the *jaunlatvieši* (Young Latvians) who tended to be intensely nationalistic and confrontational. Second, in the North American setting in the twentieth century, the term *veclatvieši* was used to describe those Latvians who had emigrated before World War I, in order to contrast them with the much larger numbers of Latvians who came to North America in the 1949-1951 period (largely as DPs--Displaced Persons, q.v.). Among the pre-World War II emigrants, the assimilation process had diminished the attachments to the ancestral homeland and the Latvian language. By contrast, the DPs remained highly nationalistic, sought to resist assimilation, and 40 years later supported in many ways the return of Latvian independence in the 1990-1991 period. These popular classifications, of course, allowed for many exceptions to the typical attitudes they were meant to characterize.

VEINBERGS, FRĪDRICHS (1844-1942). After finishing his education in law at the University of Moscow, Veinbergs returned to Riga (q.v.) in 1869 and worked as an attorney, participating actively in the expanding organizational life of Riga Latvians. He held numerous offices in the Riga Latvian Association (q.v.), founded several newspapers for which he wrote extensively, and with each decade became increasingly more conservative about

Latvian political and social problems. Despising any form of socialism, Veinbergs welcomed the punitive expeditions the czarist government sent to the Baltic to deal with the participants of the Revolution of 1905. In the years surrounding the declaration of independence during the First World War, he remained skeptical of the possibility of Latvian independence; defended, for as long as it was realistic to do so, the rights of the czarist government in the Baltic; and remained partial to the continuing Baltic German (q.v.) presence in the area, supporting the idea that the Baltic provinces (q.v.) should become a duchy affiliated with Germany.

VIDZEME (See **LIVONIA**).

VĪTOLS, JĀZEPS (1863-1948). Vītols received his primary and secondary education in Vidzeme (Livonia, q.v.) where he was born. From 1881, after starting on a lifelong career in music by entering the St. Petersburg Conservatory, he remained in that city until his return to Latvia after the independence declaration in 1918. Vītols remained at the St. Petersburg Conservatory after graduation, becoming in due course a member of its faculty. At the same time, he worked actively in St. Petersburg Latvian society and retained strong ties with Latvian life in the Baltic provinces (q.v.). Upon his return to Riga (q.v.), he helped establish the Latvian Conservatory of Music and worked as its rector and faculty member throughout almost the entire interwar period. Through these positions, he shaped the musical education of virtually all professional Latvian musicians in the interwar period. In 1944, he emigrated to Germany, where for a while in Detmold he directed a music school for Baltic DPs (q.v.). Vitols was not only a successful administrator and instructor, but also a composer, and his compositions in many genres of Latvian music proved to be models for later generations of Latvian musicians to follow.

VOSS, AUGUSTS (1916-). Of Latvian ancestry, Voss grew up in the Soviet Union and worked there in a number of Communist Party and government posts until coming to the Latvian SSR in the early 1960s to work in the Latvian Communist Party (q.v.), of which he was the first secretary from 1966 to 1984. As a loyal member of the party apparatus, Voss endorsed and implemented all policy directives from Moscow (e.g., Russification, q.v.) and thus presided over the Latvian party during most of the Brezhnev years, the so-called stagnation era. The accumulated resentments of those years among the Latvian population played an important role in the rapid collapse of the Latvian Communist Party after 1988, when the new policies of perestroika and glasnost were enunciated by Mikhail Gorbachev.

- W -

WARM LANDS MOVEMENT (Latv. SILTĀS ZEMES KUSTĪBA). A short-lived emigration of Latvian peasants from southern Livland (q.v.) to the Crimea in the early 1840s, shortly before the Crimean War. The movement was the result of rural desperation and a series of misunderstandings, when, after several years of bad harvests in the Baltic area, rumors began that free Crown land was being distributed in the Crimean region to peasants who were willing to convert to Russian Orthodoxy. After a great deal of confusion during which numerous peasants made the trek successfully while others were stopped by Livland authorities, some 15 Latvian rural "colonies" were established in the Crimea, but lasted for only about a generation.

WORLD FEDERATION OF FREE LATVIANS (Latv. PASAULES BRĪVO LATVIEŠU APVIENĪBA, PBLA). Formed in 1968, the PBLA was a linear successor of the Latvian National Council (Latviešu Nacionālā Padome, q.v.), which earlier (from 1945 on) had been the main organization of the Latvian refugees while they had "displaced person" status in postwar Germany. After its founding, the PBLA sought to unite and focus the cultural and political efforts of the various Latvian organizations (such as the American Latvian Association) that had since the late 1940s appeared in the countries to which the DPs (q.v.) had emigrated. In 1993, some of the PBLA leaders joined with political leaders in Latvia to form the Latvia's Way (*Latvijas Ceļš*, q.v.) list in order to compete in the Saeima (q.v.) (parliament) elections in June.

- Z -

ZĀLE, KĀRLIS (1888-1942). During the interwar independence period, Zāle became the most noted sculptor of public monuments in Latvia, creating, among other pieces, the Freedom Monument and the Cemetery of the Brethren, both in Riga (q.v.). He received his education as a sculptor in Kazan, Moscow, and St. Petersburg before World War I, as well as in Berlin from 1920 to 1923. In the latter part of the 1930s, he headed the Masters Workshop in the Latvian Academy of Arts and from that position influenced the subsequent work of several generations of Latvian sculptors, some of whom continued their mature work in the Soviet period of Latvian history.

ZARIŅŠ, KĀRLIS (1879-1963). Like so many others of his generation, Zariņš received his primary and secondary education in the Latvian area of the Baltic, but higher education in Russia, in his case St. Petersburg. Before World War I, he worked in Latvian organizations in the Russian capital, including the Latvian Refugee Relief Committee during World War I. He returned to Latvia in 1919 and entered the diplomatic corps of the new Latvian state. Thereafter he filled a string of diplomatic posts, including those of chargé in Stockholm, ambassador to several of the Scandinavian countries, ambassador to Estonia, and from 1933 onward ambassador to Great Britain. In May 1940, the Ulmanis (q.v.) government granted Zariņš full authority to continue acting in the name of the Latvian government if the government in Riga (q.v.) were unable to do so because of foreign occupation. Using this authority in the post-1940 period, Zariņš appointed altogether 18 consuls to serve as representatives of the de jure Latvian state in those countries that did not recognize the incorporation of Latvia into the Soviet Union. Zariņš himself remained in his post in London until his death in 1963.

ZEIFERTS, TEODORS (1865-1929). An active participant in Latvian literary circles from the late 1880s onward, Zeiferts became during his lifetime the most erudite and accomplished literary critic writing in Latvian and is usually thought of as the "father" of this genre of Latvian literary inquiry. Through his voluminous publications (which included a three-volume history of literature in Latvian [1922-1925]) he participated in shaping the development of Latvian literature (q.v.) during the crucial decades from 1890 to 1930. Zeifert's own strongly expressed views were close to those of the literary realism of the western critics Hippolyte Taine and George Brandes, and this introduced in his criticism and evaluation a note of impatience with other styles of expression.

ZEMGALE (See DUCHY OF COURLAND AND SEMIGALLIA).

ZEMGALS, GUSTAVS (1871-1939). After taking his law degree at Moscow University, Zemgals worked as an attorney in Riga (q.v.), becoming active in a number of Latvian trade and craft organizations and editing several daily newspapers. From 1917 to 1919, he served as the mayor of Riga, and after the proclamation of Latvian independence served the new government in various capacities as a deputy to the first and the fourth Saeimas (q.v.) (parliaments), as minister of finance, as minister of defense and, most notably, as president of Latvia from 1927 to 1930. In 1933, Zemgals was also president of the Baltic Union.

ZEMNIEKU SAVIENĪBA (See **AGRARIAN UNION**).

ZIEDONIS, IMANTS (1933-   ). Possibly the most revered post-World War II poet in Soviet Latvia, Ziedonis received the title of People's Poet (*Tautas dzejnieks*) in 1977 and from 1987 onward worked as the presiding officer of the Latvian Cultural Foundation. Ziedonis was a member of the post-Stalin generation of Latvian writers who were inspired by the brief intellectual thaw under Khruschev but came to intellectual maturity during the Brezhnev ("stagnation") era. Therefore his poetry and prose had to express themselves in guarded language and ambiguity so as not to offend party censors and other political authorities and to avoid the charge of "bourgeois nationalism." Ziedonis's poetry concerned itself with universal processes but also contained disguised polemical attacks on the Soviet Latvian political status quo. His prose, on the other hand, tended to be more openly celebratory of specifically Latvian uniqueness and condemnatory of the condition in which Latvians found themselves. Since 1991 and the arrival of a new period of independence, Ziedonis as an "elder statesman" of Latvian literary culture has written widely on the need for a Latvian cultural renewal and a supportive governmental cultural policy.

ZINĀTŅU AKADĒMIJA (See **ACADEMY OF SCIENCES**).

ZĪVERTS, MĀRTIŅŠ (1903-1990). Possibly the leading Latvian playwright of the twentieth century, Zīverts began to write for the Latvian stage in the late 1930s and, having emigrated to Sweden in 1944, continued his work there until his death. In Sweden he founded his own theater company. After 1988, a number of his plays were performed in Latvia when it became permissible there to read and show the work of émigré Latvian authors.

BIBLIOGRAPHY

INTRODUCTION

Because in the twentieth century Latvia is more frequently than not thought of as one of the "Baltic states," a bibliography listing works in the major Western languages about Latvia alone would be very short. Consequently, a large proportion of the titles listed below contain the term "Baltic" rather than "Latvia" or "Latvian." These "Baltic" titles were selected, however, only if a substantial proportion of their contents dealt with Latvia. On the other hand, Latvians in Latvia and in the post-World War II diaspora, when writing in the Latvian language, have produced thousands of works that in principle could have been included here but were not because the present bibliography has been compiled primarily for an audience in the English-speaking world. Only a selection of Latvian-language titles have been included, especially if they can serve as guides to additional Latvian-language titles or if they contain abstracts or summaries of their contents in the major western languages. There does not exist at this time anywhere in the world--Latvia included--what might be called a "union bibliography" listing all published material in Latvian or about Latvia and Latvians. The most complete listing of a segment of Latvian-related titles (both in Latvian or about Latvia and Latvians) is the four-volume *Latviešu trimdas izdevumu bibliogrāfija 1940-1980* (*Bibliography of Latvian Publications Published Outside Latvia 1940-1980*) listed in section I.A. below. Its coverge, of course, does not include anything published in Latvia or the outpouring of materials in Western languages since the start of the perestroika period in the Soviet Union.

For continuous coverage of historical works dealing with Latvia or Latvians the reader is directed to two types of sources. The first consists of the bibliographies, articles, abstracts, and reviews appearing in the *Journal of Baltic History* and the *Baltic Studies Newsletter*, both of which are publications of the Association for the Advancement of Baltic Studies, an organization with headquarters in

Hackettstown, New Jersey. As the names suggest, however, these publications list and review works about all three Baltic states. The second consists of the regular publications in present-day Latvia: *Latvijas vēsture* (*History of Latvia*), a semipopular publication of the University of Latvia in Riga; *Latvijas Vēstures Institūta Žurnāls* (*The Journal of the Latvian Institute of History*) and *Latvijas Zinātņu Akadēmijas Vēstis* (*Journal of the Latvian Academy of Science*), Part A, The Humanistic Sciences. Since 1990, these publications have vastly expanded their notice of books and articles about Latvia published outside Latvia, as well as the number of summaries and abstracts in Western languages (especially English) of books and articles published in Latvia. In the years from 1945 to 1990, summaries and abstracts in these publications appeared almost always in Russian or, infrequently, in German.

A fruitful source of information for entries in the present historical dictionary were the several encyclopedias in Latvian listed in section I.A. below. During the past 50 years these have appeared in two parallel series--those of the diaspora Latvians and those of what until 1991 was Soviet Latvia. The first in the diaspora series--*Latvju Enciklopēdija* (three volumes)--was published in Sweden during 1950-1951 and was edited by Arvēds Švābe, one of the most important Latvian historians of the interwar period and editor also of the 22-volume unfinished *Latviešu konversācijas vārdnīca* (*Latvian Encyclopedia*) published in Latvia in the 1930s. The second in the diaspora series--*Latvju Enciklopēdija 1962-1982*--is being published in the United States and was edited until his death by Edgar Anderson, one of the most prolific Latvian diaspora historians. Four volumes of a projected five of this encyclopedia have now been published, and, as the title indicates, it is meant to contain a chronological continuation and updating of the earlier set edited by Švābe. In Soviet Latvia, the ten-volume *Latvijas padomju enciklopēdija* (*Encyclopedia of Latvian Soviets*) appeared from 1981 to 1987, and reflected the restrictive selection principles of that period. When these had changed appreciably, a shorter two-volume *Enciklopēdiskā vārdnīca* (*Encyclopedic Dictionary*) was published in 1991, drawing for its entries on the totality of the Latvian experience, including the interwar years and the diaspora. Similar principles were used in the one-volume *Latviešu rakstniecības biogrāfijas* (*Biographies from Latvian Literature*) published in 1992 by the Institute of Literature, Folklore and Art of the Latvian Academy of Sciences. This volume resembles the very useful compilation of the interwar period--*Es viņu pazīstu : Latviešu biogrāfiskā vārdnīca* (*I Know Him : Latvian Bio-*

graphical Dictionary)--the first edition of which was published in Latvia in 1939 and the second in the U.S. in 1975.

Titles are listed in the languages in which they were published. Latvian titles are followed by an English translation.

Contents

VIII. Social
A. Folklore and Ethnography
B. Population and Demography
C. Urbanization and Migration
D. Minorities, Ethnicity, and Nationalities
E. Latvian Diaspora Communities

I. General

A. Bibliographies and Encyclopedias

Andersons, Edgars, ed. *Latvju Enciklopēdija 1962-1982* (*Latvian Encyclopedia 1962-1982*). Four volumes. Rockville, Md.: American Latvian Association, 1983 - .

Jēgers, Benjamiņš, ed. *Latviešu trimdas izdevumu bibliogrāfija* (*Bibiliography of Latvian Publications Outside Latvia*). Four volumes. Stockholm: Daugava, 1968-1988.

Jerāns, P., ed. *Latvijas Padomju Enciklopēdija* (*Latvian Soviet Encyclopedia*). Ten volumes. Rīga: Galvenā enciklopēdiju redakcija, 1981-1987.

Kundsen, Olav F. and Ovind Jaeger, eds. *The Baltic States Reborn: A Bibliography of Political Affairs in Estonia, Latvia and Lithuania.* Oslo: Norwegian Institute of International Affairs, 1992.

New Soviet and Baltic Independent Serials at the Library of Congress: A Holdings List. Washington, D.C.: Library of Congress, 1991.

von Rauch, Georg, ed. *Geschichte der deutschbaltischen Geschichts-schreibung.* Cologne and Vienna: Böhlau Verlag, 1976.

Smith, Inese and Marita V. Grunts. *The Baltic States: Estonia, Latvia, Lithuania.* World Bibliographical Series No. 161. Oxford: Clio Press, 1993.

Straumanis, Alfreds, ed. *Baltic Drama: A Handbook and Bibliog-raphy.* Prospect Heights, Ill.: Waveland Press, 1981.

Švābe, Arvēds, ed. *Latvju Enciklopēdija [Latvian Encyclopedia].* Stockholm: Trīs Zvaigznes, 1950-1955.

Vilks, Andris, ed. *Enciklopēdiskā vārdnica [Encyclopedic Dictionary]*. Two volumes. Riga: Latvijas Enciklopēdijas Redakcija, 1991.

Zeps, Valdis, comp. *Baltica In Microform*. Madison, Wisc.: AABS, 1983.

B. General Information

Anderson, Edgar. *Latvia: Past and Present*. Waverly, Iowa: Latvju Grāmata, 1968.

The Baltic States. London: Royal Institute of International Affairs, 1938.

The Baltic States. London: Economist Intelligence Unit, 1990.

Die Baltische Nationen: Estland, Lettland, Litauen. Cologne: Markus, 1991

Dini, Pietro U. *L'annello baltico: profilo delle nazioni baltiche Lituania, Lettonia, Estonia*. Genoa: Marietti, 1991.

Flint, David. *The Baltic States: Estonia, Latvia, Lithuania*. Brookfield, Conn.: Millbrook Press, 1992.

Plasseraud, Yves, ed. *Les pays baltes: Estonie, Lettonie, Lituanie*. Paris: Autrement, 1991.

Rutkis, J. *Latvia: Country and People*. Stockholm: Latvian National Foundation, 1967.

Statistical Yearbook of Latvia. State Committee for Statistics of the Republic of Latvia. Riga, 1992- (annual).

Stewart, Gail. *The Baltic States*. New York: Crestwood House, 1992.

C. Guides

The Baltic States: A Reference Book. Tallin: Estonian Encyclopedia Publishers, 1991.

Hoh, Peter and Rainer Hoh. *Baltikum Handbuch: Litauen, Lettland, Estland mit Kaliningrad*. Bielefeld: Peter Rump Verlag, 1992.

Kalnins, Ingrida. *A Guide to the Baltic States*. Merrifield, Va.: Inroads, 1990.

Sakk, V. *Baltische Sowjetrepubliken: Impressionen aus Litauen, Lettland, und Estland*. Leipzig: Brockhaus, 1989.

D. Travel and Description

Addison, Lucy. *Letters from Latvia*. London: Macdonald, 1986.

Bailey, S. F. "Sailing Through Baltic History." *Contemporary Review*, vol. 260 (1992), pp. 24-29.

Benton, Peggy. *Baltic Countdown: A Nation Vanishes*. London: Centaur Press, 1984.

Ivask, Ivar. "A Home In Language and Poetry: Travel Impressions from Estonia, Latvia, Lithuania, and Russia." *World Literature Today*, vol. 63 (1989), pp. 391-405.

Mrazkova, Daniela. "Many Nations, Many Voices." *Aperture*, Fall 1986, pp. 24-33.

Tanner, Marcus. *Ticket to Latvia: A Journey from Berlin to the Baltic*. London: J. M. Dent, 1989.

Thomson, Clare. *The Singing Revolution: A Political Journey Through the Baltic States*. London: Michael Joseph, 1992.

Vesilind, Priit J. "The Baltic Nations." *National Geographic*, November 1990, pp. 2-37.

II. Cultural

A. Art, Architecture, and Music

Apkalns, Longins. *Lettische Musik*. Wiesbaden: Breitkopf und Hartel, 1977.

Bockler, Erich, ed. *Beiträge zur Geschichte der baltischen Kunst*. Giessen: W. Schmitz, 1988.

Ivanovs, M., comp. *Latvian Painting: Pre-Soviet Period*. Riga: Liesma, 1981.

Kaiser, Kay. *The Architecture of Gunārs Birkerts*. Washington, D.C.: American Institute of Architects Press, 1989.

Nefedova, Irina, comp. *Masterpieces of Latvian Painting*. Riga: Liesma, 1988.

Siliņš, Jānis. *Latvijas māksla 1800-1914* [*The Art of Latvia 1800-1914*]. Two volumes. Stockholm: Daugava, 1979-1980.

----------. *Latvijas māksla 1915-1940* [*The Art of Latvia 1915-1914*]. Three volumes. Stockholm: Daugava, 1988-1993.

Unerwartete Begegnung: Letttische Avantgarde 1910-1935: Der Beitrag Lettlands zur Kunst der europaischen Moderne. Neue Gesellschaft für bildende Kunst. Cologne: Wienand Verlag, 1990.

Vasiljev, Yuri, ed. *The Dom Cathedral Architectural Ensemble in Riga*. Leningrad: Aurora Art Publishers, 1980.

B. Linguistics and Literature

a. Linguistics and Language

Eiche, Aleksandra. *Latvian Declinable and Indeclinable Participles*. Stockholm: Almqvist and Wiksell, 1983.

Gaters, Alfreds. *Die lettische Sprache und Ihre Dialekte*. The Hague: Mouton, 1977.

Metuzale-Kangere, Baiba. *A Derivational Dictionary of Latvian*. Hamburg: Helmut Buske, 1985.

---------------, ed. *Symposium Balticum: A Festschrift to Honor Professor Velta Rūķe-Draviņa*. Hamburg: H. Buske, 1990

Plakans, Andrejs. "From A Regional Vernacular to the Language of a State: The Case of Latvian." *International Journal of the Sociology of Language*, Nos. 100/101 (1993), pp. 203-219.

Ruke-Dravina, Velta. *Place Names in Kauguri County, Latvia: A Synchronic-Structural Analysis of Toponyms in an Ancient Indo-European and Finno-Ugric Contact Area*. Stockholm: University of Stockholm, 1971.

------------------. *The Standardization Process in Latvian: 16th Century to the Present*. Stockholm: University of Stockholm, 1977.

Soikane-Trapane, Mara. *Latvian Basic and Topical Vocabulary*. Rockville, Md.: American Latvian Association, 1984.

Stolz, Thomas. *Sprachbund im Baltikum: Estnisch und Lettisch im Zentrum einer sprachlichen Konvergenzlandschaft*. Bochum: N. Brockmeyer, 1991.

Zeps, Valdis. *The Placenames of Latgola: A Dictionary of East Latvian Toponyms*. Madison: Baltic Studies Center, 1984.

b. Literature

Andrups, Janis and Vitauts Kalve. *Latvian Literature: Essays*. Stockholm: Zelta Ābele, 1954.

Anerauds, Janis, ed. *Amberland: Selections from Latvian Poetry and Prose*. Riga: Liesma, 1967.

Cedrins, Inara, ed. *Contemporary Latvian Poetry*. Iowa City: University of Iowa Press, 1984.

Ekmanis, Rolfs. *Latvian Literature Under the Soviets, 1940-1975*. Belmont, Mass.: Nordland Publishing Company, 1978.

Lesins, Knuts. *The Wine of Eternity: Short Stories from the Latvian*. Minneapolis: University of Minnesota Press, 1957.

Nollendorfs, Valters. "Teaching Language and Literature in Latvia: The Return of a Native as a Fulbright." *Profession 91*. New York: Modern Language Association, 1991, pp. 17-21.

Rubulis, Aleksis, ed. *Baltic Literature: A Survey of Finnish, Estonian, Latvian, and Lithuanian Literatures*. Notre Dame: University of Notre Dame Press, 1970

--------------. *Latvian Literature*. Toronto: Daugavas Vanags Publishers, 1964.

Stahnke, Astrida B. *Aspazija: Her Life and Her Drama*. London: University Press of America, 1984.

Vikis-Freibergs, Vaira, ed. *Linguistics and Poetics of Latvian Folk Songs*. Montreal: McGill-Queen's University Press, 1989.

Ziedonis, Arvids, Jr. *The Religious Poetry of Janis Rainis: Latvian Poet*. Waverly, Iowa: Latvju Gramata, 1969.

----------------. *A Study of Rudolfs Blaumanis*. Hamburg: Helmut Buske, 1979.

Ziedonis, Arvids, Jr. et al., eds. *Baltic Literature and Linguistics*. Columbus, Ohio: AABS, 1973.

C. Education

Kenez, Csaba Janos, ed. *Zur gegenwärtigen Lage des Bildungswesens in den baltischen Sowjetrepubliken Estland und Lettland*. Marburg: J. G. Herderinstitut, 1986.

Namsons, Adrivs. "Die Sowjetisierung des Schul- und Bildungswesens in Lettland von 1940 bis 1960." *Acta Baltica*, vol. 1 (1960-61), pp. 148-167.

D. Religion

Cherney, Alexander. *The Latvian Orthodox Church*. Welshpool, Wales: Stylite Publishing, 1985.

Neubert, K. H. *Im Banne Moskaus: Die Evangelisch-lutherische Kirche in den Russischen Ostseeprovinzen*. Berlin: H. Klein, 1888.

Rozitis, Elmars. "Die evangelisch-lutherische Kirche in Sowjetlettland." *Acta Baltica*, vol. 1 (1960-61), pp. 93-109.

Sapiets, M. "'Rebirth and Renewal' in the Latvian Lutheran Church." *Religion in Communist Lands*, vol. 16, no. 3 (1988), pp. 237-249.

III. Economic

A. General

Bohnet, A. and N. Penkaitis. "A Comparison of Living Standards and Consumption Patterns Between the RSFSR and the Baltic Republics." *Journal of Baltic Studies*, vol. 19, no. 1 (1988) pp. 22-48.

Dreifelds, Juris. "Belorussia and the Baltics," in *Economics of Soviet Regions*, edited by I. S. Koropeckyj and Gertrude Schroeder. New York: Praeger, 1981, pp. 325-385.

Gotz, Roland. *Die Wirtschaft des Baltikums*. Cologne: Bundesinstitut fur Ostwissenschaftliche und Internationale Studien, 1990.

King, Gundar. *Economic Policies in Occupied Latvia*. Tacoma, Wash.: Pacific Lutheran University Press, 1965.

Kolde, Endel Jakob. "Structural Integration of the Baltic Economies into the Soviet System." *Journal of Baltic Studies*, vol. 9, no. 2 (1978), pp. 164-176.

Latvia: An Economic Profile. Washington, D.C.: U.S. Government Printing Office, August 1992.

Latvia: The Transition to a Market Economy. A World Bank Country Study. Washington, D.C.: The World Bank, 1993.

Neuschaffer, Hubertus. *Kleine Wald- und Forstgeschichte des Baltikums, Lettland und Estland: Ein Beispiel europäischer Integration und kultureller Wechselwirkungen*. Bonn: Kulturstiftung der deutschen Vertriebenen, 1991.

Van Arkadie, Brian and Mats Karlson. *Economic Survey of the Baltic States*. New York: New York University Press, 1992.

Viksnins, George J. "Current Issues of Soviet Latvia's Economic Growth." *Journal of Baltic Studies*, vol. 7, no. 4 (1976), pp. 343-351.

------------------. "Evaluating Economic Growth in Latvia." *Journal of Baltic Studies*, vol. 12, no. 2 (1981), pp. 173-188.

B. Agriculture

Boruks, Arturs. *Zemnieks, zeme, un zemkopība Latvijā no senākiem laikiem līdz mūsdienām* [*Farmers, Land, and Farming in Latvia from the Earliest Times to the Present*]. Riga: Grāmatvedis, 1995.

Feiferis, Inesis. "Agrarian Reform in Latvia." in *Agricultural Transformation and Privatization in the Baltics*. Report 92-BR7 of the Center for Agricultural and Rural Development, Iowa State University, Ames, Iowa, December 1992.

Labsvirs, Janis. *The Sovietization of the Baltic States: Collectivization of Latvian Agriculture 1944-1956*. n.p.: Taurus, 1989.

Namsons, Andrivs. "Die Entwicklung der Landwirtschaft in Sowjetlettland." *Acta Baltica*, vol. 9 (1969), pp. 135-176.

----------------. "Die Umgestaltung der Landwirtschaft in Lettland." *Acta Baltica*, vol. 2 (1962), pp. 57-92.

Plakans, Andrejs. "Agrarian Reform in the Baltic States Between the World Wars: The Historical Context," in *An Overview of Rural Development Strategies for the Baltics*. Report 93-BR9 of the Center for Agricultural and Rural Development, Iowa State University, Ames, Iowa, March 1993, pp. 1-14.

Tabuns, Aivars. "Agricultural Education and Training in Latvia: Changes and Problems," in *An Overview of Rural Development Strategies for the Baltics*. Report 93-BR9 of the Center for Agricultural and Rural Development, Iowa State University, Ames, Iowa. March 1993, pp. 41-46.

Zile, Roberts. *Changing Ownership in Latvia Through Agrarian Reform*. Report 92-BR5 of the Center for Agricultural and Rural Development, Iowa State University, Ames, Iowa, September 1992.

C. Industry, Commerce, and Business

Hanson, P. "Centre and Periphery: The Baltic States in Search of Economic Independence." *Journal of Interdisciplinary Economics*, vol. 4 (1992), pp. 249-267.

Namsons, Andrivs. "Neue Errungenschaften in der Industrie Lettlands." *Acta Baltica*, vol. 9 (1969), pp. 81-134.

D. Technology

Irbitis, Karlis. *Of Struggle and Flight: The History of Latvian Aviation*. Stittsville, Ont.: Canada's Wings, Inc. 1986.

Rimmington, Anthony. *Technology and Transition: A Survey of Biotechnology in Russia, Ukraine, and the Baltic States*. Westport, Conn.: Quorum Books, 1992

Stakle, Janis. "Die Eisenbahnen und das Transportwesen Lettlands in der Zeit von 1940-1970." *Acta Baltica*, vol. 15 (1975), pp. 175-210.

E. Labor and Labor Conditions

Oxensteirna, Susanne. "Labor Market Policies in the Baltic Republics." *International Labour Review*, vol. 130 (1991), pp. 255-273.

IV. Historic

A. General

Bilmanis, Alfreds. *Baltic Essays*. Washington, D.C.: Latvian Legation, 1945.

----------------. *A History of Latvia*. Princeton: Princeton University Press, 1951.

Carson, George B., ed. *Latvia: An Area Study*. Human Relations Area Files, no. 41. New Haven, Conn.: Yale University Press, 1956.

Mangulis, Visvaldis. *Latvia In the Wars of the 20th Century*. Princeton Junction, N.J.: Cognition Books, 1983.

Meissner, Boris, ed. *Die Baltische Nationen: Estland, Lettland, und Litauen*. Cologne: Markus Verlag, 1990

Plakans, Andrejs. *The Latvians: A Short History*. Stanford: Hoover Institution Press, 1995.

von Rauch, Georg. *The Baltic States. Estonia, Latvia, and Lithuania: The Years of Independence 1917-1940*. Berkeley: University of California Press, 1974.

Spekke, Arnolds. *A History of Latvia: An Outline*. Stockholm: M. Goppers, 1957.

Vardys, V. Stanley and Romuald J. Misiunas, eds. *The Baltic States in Peace and War 1917-1945*. University Park: Pennsylvania State University Press, 1978.

Ziedonis, Arvids, William R. Winter, and Mardi Valgemae, eds. *Baltic History*. Columbus, Ohio: AABS, 1974

B. Archaeology and Prehistory

Gimbutas, Marija. *The Balts*. New York: Praeger, 1963.

C. The Medieval Centuries

Abers, Benno. "Zur päpstlichen Missionspolitik in Lettland und Estland zur Zeit Innocenz III." *Commentationes Balticae*, vol. 4-5 (1958).

Biezais, H. *Die Gottesgestalt der lettischen Volkreligion*. Stockholm: Almqvist and Wiksell, 1961.

Bilkins, Vilis. "Die Autoren der Kreuzzugszeit und das deutsche Milieu Livlands und Preussens." *Acta Baltica*, vol. 14 (1975).

Brockmann, Hartmut. *Der Deutsche Orden: Zwölf Kapitel aus seiner Geschichte*. Munich: Beck, 1981.

Brundage, James A. "Hunting and Fishing in the Law and Economy of Thirteenth Century Livonia." *Journal of Baltic Studies*, vol. 13 (1982), pp. 3-11.

Christiansen, Eric. *The Northern Crusades: The Baltic and the Catholic Frontier 1100-1525*. London: Macmillan, 1980.

The Chronicle of Balthasar Russow: a Forthright Rebuttal by Elert Kruse; Errors and Mistakes of Balthasar Russow by Heinrich Tisenhausen, translated and edited by Jerry C. Smith, Juergen Eichhoff, and William L. Urban. Madison, Wisc.: Baltic Studies Center, 1988.

The Chronicle of Henry of Livonia, edited and translated by James A. Brundage. Madison: University of Wisconsin Press, 1961.

Gli inizi del cristianesimo in Livonia-Lettonia. Vatican City: Libreria Editrice Vaticana, 1989.

Hellmann, Manfred, ed. *Studien über die Anfänge der Mission in Livland.* Sigmaringen: Jan Thordbecke, 1989.

Indriķa hronika [*Chronicle of Heinrich of Livonia*] translated by A. Feldhuns. Introduction by E. Mugurēvičs. Riga: Zinatne, 1993.

The Livonian Rhymed Chronicle, translated by Jerry C. Smith and William Urban. Bloomington, Ind.: Indiana University Press, 1977.

Niitemaa, Vilho. *Der Binnenhandel in der Politik der livländischen Städte im Mittelalter.* Helsinki, 1952.

----------------. *Die undeutsche Frage in der Politik der livländischen Städte im Mittelalter.* Helsinki, 1949.

Salomon Hennings Chronicle of Courland and Livonia, translated and edited by Jerry Smith, J. War Jones, and William Urban. Dubuque, Iowa: Kendall Hunt Publishing, 1991.

Spekke, Arnolds. *The Ancient Amber Routes and The Geographical Discovery of the Eastern Baltic.* Stockholm: M. Goppers, 1957

----------------. *The Baltic Sea in Ancient Maps.* Stockholm: M. Goppers, 1957.

Urban, William. *The Baltic Crusade.* First edition--Dekalb, Ill.: Northern Illinois University Press, 1975; second edition--Chicago: Lithuanian Research and Studies Center, Inc., 1994.

---------------. *The Livonian Crusade*. Washington, D.C.: University Press of America, 1981.

D. The Early Modern Centuries

Angermann, Norbert, ed. *Deutschland-Livland-Russland, ihre Beziehung vom 15. bis 17. Jahrhundert*. Luneburg: Nordostdeutsches Kulturwerk, 1988.

------------------, ed. *Wolter von Plettenberg: Der Grösste Ordenmeister Livlands*. Luneburg: Nordostdeutsches Kulturwerk, 1985.

Dunsdorfs, Edgars. *Latvijas vesture 1600-1710 [History of Latvia 1600-1710]*. Stockholm: Daugava, 1962.

---------------. *The Livonian Estates of Axel Oxenstierna*. Stockholm: Almqvist and Wiksell, 1981.

Dunsdorfs, Edgars and Arnbolds Spekke. *Latvijas vesture 1500-1600 [History of Latvia 1500-1600]*. Stockholm: Daugava, 1964.

Germanis, Uldis. "Die Agrargesetzgebung auf den herzöglichen Domänen Kurlands zur Zeit Birons." *Acta Baltica*. Vol. XVI (1976).

Kirby, David. *Northern Europe in the Early Modern Period: The Baltic World 1492-1772*. London: Longman, 1990.

Lindquist, Sven-Olof, ed. *Economy and Culture in the Baltic 1650-1700*. Visby: Gotlands Fornsal, 1989.

Mattiesen, Otto Heinz. *Die Kolonial- und Überseepolitik der Kurländischen Herzoge im 17. und 18. Jahrhundert*. Berlin: Kohlhammer, 1940.

E. The Russian Imperial Era (18th-20th Centuries)

The Baltic Countries 1900-1914. Stockholm: University of Stockholm, 1990.

Bukss, Mikelis. *Die Russifizierung in den baltischen Ländern*. Munich: Latgaļu izdevniecība, 1964.

Dunsdorfs, Edgars. *Latvijas vēsture 1710-1800* [*History of Latvia 1710-1800*]. Stockholm: Daugava, 1973.

Ezergailis, Andrievs and Gert von Pistohlkors. *Die Baltischen Provinzen Russlands zwischen den Revolutionen vom 1905 und 1917.* Cologne: Bohlau Verlag, 1982.

Johansons, Andrejs. *Latvijas kultūras vēsture 1710-1800* [*History of Latvian Culture*]. Stockholm: Daugava, 1975.

Liebel-Weckowicz, Helen. "Nations and Peoples: Baltic-Russian History and the Development of Herder's Theory of Culture." *Canadian Journal of History*, vol. 21 (1986), pp. 1-23.

Loit, Aleksander, ed. *National Movements in the Baltic Countries During the 19th Century.* Stockholm: University of Stockholm, 1985.

von Hehn, Jurgen. *Die lettisch-literärische Gesellschaft und das Lettentum.* Berlin, 1938.

Henriksson, A. *The Tsar's Loyal Germans: The Riga German Community: Social Change and the Nationality Question, 1855-1905.* Boulder, Colo.: East European Monographs, 1983.

Plakans, Andrejs. "The Latvians." in *Russification in the Baltic Provinces and Finland, 1955-1914.* Edited by Edward Thaden. Princeton: Princeton University Press, 1981.

----------------. "Peasants, Intellectuals, and Nationalism in the Russian Baltic Provinces, 1820-1890." *Journal of Modern History* vol. 46 (1974), pp. 445-475.

Raun, Toivo U. "The Latvian and Estonian National Movements, 1860-1914." *The Slavonic and East European Review*, vol. 64, no. 1 (1986), pp. 66-80.

----------------. "The Revolution of 1905 in the Baltic Provinces and Finland." *Slavic Review*, vol. 43 (1984), pp. 453-467.

Svabe, Arveds. *Latvijas vēsture 1800-1914* [*History of Latvia 1800-1914*]. Stockholm: Daugava, 1958.

Thaden, Edward C. "The Baltic National Movements During the Nineteenth Century." *Journal of Baltic Studies,* vol. 16 (1985) pp. 411-421.

----------------. "Estland, Livland, and the Ukraine: Reflections on Eighteenth Century Regional Autonomy." *Journal of Baltic Studies,* vol. 12 (1981), pp. 312-217.

----------------. *Russia's Western Borderlands, 1710-1870.* Princeton: Princeton University Press, 1984.

Thimme, Heinrich. *Kirche und nationale Frage in Livland während der ersten Hälfte des 19. Jahrhunderts.* Königsberg, 1938.

Viese, Saulcerite. *Krisjanis Barons: The Man and His Work.* Moscow: Raduga, 1985.

F. World War I and Interwar Independence (1914-1940)

Aizsilnieks, Arnolds. *Latvijas saimniecības vēsture 1914-1945 [History of the Latvian Economy 1914-1945].* Stockholm: Daugava, 1968.

Andersons, Edgars. *Latvijas vēsture 1914-1920 [History of Latvia 1914-1920].* Stockholm: Daugava, 1967.

----------------. *Latvijas vēsture 1820-1940: Arpolitika [History of Latvia: Foreign Policy].* Two volumes. Stockholm: Daugava, 1982.

The Baltic in International Relations Between the Two World Wars: A Symposium. Stockholm: University of Stockholm, 1988.

Buchan, John, ed. *Baltic and Caucasian States.* London, n.d. (c.1923).

Crowe, David. "Germany and the Baltic Question in Latvia 1939-1940." *East European Quarterly,* vol. 26 (1992), pp. 371-389.

Ezergalis, Andrew. *The Latvian Impact on the Bolshevik Revolution: The First Phase, September 1917-April 1918.* Boulder, Colo.: East European Monographs, 1983.

----------------. *The 1917 Revolution in Latvia.* Boulder, Colo.: East European Quarterly, 1974.

Germanis, Uldis. "The Idea of an Independent Latvia and Its Development in 1917," in *Res Baltica*, edited by A. Sprūdžs and A. Rūsis. Leyden: A. W. Sijthoff, 1968, pp. 27-87.

Graham, M. W. *The Diplomatic Recognition of the Border States.* Berkeley, Calif.: University of California Press, 1939-1941. Publications of the University of California at Los Angeles in Social Sciences. Volume 3. Latvia.

Hovi, Olavi. *The Baltic Area in British Policy 1918-1921.* Helinski: Finnish Historical Society, 1980.

Krupnikov, P. *Lettland und die Letten im Spiegel deutscher und deutschbaltischer Publizistik, 1895-1950.* Hannover: H. von Hirschheydt, 1989.

Loeber, Dietrich Andre, ed. *Diktierte Option: Die Umsiedlung der Deutschbalten aus Estland und Lettland 1939-1941: Dokumentation.* Neumunster: Karl Wachholz, 1972.

Mendelsohn, Ezra. *The Jews of East Central Europe Between the World Wars.* Bloomington: Indiana University Press, 1983.

Page, Stanley W. *The Formation of the Baltic States: A Study of the Effects of Great Power Policies on the Emergence of Lithuania, Latvia, Estonia.* Cambridge, Mass.: Harvard University Press, 1959. Reprinted 1970, New York: Howard Fertig.

Popoff, George. *The City of the Red Plague.* London: George Allen and Unwin, 1932.

von Rauch, Georg. *The Baltic States: The Years of Independence: Estonia, Latvia, and Lithuania.* Stanford: University of California Press, 1974.

Silde, Adolfs. *Latvijas vēsture 1914-1940 [History of Latvia 1914-1940].* Stockholm: Daugava, 1976.

Vardys, V. Stanley and Romuald Misiunas, eds. *The Baltic States In Peace and War, 1917-1945.* University Park: Pennsylvania State University Press, 1978.

G. Soviet and German Occupation (1940-1945)

Bilmanis, Alfreds. *Latvia Under German Occupation*. Washington, D.C.: Latvian Embassy, 1943.

Ezergailis, Andrew. "Anti-Semitism and the Killing of Latvia's Jews." in *Anti-Semitism in Times of Crisis*, edited by Sander L. Gilman and Steven T. Katz. New York: New York University Press, 1991.

-----------------. *The Holocaust in Latvia, 1941-1944: The Missing Center*. Riga: The Historical Institute of Latvia, in association with the United States Holocaust Museum, 1996.

Hiden, John, ed. *The Baltic and the Outbreak of the Second World War*. Cambridge: Cambridge University Press, 1992.

Hough, W. J. "The Annexation of the Baltic States and Its Effect on the Development of Law Prohibiting Forcible Seizure of Territory." *New York Law School Journal of International and Comparative Law,* vol. 6 (1985), pp. 300-533.

Kaufmann, Max. *Die Vernichtung der Juden Lettlands*. Munich: Deutscher Verlag, 1947.

Kavass, Igor I. and Adolph Sprudzs, eds. *Baltic States: A Study of their Origin and National Development, Their Seizure and Incorporation into the USSR*. New York : William Hein, 1972.

Levin, Dov. "Arrests and Deportations of Latvian Jews by the USSR During the Second World War." *Nationalities Papers*, vol. 16, no. 1, 1988, pp. 50-70.

--------------. "The Jews and the Sovietization of Latvia, 1940-41." *Soviet Jewish Affairs*, vol. 5, no 1., 1975.

Littlejohn, David. *Foreign Legions of the Third Reich*. Vol. 4. *Poland, Ukraine, Bulgaria, Romania, Free India, Estonia, Latvia, Lithuania, Finland, and Russia*. San Jose, Calif.: James Bender, 1987.

Michelson, Frida. *I Survived Rumbuli*. New York: Holocaust Library, 1979.

Mylliniemi, Seppo. *Die Neuordnung der Baltischen Länder 1941-1944*. Helsinki: Societas Historica Finlandiae, 1973.

Neulen, Hans Werner. *An deutscher Seite: Internationale Freiwillige von Wehrmacht und Waffen-SS*. Munich: Universitas, 1985.

Press, Bernard. *Judenmord in Lettland 1941-1945*. Berlin. 1988. Second edition 1992.

Silgailis, Arthur. *Latvian Legion*. San Jose, Calif.: James Bender, 1986.

Vairogs, Dainis. *Latvian Deportations 1940-Present*. Rockville, Md.: World Federation of Free Latvians, 1986.

H. The Soviet Period (1945-1985)

Allworth, E., ed. *Nationality Group Survival in Multi-Ethnic States: Shifting Support Patterns in the Soviet Baltic Region*. New York: Praeger, 1977.

Bonosky, Phillip. *Devils in Amber: The Baltics*. New York: International Publishers, 1992.

Clem, Ralph S. ed. *The Soviet West: Interplay Between Nationality and Social Organization*. New York: Praeger, 1975. Essay on Latvians by Mary Ann Grossman.

Dreifelds, Juris. "Latvian National Demands and Group Consciousness Since 1959," in *Nationalism in the USSR and Eastern Europe in the Era of Brezhnev and Kosygin*, edited by J. Simmonds. Detroit: University of Detroit Press, 1977, pp. 136-156.

Harned, Frederick. "Latvians," in *Handbook of Major Soviet Nationalities*, edited by Zev Katz. New York : Free Press, 1975.

Kalnins, Bruno. "How Latvia Is Ruled: The Structure of the Political Apparatus." *Journal of Baltic Studies*, vol. 8 (1977), pp. 70-78.

Karklins, Rasma. *Ethnic Relations in the USSR: The Perspective From Below*. Boston, Mass.: Allen and Unwin, 1986.

Küng, Andres. *A Dream of Freedom: Four Decades of National Surival versus Russian Imperialism in Estonia, Latvia, and Lithuania 1940-1980*. Cardiff, Wales: Boreas, 1981.

"Letter by Seventeen Latvian Communists," in *Samizdat*, edited by G. Saunders. New York, 1974, pp. 427-440.

Loeber, Dietrich A., V. Stanley Vardys, and Laurence P. Kitching, eds. *Regional Identity Under Soviet Rule: The Case of the Baltic States*. Hackettstown, N.J.: AABS, 1990.

Maley, William. *The Politics of Baltic Nationalism*. Canberra, Australia: Research School of Pacific Studies, 1990.

Misiunas, R. J. "Baltic Nationalism and Soviet Language Policy: From Russification to Constitutional Amendment," in *Soviet Nationality Policies: Ruling Ethnic Groups in the USSR*. London: Mansell, 1990, pp. 206-220.

----------------. "The Baltic Republics: Stagnation and Strivings for Sovereignty," in *The Nationalities Factor in Soviet Politics and Society*. Boulder, Colo.: Westview Press, 1990, pp. 204-227.

Misiunas, R. J. and Rein Taagepera. *The Baltic States: Years of Dependence 1940-1980*. Berkeley: University of California Press, 1983; expanded and updated edition, 1993.

-------------------------. "The Baltic States: Years of Dependence 1980-1986." *Journal of Baltic Studies*, vol. 20 (1986), pp. 65-88.

Nielsen-Stokkeby, Bernd. *Baltische Erinnerungen: Estland, Lettland, Litauen zwischen Unterdruckung und Freiheit*. Bergisch Gladbach: Gustav Lubbe Verlag, 1990.

Penikis, John J. "Latvian Nationalism: Preface to the Dissenting View." in *Nationalism in the USSR and Eastern Europe in the Era of Brezhnev and Kosygin*, edited by J. Simmond. Detroit: University of Detroit Press, 1977, pp. 157-161.

Shtromas, Alexander. "Soviet Occupation of the Baltic States and their Incorporation into the USSR: Political and Legal Aspects." *East European Quarterly*, vol. 19 (1985), pp. 289-304.

Silde, Adolfs. *Resistance Movement in Latvia.* Stockholm: Latvian National Foundation, 1972.

Smith, G. E. "The Impact of Modernisation on the Latvian Soviet Republic." *Coexistence,* vol 6 (1979), pp. 45-64.

------------. "Die Probleme des Nationalismus in den drei Baltischen Sowjet Republiken Estland, Lettland, und Litauen." *Acta Baltica,* vol. 21 (1981) , pp. 143-177.

Trapans, Andris. *Soviet Miltary Power in the Baltic Area.* Stockholm: Latvian National Foundation, 1986.

Vizulis, I. J. *Nations Under Duress. The Baltic States.* Port Washington, N. Y.: Associated Faculty Press, 1985.

Widmer, Michael J. "Nationalism and Communism in Latvia: The Latvian Communist Party Under Soviet Rule." Ph.D. diss. Harvard University, Cambridge, Mass., 1969.

Zagars, E. *Socialist Transformation in Latvia, 1940-1941.* Riga: Zinatne, 1978.

I. Current History (1985--)

Alexeyeva, Ludmilla. *Soviet Dissent: Contemporary Movements for National, Religious, and Human Rights.* Middletown, Conn.: Wesleyan University Press, 1985. Chapter 4: The Latvian National-Democratic Movement.

Bitzinger, Richard A. "The Baltic: a Changing Security Situation," *Scandinavian Studies,* vol 64 (1992), pp. 606-613.

Clemens, Walter C., Jr. *Baltic Independence and Russian Empire.* New York: St. Martins Press, 1991.

Cullen, Robert. *Twilight of Empire: Inside the Crumbling Soviet Bloc.* New York: Atlantic Monthly Press, 1991.

Dalhoff-Nielsen, Peter. *Baltisk opbrud: Estland, Letland och Litauens forvandling efter glasnost.* Copenhagen: Vindrose, 1990.

Dreifelds, Juris. *Latvia in Transition.* New York: Cambridge University Press, 1996.

--------------------. "Latvian National Rebirth." *Problems of Communism* , No. 4 (1989), pp. 77-95.

Gerner, Kristian. *The Baltic States and the End of the Soviet Empire.* London: Routledge, 1993.

Graw, Ansgar. *Der Freiheitskampf im Baltikum.* Erlangen: Straube, 1991.

Heuvel, Martin P. van den. *David versus Goliath: het vrijheidsstreven van Estland, Letland, Litouwen.* Baarn: Anthos, 1989.

Leber, Jeri. "The Baltic Revolt." *New York Review of Books*, March 28, 1991.

Lieven, Anatol. *The Baltic Revolution: Latvia, Lithuania, Estonia, and the Path to Independence.* New Haven: Yale University Press, 1993.

Mercier, P. R. *Aspects des luttes sociales en URSS: le mouvement démocratique des Arméniens, les Baltes, et la question de l'état de droit.* Paris: P. Bouchereau, 1989.

Plotnieks, Andris. "The Evolution of the Soviet Federation and the Independence of Latvia." in *Soviet Federalism, Nationalism, and Economic Decentralisation,* edited by Alistair McAuley. New York: St. Martins Press, 1991.

Raun, Toivo U. "Perestroika and Baltic Historiography." *Journal of Soviet Nationalities*, vol. 2, no. 2 (1911), pp. 52-62.

Shtromas, Alexander. *The Soviet Method of Conquest of the Baltic States: Lessons for the West.* Washington, D.C. : Washington Institute for Values in Public Policy, 1986.

Silde, Adolfs. "Die Entwicklung der Republik Lettland." in *Die Baltischen Nationen: Estland, Lettland, Lituaen.* Cologne: Markus Verlag, 1990.

Smith, Graham. "Latvians." in *The Nationalities Question in the Soviet Union*, edited by Graham Smith. London: Longmans, 1990, pp. 54-71.

Sprudzs, Adolfs, ed. *The Baltic Path to Independence: An International Reader of Selected Articles*. Buffalo, N.Y.: William S. Hein and Co., 1994.

Taagepera, Rein. "Citizens' Peace Movement in the Soviet Baltic Republics." *Journal of Peace Research,* vol. 23 (1986), pp. 183-192.

Terauda, Vita. *The Rise of Grass Roots Environmental Groups Under Gorbachev: A Case Study of Latvia*. Washington, D.C.: Johns Hopkins University-SAIS, 1989.

Trapans, J. A. "Averting Moscow's Baltic Coup." *Orbis,* vol. 35, no. 3 (1991), pp. 427-439.

--------------- . *Impatient for Freedom: The Baltic Struggle For Independence*. London: Institute for European Defence and Strategic Studies, 1990. European Security Study No. 8.

---------------. *Toward Independence: The Baltic Popular Movements*. Boulder, Colo.: Westview Press, 1991.

Vizulis, J. I. *The Molotov-Ribbentrop Pact of 1939: The Baltic Case*. New York: Praeger, 1990.

V. Juridical

Constitution of the Republic of Latvia. Stockholm: Latvian National Foundation, 1984.

Economic Legislation of the Republic of Latvia in English. Riga: Department of Foreign Economic Relations, Council of Ministers, 1991-1992.

Uibopuu, Henn-Juri. *Die Verfassungs- und Rechtsentwicklung der baltischen Staaten 1988-1990*. Cologne: Bundesinstitut für Ostwissenschaftliche und Internationale Studien, 1990.

Zile, Zigurds. "Legal Thought and the Formation of Law and Legal Institutions in the Socialistic Soviet Republic of Latvia 1917-1920." *Journal of Baltic Studies*, vol. 7, no. 3 (1977), pp. 195-204.

VI. Political

A. Domestic

Dellenbrandt, J. A. "The Re-Emergence of Multi-Partism in the Baltic States," in *The New Democracies in Eastern Europe: Party Systems and Political Cleavages.* Edited by Sten Berglund and J. A. Dellenbrandt. London: Edward Elgar, 1992, pp. 75-106.

Kerner, Manfred. *Die Unabhängigkeit der baltischen Staaten in Historischer Bilanz und als aktuelle Perspektive: Betrachtungen und Geschpräche zu kontroversen Fragen der Innen- und Aussenpolitik Litauens, Lettlands, and Estlands sowie zum Stand der Wissenscahftlichen Forschung.* Berlin: Berghofs-Stiftung, 1990

Presidential Elections and Independence Referendums in the Baltic States, The Soviet Union, and Successor States: A Compendium of Reports. Washington, D.C.: Commission on Security and Cooperation in Europe, 1992.

Ziedonis, Arvids, Rein Taagepera, and Mardi Valgemae, eds. *Problems of Mininations: Baltic Perspectives.* San Jose, Calif.: AABS, 1973.

B. Foreign Relations

Bilmanis, Alfred, ed. *Latvian-Russian Relations: Documents.* Washington, D.C.: Latvian Legation, 1978.

Comprehensive Security for the Baltic: An Environmental Approach. Oslo: International Peace Research Institute, 1989.

Hiden, J. W. *The Baltic States and Weimar Ostpolitik.* Cambridge: Cambridge University Press, 1987.

Loit, Aleksander and John Hiden, eds. *The Baltic In International Relations Between the Two World Wars.* Stockholm: University of Stockholm, 1988.

Mangulis, Visvaldis. *Latvia in the Wars of the Twentieth Century.* Princeton Junction, N. J.: Cognition Books, 1983.

Rogers, H. I. *Search for Security: A Study in Baltic Diplomacy 1920-1934.* Hamden, Conn.: Archon Books, 1975.

Tarulis, A. N. *Soviet Policy Toward the Baltic States 1918-1940.* Notre Dame, Ind.: University of Notre Dame Press, 1959.

VII. Scientific

Academies of Science in the Constituent Republics of the Former Soviet Union: A Current Appraisal. London: The Royal Society, 1992.

Latvian Research: An International Evaluation. Copenhagen: Danish Research Councils, 1992.

Priednieks, J. et al. *Latvian Breeding Bird Atlas 1980-1984.* Riga: Zinātne, 1990.

Voigt, Klaus. "The Baltic Sea: Pollution Problems and Natural Environmental Changes." *Impact of Science on Society,* nos. 3-4 (1983), pp. 413-420.

VIII. Social

A. Folklore and Ethnography

Ambains, Ojars, ed. *Lettische Volksmärchen.* Berlin: Akademie-Verlag, 1977.

Berzins, Ludis. "Metrik der lettischen Volkslieder." *Magazin der Lettisch-literarische Gesellschaft* , vol. 19, 1896. (Riga)

Berzins, Valdis, Imants Freibergs, Kristine Konrade, Guntis Strazds, and Vaira Vike-Freiberga. *The Boston - Montreal Data Base of Latvian Folks Songs.* Montreal: University of Montreal, 1982.

Berzkalne, Anna. *Typenverzeichnis lettischer Volksromanzen in der Sammlung Kr. Barons' "Latvju Dainas."* Helsinki: University of Helsinki, 1938. Folklore Fellows Communications 123.

Bielenstein, August von. *Die Holzbauten und Holzgeräte der Letten: Ein Beitrag zur Ethnographie, Kulturgeschichte, und Archeologie der Völker Russlands im Westgebiet.* St. Petersburg, 1907-1918 reprint Hannover-Dohren, Germany: Harro von Hirschheydt, 1969.

Biezais, Haralds. *Die Hauptgöttinen der alten Letten.* Uppsala: Almqvist and Wiksell, 1955.

----------------. *Lichtgott der alten Letten.* Stockholm: Almqvist and Wiksell, 1976.

Bisenieks, Valdis. *Lettische Volkslieder: Methodische Ausarbeitung.* Riga: State University of Latvia, 1985.

Brambats, K. "Die lettische Volkspoesie in musikwissenschaftlicher Geschichte." *Musik des Ostens,* vol 5 (1965).

Carpenter, Rita Gale. *A Latvian Story Teller.* New York: Arno Press, 1980.

Dunkele, Irene. *Zur Struktur der lettischen Volkslieder "Pūt vējiņi".* *Ein Lied in Tradition und Expansion seit 1800.* Stockholm: Almkvist and Wiksell, 1984.

Johansons, A. *Der Schirmherr des Hofes im Volksglauben der Letten.* Stockholm: Almqvist and Wiksell, 1964.

Jonval, Michel. *Les chansons mythologiques lettones.* Paris: Picart, 1929.

Katzenellenbogen, Uriah. *The Daina: An Anthology of Lithuanian and Latvian Folk Songs.* Chicago: Lithuanian News Publishing Company, 1935.

Kratins, Ojars. "An Unsung Hero: Krišjānis Barons and His Lifework in Latvian Folk Songs." *Western Folklore,* vol. 20 (1961), pp. 239-255.

Ligers, Ziedonis. *Latviešu etnogrāfija [Latvian Ethnography].* Bayeaux, France: Apgads Tauta, 1952. Vol. 1.

Mannhardt, Wilhelm. "Die lettischen Sonnenmythen." *Zeitschrift für Ethnologie,* vol 7 (1875), pp. 73-104, 209-244, 282-330.

Rathfelders, Hermanis. "Die Letten, ihre Sprache und Tradition in Volksliedern." *Acta Baltica* . Vol. XI (1972).

Rubulis, Aleksis, ed. *Latvian Folktales*. Grand Rapids, Mich.: Aka, 1982.

Strods, Heinrihs, ed. *Latviešu etnogrāfija [Latvian ethnography]*. Riga: Zinatne, 1969.

B. Population and Demography

Dreifelds, Juris. "Characteristics and Trends of Two Demographic Variables in the Latvian SSR." *Bulletin of Baltic Studies,* vol. 8 (1971), pp. 10-17.

Krūmiņš, Juris. *Iedz īvotāju mūža ilgums: tendences un palielināšanās problēmas [Longevity: Tendencies and the Problems of Increase]*. Riga: Latvijas Universitāte, 1993.

Krūmiņš, Juris and Pēteris Zvidriņs. "Recent Mortality Trends in the Three Baltic Republics." *Population Studies*, vol. 46 (1992), pp. 259-273.

Namsons, Andrivs. "Nationale Zusammensetzung und Struktur der Bevölkerung Lettlands nach den Volkszählungen von 1935, 1959, und 1970." *Acta Baltica*, vol. 11 (1971), pp. 61-68.

Parming, Tönu, "Population Processes and the Nationality Issue in the Soviet Baltic." *Soviet Studies*, vol. 32, no. 3 (1980), pp. 398-414.

Smith, G. E. "Soziale und Geographische Veränderungen in der Bevölkerungs-struktur von Estland, Lettland, und Litauen 1918-1940." *Acta Baltica*, vol. 1920 (1979/80), pp. 118-181.

C. Urbanization and Migration

Brubaker, W. Rogers. "Citizenship Struggles in Soviet Successor States." *International Migration Review*, vol. 26 (1992), pp. 269-291.

Corrsin, Stephen B. "The Changing Composition of the City of Riga 1867-1913." *Journal of Baltic Studies*, vol. 13, no. 1 (1982).

Grava, Sigurd. "The Urban Heritage of the Soviet Region: The Case of Riga, Latvia." *Journal of the American Planning Association*, vol. 59 (1993), pp. 9-30.

Namsons, Andrivs. "Die bürgerliche Bewegung in Sowjetrussland und in den baltischen Ländern." *Acta Baltica*, vol. 14 (1974), pp. 138-183.

----------------. "Stadtentwicklung und Siedlungsformen in Lettland." *Acta Baltica*, vol. 7 (1967), pp. 131-169.

D. Minorities, Ethnicity, and Nationalities

Allworth, Edward, ed. *Nationality Group Survival in Multi-Ethnic States: Shifting Support Patterns in the Soviet Baltic Region.* London: Praeger, 1977.

Bobe, Mendel, ed. *Jews In Latvia.* Tel Aviv: Association of Estonian and Latvian Jews in Israel, 1971.

Gordon, Frank. *Latvians and Jews Between Germany and Russia.* Stockholm: Memento, 1990.

Karklins, Rasma. *Ethnic Relations in the USSR: The Perspective From Below.* Boston: Allen and Unwin, 1986.

------------------. *Ethnopolitics and Transition to Democracy: The Collapse of the USSR and Latvia.* Washinton, D.C. and Baltimore, Md.: Woodrow Wilson Center Press and the Johns Hopkins University Press, 1994.

Levin, Dov. "On the Relations between the Baltic Peoples and Their Jewish Neighbors Before, During, and After World War II." *Holocaust and Genocide Studies*, vol. 5, no. 1 (1990), pp. 53-56.

Smith, Graham, ed. *The Nationalities Question in the Soviet Union.* London: Longman, 1990.

Uibopuu, Henn-Juri. "Dealing With the Minorities: A Baltic Perspective." *The World Today*, vol. 48, no. 6 (1992), pp. 108-112.

E. Latvian Diaspora Communities

Anderson, Edgar. "Latvians." in *Harvard Encyclopedia of American Ethnic Groups*, edited by Stephan Thernstrom. Cambridge: Harvard University Press, pp. 638-642.

Birskys, Betty et al. *The Baltic Peoples in Australia: Lithuanians, Latvians, Estonians.* Melbourne: A.E. Press, 1986.

Janitens-Brizgalis, Ausma. *Latvians in Alberta: A Study.* Edmonton: University of Alberta, 1980.

Karklis, Maruta et al., eds. *The Latvians In America, 1640-1973: A Chronology and Fact Book.* Dobbs Ferry, N.Y.: Oceana Publishers, 1974.

Putnins, Aldis. *Latvians in Australia: Alienation and Assimilation.* Canberra: Australian National University Press, 1981.

ABOUT THE AUTHOR

Andrejs Plakans is professor of history at Iowa State University, Ames, Iowa. He is the author of *Kinship in the Past: An Historical Anthropology of European Family Life 1500-1900* (Basil Blackwell, 1984), and *The Latvians: A Short History* (Hoover Institution Press, 1995), and coeditor (with Tamara Hareven) of *Family History at the Crossroads: Linking Familial and Historical Change* (Princeton University Press, 1987). Born in Riga, Latvia, in 1940, he received his B.A. degree in history at Franklin and Marshall College, Lancaster, Pennsylvania, and his M.A. and Ph.D. degrees from Harvard University. He has taught at Boston College, the University of Pittsburgh, the University of California--Riverside, the University of Washington, and the University of Latvia in Riga. A past president of the Association for the Advancement of Baltic Studies, he has also served on committees of the American Association for the Advancement of Slavic Studies, the American Historical Association, and the Social Science History Association. In 1992, he was a fellow at the Woodrow Wilson International Center for Scholars, Washington, D.C., and since 1990 has been a foreign member of the Academy of Sciences of Latvia.